THE ANDHRA CULTURE DURING THE KAKATIYAN TIMES

By

Dr. Mrs. V. ANILA KUMARI

EASTERN BOOK LINKERS
DELHI :: INDIA

Publishers :
EASTERN BOOK LINKERS
5825, New Chandrawal, Jawahar Nagar,
Delhi-110007 Ph.: 2520287

First Edition : 1997

ISBN : 81-86339-15-9

Rs : 800.00

Laser typesetting & Printing at :
Unique Print Media,
Vijay Nagar, Delhi-110009

CONTENTS

Foreword

Culture is the mirror which captures the image of civilization. Culture is a process in which human aspirations, ideals, material facts and social progress are transmitted from time to time. It is of two kinds- indeological and material. Ideological culture is that which reflects ideas pertaining to philosophy, religion, forms of worship, ethical behaviour of the society and moral norms that regulate the human life. The material culture is that which is represented by human achievements in the fields of art, architecture, music, dance, ornaments, dress, games, conveyances and weaponry and all that which forms a part of civlization.

Civilizations may perish, but the imperishable remains of every civlization become a subject matter for study by historians and archeologists. Indian culture is so rich and varied that every time a historian lays his or her hand on it to unravel the mysteries, it still gives further scope for investigation. The more a historian probes the deeper and varied facets come to light. The tools with which a historian probes into the complexity of civilization are the contemporary literature, epigraphy, iconography, artefacts, monuments and all that of which is consequential.

Several scholars such as Late Sri Survaram Pratapa Reddy, Khandavalli Lakshmi Ranjanam, Balendu Sekharam have worked previously on the socio-cultural aspects of Mediaeval Andhra mainly basing on the contemporary literature. Prof. Late. R. Narasimha Rao, Prof. Alladi Vaidehi and Sri B.N. Sastri have worked on the socio-political and economic aspects basing on literature as well as on epigraphical sources. Here is for the first time we have an authoritative and distintive contribution by Dr. Mrs. Anila Kumari on the great Kakatiyan culture based on much wider yet substantial foundation of contemporary literature combined with epigraphy, architecture and more importantly sculpture. Her personal knowledge of even minute architectural and artistic details of Kakatiyan monuments and sculpture as reflected in this work are enough proof of her tedious and tiresome peregrinations for collection of research material and photography to all parts of Andhra wherever they are available.

Material culture as reflected in architecture art, music, dance, drama, costumes, hair styles, jewellery, games amusements and such other socio-cultural aspects are discussed with personal knowledge and full authority. Confined to the parameters of methodology and scope which a historian documents his or her results of research, Dr. Mrs. Anila Kumari ably defined the boundaries of her field work.

In the culture history of India, the role played by the Kakatiyas of Warangal (1050-1323 A.D.) is highly significant and favourably emulate with those of the contemporary dynasties like Hoyasalas, Cholas, Eastern Gangs etc., Right from the times of Mauryas through Satavahanas, Ikshvakus Vishnukundins, Badami Chalukyans, religious art was liberally patronised in one form or the other. Temple construction though from the point of religion is a pious activity has an enoromous significance in terms of social and cultural activity, What kind of cultural activity is preferable for the society? It may be any kind of socio-cultural activity that promotes harmony among people, that brings all sections of people together and that makes people contented and that which fosters economic prosperity is preferable. The Kakatiyan rulers are second to none in achieving this noble goal.

The great religions of India-Buddhism, Jainism and Hinduism were liberally patronised by the royalty and nobility. The religious doctrines and practices are not just dogmas tutored to the people but are life sustaining divine doctrins. A temple is a citadel for social and cultural activities. Various aspects of contemporary dance forms, social life, war machinery were frozen on the stone beams, lintels, pillars of temples with a view to perpetuate the aesthetic values that were ingrained in the society. The mighty Kakatiyan Emperors like Prola, Beta, Rudra, Ganapati, Rudramadevi and Prataparudra had not only ruled the kingdom effectively but also contributed immensely to architecture, art, literature, dance, drama, and other aspects of social life. It is the ideas that reflect in institutions and it is the institutions that get concretised in the dexterous hands of architects and it is those concretised forms that were brought to lime-light by the archaeologists.

The present writer Dr. Mrs Anila Kumari, now happily settled in U.S.A. is a well known scholar with an excellent back ground of Museology and Archaeology. Her long association with the world famous Salarjung Museum at Hyderabad gave her a unique opportunity of not only studying the priceless antiquities exhibited therein but also meeting and guiding eminent personalities from all over the world around the galleries of the Museum. Being the daughter of an eminent archaeologist, Dr. V.V.Krishna Sastri, who was formerly Director, Department of Archeology and Museums, Government Oriental Manuscripts Library and State Archives, she learnt her primary lessons in field Archeology as infant tagging behind her father to the sites under excavation at Nagarjuna Konda, Yelleswarm, Peddabankur and Kotilingala besides various monuments of different periods. As a research scholar, she was the disciple of Prof. B.K. Gururaja Rao, a reputed scholar in his own right end a known disciplinarian. She also received guidance from Dr. M.L.Nigam, Dr. Y.Gopala Reddy, Prof. S. Nagaraju. It is no wonder that Anila Kumari did an excellent job in unfolding before us in a very neat and lucid style, the cultural fabric of Andhra during the Kakatiyan times as it is emobodied in architecture, sculpture, dance, drama and other facets. I have no hesitation at all to state that this book is a most valuable contribution which caters to all those researchers and general readers who are interested in undertstanding the Andhra culture of the Kakatiyan times in a deeper and detailed way.

—Prof. G. Sundararamayya

Dept. of Indian Philosophy and Culture.

Andhra University

VISHAKHAPATNAM

Preface

The present dissertation embodies the study of the author on the socio-cultural aspects of the Kakatiya times, approximately from 1000 to 1323 A.D., as reflected in the vast mass of extant contemporary literature, either published or unpublished, on the priceless sculptural wealth available in the temples or lying scattered on the open spacious ground inside the fort of Warangal and on those exhibited in the various Archaeological Museums under the control of the Department of Archaeology and Museums and the Birla Archaeological and Cultural Rasearch Institute, Hyderabad.

Previously several scholars of repute have worked on the political and economic aspects of this period. Mention may be made of Prof. M. Rama Rao, more recently, Prof.R.Narasimha Rao, who made intensive study of the medieval history of Andhra Desa, mostly on the aforesaid topics. Late Sri Suravaram Pratapa Reddy, Prof.Lakshmiranjanam, Sri Balendusekharam, Sri Mallampalli Somasekhara Sarma, Sri B.N.Sastry have done pioneering work on the cultural history of Andhra Desa through the ages. Prof. Radhakrishna Sarma brought all the important temples in Telangana region into limelight through his book entitled "The Temples of Telingana". As such, it is found necessary to focus mainly on the Kakatiyan age which witnessed the flowering of various aspects of Andhra culture, the fragrance of which permeated throughout South India during the subsequent periods.

This work deals with the cultural aspects like architecture, art, music, dance, drama besides discussing the other social facets such as costumes, hair-dresses, foot-wear, jewellery, ornaments, coiffure, games, amusements, conveyances, weapons of offence and defence and lastly flora and fauna.

In course of my field work in the Districts of Warangal, Kareemangar, Khamanm, Nalgonda and Mahboobnagar, I acknowledge the help received from Sri A.Someswara Rao, a historian of Warangal and Sri Thakur Rajaram Singh, Advocate from Kareemangar District.

I am grateful to Dr.M.S.Nagaraja Rao, Director-General, Archeaological Survey of India Dr.V.V.Krishna Sastry, Director, Dept. of Archaeology and Museums Govt. of Andhra Pradesh, Hyderabad Dr. Kamalakar, Director, Birla Archaeological and Cultural Research Institute, Hyderabad for permitting me to study the relevant monuments, sculptures and antiquities exhibited in the Museums. My sincere thanks are also due to Dr.M.L.Nigam, Director,

Salarjung Museum, without whose encouragement and inspiration this work would not have seen the light of the day. I am beholden to Sri P.Sitapatai,I.A.S.,for the award of research fellowship from the State Archives, to Sri R.Parathasarathy, I.A.S., former Commissioner of State Archives for his coperation in the study of the manuscripts and in the collection of material from the library, to Dr.V.V.L.Narasimha Rao, the then Director, Oriental Manuscripts Library, Hyderabad for according permission to study the rare manuscripts and books.

I gratefully acknowledge the cooperation I have received from some of the staff members of the Department of Archaeology, and Museums-Hyderabd, namely Dr. B.Subramanyam, Sri K.Raghunath, Sri V.Yellaiah and Sri J.V.S.Sainath, Sri G.Narasimha Rao, Sri E.S.Nagi Reddy, Asst. Sthapati, and Sri B.Narayana, Conservation Assistant. I also owe my thanks to Smt.Kusuma Kumari, Research Officer, State Archives for help in procuring material from the manuscripts hall, to Smt.Varalakshmi, Librarian in the State Department of Archaeology, Sri K.Ramesh, Librarian, Salarjung Museum for providing library facility. I am obliged to Mr.Syed Habeebuddin and Sri Surya Bhaskar for their excellent job in typing the manuscripts.

I express my deep sense of gratitude to Dr.B.K. Gururaja Rao, Professor, Department of Ancient Indian History and Archaeology, University of Mysore who through his parental guidance, critical appraisal and invaluable comments, is solely responsible for shaping this thesis.

I am also grateful to Prof.A.V.Narasimha Murthy, Head of the Dept. of Ancient History and Archaeology, University of Mysore and the authorities of the University of Mysore for permitting me to register for doctoral research and publish the thesis.

CHAPTER-I

INTRODUCTION

The scope of the study:

The rule of the *Kākatiyas* of Warangal (1050-1323 A.D.) may be considered as the most magnificent period in the cultural history of Andhra Pradesh. The long reign witnessed the erection of several exquisite monuments in the shape of temples, forts, tanks etc. Some of the temples may unhesitatingly be rated amongst the greatest monuments of India. Any student of the medieval Indian art cannot afford to ignore these exquisite architectural creations. The two contemporary South Indian dynasties, namely the Hoyasālas of Dwarasamudra and Kākatiyas of Orugallu (Warangal) vied with each other in patronising fine arts, such as music, dance, sculpture and architecture. They had in fact, carried forward the great traditions left behind by the Chālukyas, yet evolving their own individual styles.

It was a period of culmination for music, dance, sculpture, painting and various other fine arts. This is due to the uninterrupted prosperity of Deccan in general and Andhra in particular from the times of the Satavāhanas. The kings have gone into oblivion, the dynasties have ended, but the steady progress of culture was never impeded. It was homogeneous, deep rooted and carried forward, whether it be by the Satavāhanās, Ikshvākus, Vishnukundins, or Badāmi Chālukyās. The uninterrupted stream of culture began like a small rivulet cut across rugged plains and plateaus, rocks and hills taking several tributaries into the main stream and finally became a mighty river to join the sea of Indian culture.

It was a populous and wealthy society which did not bother too much for searching food and daily needs, but engaged itself in singing, dancing, carving and painting. The population was limited, according to the modern standards, but the crops were abundant due to construction or repairs of several huge tanks, existing even today like those situated at Palampet, Pakhal, Laknavaram and Bhadrakali etc.

It is to extricate the details of this cultural glory of the Andhras, and the interesting and absorbing facets of their history that an attempt is being made now. No doubt earlier scholars have probed into the history of this dynasty; Dr. Parabrahma Sastry has in yester years probed into and reconstructed the political history of the Kakatiyas.[1] Rama Rao had made a study of the temple architecture under these kings.[2] Other scholars have provided some general accounts of the history of Andhra during the period under consideration.[3] But no systematic account of the life of the people of Andhradesa during the period as could be gleaned from the literature, epigraphs and more sumptuously from the temple sculptures has been made available so far. This study, as could be seen from the foregoing pages underlines the rich and vivid culture, social life and traditions of the Andhras as part of a wider panorama of the Deccan in the early medieval times and represents the best phase of the Hindu culture before the penetration of Islam. The author hopes to have considerably filled this gap by this research venture.

The sources of study:

For a study of the Kākatiyan society and its cultural achievements, there are three main sources of information. Firstly, the sculptures strewn around some of the important temples, like the Thousand Pillared temple at Hanumakonda, the loose sculptures-some intact and some fragmentary - of the great temple destroyed under the hands of the iconoclastic vandals, now sprawling on the bare ground in the middle of the Warangal fort, those found at Katakshapur, Jakaram, Palampet, Ghanpur, Pillalamarri, Nāgulapadu, Niḋikonda, Kondaparti, Ramanujapuram, Pangal, Nagunur, Manthani, Dharmapuri, Bejjanki, Kusumañchi, Umamaheśwaram, Ryāli etc. It is necessary to take the readers around some of the magnificent edifices of the Kākatiyās regarding their situation, chronology and artistic excellence, so that the following chapters of this work are better understood.

1. Hanumakonda : The Hanumakonda temple situated in the middle of Hanumakonda town, is dated to the time of Kakatiya Rudradeva (1163 A. D.)[4] This *trikuta* temple locally known as the Thousand pillared temple, consists of exquisite carvings of *Nritta* Narasiṁha, Natarāja, musicians, drummers, *chauri* bearers which can be classified as some of the best specimens in the annals of plastic art of India. 2. The sculptures in Warangal fort, variously known as Orugallu, Ekasilanagara, and Andhra-nāgari, the celebrated capital of the illustrious Kākatiya dynasty, which ruled over Andhradesa between 1000 A.D. to 1323 A.D. It was a great centre of literary and cultural activity during the 12th, 13th, 14th centuries A.D. An extensive fort, a *staladurga,* is still intact due to the renovations carried out by the

1. Sastry, P.V.P., *The Kākatiyas,* A.S.No. 51. Hyderabad.
2. Rama Rao, M., *The Select Temples of Kakatiyas,* Tirupati.
3. Gopalakrishna Murthy, S.,The Sculpture of the Kakatiyas, A.S.No.34, Hyderabad.
4. Venkataramanayya, N., *Inscriptions of Andhra Pradesh, Warangal district,* E.S. No. 6, Hyderabad.

later Muslim kings. The extant temples i.e. Saṁbhuni gudi, Venkateśwara temple and other unearthed *maṇḍapas,* sculptures and *toraṇas* are the best testimonials for the last phase of the glorious art of the Kākatiyās.

3. Temples at Katakshapur: Katakshapur is a temple village situated about a mile in the interior to the left of the Warangal-Mulugu road in the Warangal district. There are two temples, one dedicated to Chennakeśava and the other to Śiva.

4. Temple at Jakaram: Jakaram temple is a fine example of early Kakatiya architecture which is situated further down the Warangal-Mulugu road, outside the village Jakaram. It is about 200 meters from the road towards west.

The temples of Katakshapur and Jakaram are endowed with the earliest art traditions of the Kakatiyas. Unfortunately, the temples are badly damaged by vandals. Inside the garbhagriha of Keśava temple at Katakshapur is a low *vedi* with a carved *prabha* but the Dhruva Bera was shifted to the State Museum, Hyderabad.

5. Palampet: Palampet is a small village in the Mulugu taluk of the Warangal District, situated about 64 kms., north-west of Hanumakonda in the Warangal District of Andhra Pradesh. The inscription in the Rudreśvara temple is dated to the reign of Gaṇapatideva. The temple was built by the famous Kakatiya General, Recharla Rudra in 1213 A.D.[1]

The Rudreśvara temple more popularly known as Ramappa temple is unique and a solitary example of the middle phase of Kakatiyan art. The *adhisthāna* mouldings, wall sculptures, bracket figures, the exquisitely carved pillars, ceiling panels are examples of the finest workmanship of the Kakatiya sculptors.

6. Ghanpur: The Ghanpur group of temples are situated 8 kms., north-east of Palampet and 72 kms north-east of Warangal in Andhra Pradesh. The main shrine, dedicated to Śiva, is in the middle of a mud fort. All the temples are in a dilapidated condition. The door-jamb decoration of *Nāgini* and other dancers, *alasa kanyas* and *madanikas* are anatomically more proportionate and artistically more refined than those at Palampet.

7. Pillalamarri : Pillalamarri is a small village situated about three miles to the north-east of Suryapet, the headquarters of a taluk in the Nalgonda district of Andhra Pradesh. The village contains three temples which are good examples of Kakatiya architectuure. The *trikūṭa* temple of Namesvara was built by Nami Reddy in 1195 A. D. Erakasani, wife of Beti Reddy, built another beautiful temple in Pillalamarri and installed a linga by name Erakeśvara in 1208 A.D. This is a fine temple built on a double

1. Srinivasachari, P., Ramappa and other Temples of Palampet, Hyderabad, P. 15.

platform with three porches and a *Vimana*. It is a complete temple, like the great temple at Palampet.

8. Nagulapadu: The village of Nagulapadu is situated in the Suryapet Taluk of the Nalgonda District. There are two main temples at Nagulapadu, situated close to one another. The temple inscriptions are dated to 1234 A.D. and 1258 A.D. The Nagulapadu temple is described as the gem of the Kakatiya architecture.[1] The carved panels of the ceiling contains *Pārvati-Kalyānaṁ, Samudra Mathana* and scenes from *Rāmāyna*, such as *Rama- Rāvana Yuddha, Sapta Talachedana* and *vānaras* constructing a bridge over the sea etc.

9. Nidikonda : The village Nidikonda is situated at a distance of 8 kms., from Jangaon in Warangal district. Important among the ruins in the village are Kummarigullu temple, Śiva temple and Narasimhaswāmi temple. The Kummarigullu temple with a *trikuta* plan was built by Kundamāmba, wife of Natawādi Rudra and a sister of Kakatiya Gaṇapati deva, consecrated the temple to Gods Mahādeva, Sūrya and Ganapati in the year 1219 A.D.[2] In the inscription found at Nidikonda, it is said that she also built temples for Śiva at Śrīsailam, Kaleswaram, Jidikallu and Manthrakuta (Manthani).[3] Among the narrative panels, *Tārā vilāpaṁ* is a unique example of sentiment frozen in rock.

10. Kondaparti : The village Kondaparti is situated in the Warangal District at a distance of 8 kms., from the Warangal Railway station. The first inscription is of the time of the Kakatiya Gaṇapatideva and is dated 1203 A.D. The Chaundesvara temple, built by *Chaunda-Senani* of Ganapatideva consists of dancing figures, portrait sculpture of Chaunda *Senapati* etc.

11. Ramanujapuram: This is a unique *Pañchāyatana* temple in Telangana region and is situated in Mulugu talk of Warangal district. It has five shrines. Two shrines having *garbhagriha* and *antarāla* are situated on each side (east and west) and one on the north. Connecting them are two *Sabhāmaṇḍapas*.

12. Panugallu: The village of Panugal or Panugallu is situated about 3 kms., north of Nalgonda town, a district headquarters. The village was an important pilgrim and political centre during the times of the Chālukyās of Kalyāna and continued to be so during the Kakatiya period. An inscription in the court of Pacchala Somesvara temple dated to 1124 A.D. was issued by the mother of Kanduri Choda Bhima.[4] The Chaya Somesvara and the Pacchala Somesvara are the two important temples situated in Panugal. Both the temples must have been constructed by the chiefs of the Kanduri Choda family, who ruled over the regions of Atmakur, Markapuram, Dornala in

1. Ibid, Annual Report, 1927-28,Hyderabad Archaeological series, P.18
2. Venkataramanayya, N., Op.cit., p.84
3. Venkartaramanayya, N., Ibid.
4. Radhakrishna Sarma, M., *Temples of Telangana*, p. 85

Kurnool District and over the modern districts of Mahboonagar, Nalgonda, Khammam in the Telangana region. The Kanduri Chodas were feudatories under the Kalyana Chalukyas and later to Kakatiyas and subsequently became independent rulers. The wall sculptures over the rebuilt Pacchala Somesvara temple are highly refined and belong to a transitory phase, Chalukya to Kakatiya. The Ashṭhadikpalas, dancing Ganesha, Natarāja Śiva, Sālabhanjika and other Alasakanyas display a lucid evolution of individual style and at the same time exhibiting a closer impact of Chalukya-Kakatiya idiom.

13. Nagunur : The village of Nagunur is situated 9 Kms., north-west of Karimnagar in Andhra Pradesh. That it was an important political and religious centre in the medieval times is borne out by the references in the inscriptions and by the ruins of several temples in the Kakatiya idiom.

14. Manthani : Manthani in Karimnagar district played an important role in the religious history of the Kakatiyas. Today there are several ruined Kakatiya temples in the town.

15. Dharmapuri : Dharmapuri is situated in the Jagtial taluk of Karimnagar district and is about 48 kms., from Jagtial town. The most important temple in Dharmapuri is dedicated to Narasiṁha consisting of dancing figures of Natarāja, Ganeśa, Bhu-Varaha, Siva Parvati, several bold reliefs of pillared *mandapas* which are good specimens for study.

16. Bejjanki : Bejjanki or Bejavanka is a small village 18 kms., south of Karimnagar. There is a temple dedicated to Siva situated on the top of a hill. At the mid-level of the hill there is a big tunnel cut through the granitic rock through which rain water is drained down the hill. The four central pillars of the *mantapa* of the temple are richly carved with, hunters, huntresses, dancers and tribals with leaf-garments and are exemplary of the plastic art.

17. Kusumanchi : Kusumanchi is about 20 kms., west of Khammam in Khammam District of Andhra Pradesh. Noteworthy among the temples at Kusumanchi are those of Gopalaswami and Mukteśvara.

Apart from the above temples, there are other Kakatiya temples at Bodhan, Kothapalli, Ainolu, Moglicherla, Garla, Pantangi, Punnolu, Dharmasagaram, Umamahesvaram, Ryali etc.

The sculptures, pillars and a reconstructed *mandapa* exhibited at the State Museum, Hyderabad, provide additional source of information. The State Department of Archaeology and Museums has a considerable collection of sculptures brought from Warangal and Karimnagar regions. An exquisite idol of Goddess Annapūrṇa brought from Kasipet in Karimnagar district, two figures of Chennakesava, one from Visnur and the other from Katakshapur, the *Madanika* figures from Ghanpur, the idol of Bhiskshatana Murthy from Umamahesvaram are some of the best specimens of Kakatiya art available in the State Museum, Hyderabad. Further, there are some sculptures in the Kakatiya idiom in the Victorica Jubilee Museum Vijayawada, the Khajana Building Museum, Golconda, Gandhi Centenary Museum, Karimnagar and Government Archaeological Museum at Pillalamarri near Mahaboobnagar. Some good Kakatiya sculplutures are exhibited in the Birla Archaeological Museum at Malakpet, Hyderabad.

Another important source of information is the contemporary Telugu literature, which throw invaluable light on the social and cultural conditions, customs, fine arts and various other analogous aspects. The works like *Mahābhārata* by Nannaya, *Kumara Sambhava* by Nannechoda, *Sivatatva Sāraṁ* of Mallikārjuna Pandita ; *Basava Purāṇa* and *Paṅditarādhya Charitra* of Palkurki Somanatha, *Kridabhiramam* of Vinukonda Vallabharaya (Srinatha ?), *Palnati vīra Charitra* of Srinatha, *Nṛitta-Ratnāvali* of Jaya Senāni, *Ranganatha Rāmāyaṇa* of Ranganatha, *Simhāsana Dvatrimsika* of Koravi Goparaju, are some of the principal works consulted. From among these we may now discuss more important works which provide the ground work for a study of socio-cultural aspects.

Kumāra Saṁbhava of Nannechoda: There are differences of opinion regarding the date of this work; however the most agreeable date is 1130 - 1150 A.D.[1] Though the work is a faithful translation of the celebrated *Kumāra Saṁbhava* of Kālidāsa, the Telugu work of Nannechoda is considered to be of a very high literary merit. Information regarding various methods of swimming, costumes, sports and games prescribed to the girls, music and dance has been culled out from this work.

Basava Purāna and Paṅditārādhya Charitra by Palkurki Somanatha: Some critics are of the opinion that Somanatha hailed from the Kannada Desa and some argue that he was a native of Palkurki situated about 40 kms., from Warangal and 10 kms., from Bommera, the native place of Potana who composed Andhra Mahābhāgavataṁ. Palkurki is an important early historical site. There are also medieval temples at this place dedicated to Siva and Narasimha. As regards the date, opinions differ. Some feel that he lived during 12th-13th centuries *A.D.*[2] *(1190-1260)*. However Mallampalli Somasekhara Sarma, a profound Telugu historian, believed that he lived between 1290-1320 A.D.[3] and was contemporary of Prataparudra, the last king of the Kakatiya line. As far as the source material is concerned *Basavapurāṇa* provides information on the contemporary .socio religious conditions, costumes, textiles etc.

Paṇditārādhya Charitra, also authored by Somanatha, is a great work on Saivism in which the efficacy of the worship of Śiva and various episodes revolving round Śaivism are narrated. He also discusses and refutes various

1. *Kumarasambhavam By Nannechoda,* P.4
2. *Basava Puranam by Pālakurki Somanatha,* p.31
3. Ibid Op.cit., p.32

schools of religious philosophy, such as the Vedic, Karma, Kala-mukha, Sankhya, Yoga, Charvaka, Pancharatra, Bauddha, Jaina etc., as against Saiva. A fund of information has been collected from this work regarding music, dance, flora, and fauna, dress, ornaments etc. In short, it is a compendium of various cultural facets of the contemporary society.

Another work of great importance is *Krīdābhirāmaṁ* by Vinukonda Vallabharaya.[1] The work consists of 294 verses interspersed with prose. This is a unique work without comparison, providing information about the contemporary society in general and Warangal in particular during the time of Pratāparudradeva, the last king of the line. It runs like a modern documentary film on the life style as existed at Warangal, during the time of the Kakatiyas. The main difference between other works and *Krīdābhirāmaṁ* lies in presentation of material which is nearer to truth than being loaded with flights of imagination. The description is sometimes interlaced with obscene narratives, yet the book literally drags the reader to the streets of contemporary Warangal and Hanumakonda. No doubt, there is a controversy regarding the authorship, whether it was composed by Vallabharāya or by the most famous Telugu poet, Śrinātha, but regarding the date of the composition there is no scope for controversy. The vigorous style, diction and encyclopaedic knowledge about various aspects of Indian culture led most critics to believe that it was composed by a poet no less than Srinatha himself.

Regarding the material available in this work, we find mention of various methods and auspicious movements for entering the town of Orugallu (Warangal) the omens, the suburb of basket makers, description of a low caste lady from Karnataka, the'*Maila santha*' where meat, cereals and condiments for removing unwanted hair are sold, about *Rangavalli*, about balls of dung decorated with saffron and flowers known as *Gobbillu*, about gambling and its bad effects, scented oils for hair, about a lady sitting on a rotating oil mill, about a suburb in which military barracks were situated, a tailor making fun with the girls who came to get their blouses stitched, the tempting posture of a squatting lady while pulverising saffron, about the main gateway of Warangal fort and the moat around the fort, the elephants, horses, chariots etc., about the suburb of prostitutes, the Śivālayaṁ street where a songster recites the deeds of the Palanāti heroes, the cock-fights, the pictures of the heroes of Palnadu found on the plaque above a raised platform, about the temple of the nude Goddess Ekavīra Devi, the Mother of Parasurama, Kākatamma a famous deity of the Kakatiya period, about Mailarabhatas, about the Gondli type of *desi* dance form, worship of Mailara deva, the temples of Bhairava, Chāmundi, Vīrabhadra etc., a Buddhist monastery then the temples of Pāṅdavās, the mosque of the Muslims, the

1. Umakanta,Pandita *Palnātivira Charitra,* p.1

Svayambhu temple, bell tolling sixteen times for telling the time from the palace of the king to indicate noon, visit to Māchāla Devi, a courtesan of Prataparudra and about the description of her painting gallery consisting of several pictures, the main theme of which being illegal sex, about the fair at Srikakulam in Krishna district, illegal sex orgies at the above fair and about the ram fights etc.

Palnātiveera Charitra: As one indian writer has remarked "Unhappy is the nation that has no history and happy the nation that can hear the ballads commemorating the adventures of her warriors sung with fervour......" [1] *Palnativeera Charitra* or the history of Palnāti heroes is a historical account of the fratricidal war that occurred during 1182 A.D.[2] around the village Kāryaṁpūdī in the present Palnad talk of Guntur district in Andhra. It was fought between two princes of the same family, Haihayas, but participated by several other kings such as the Rudradeva of Warangal, Bhīmadeva of Dharanikota (Amarāvathi), Vira Ballāla of Dwārasamudra, Kamavibhu of Malva, Prachideva of Bengal, Baladeva Purushottama of Orissa and other kings from Kalyana, Gujarat, Pandya, Kerala etc.[3]

Palnātiveera Charitra was composed by Srinatha in *Dvipada* metre (couplet).[4] The story begins with the preparations by Malideva Rāja and Brahmanaidu to start on their journey to the battle of Palnadu. It mentions about the various pet names given to bulls yoked to draw carts to the battle, then Malidevarāja and others reaching Tripurantakam, near Śrīsailam, on their way to the battle ground at Kāryaṁpūdi, then Nalagāma, the opposing prince proceeding to the battle on an elephant back, arrival of kings from different places and meeting Nalagāma, then the story of Bālachandra, the hero *par excellence* compared to Abhimanyu of *Mahābhārata*, who was the only son of Brahmanāyudu, Bālachandra playing with tops, ladies taking pleasure to see Balachandra playing tops,Bālachandra first meeting his courtesan, then Manchala - his wife - who wishing him good, hands over a sword and sends him to battle. The work also provides information on cock fights, a classical dance concert, music and musical instruments, games and amusements, performance of *Vratas*, jewellery, arms and weapons, social customs, food habits, costumes,different arrays (*vyuhas*) in the battle field and the paraphernalia required for the battle etc.

Srinatha was the 'Director of Education', *Vidyādhikāri* under the Reddys of Koṅdavīdu and must have lived from the last quarter of the 14th century and upto the middle of 15th century A.D. On the basis of some inscriptions it is believed that he become the *Vidyādhākāri* (Director of Education) during

1. Umakanta,Pandita *Palnātivira Charitra*, p.1
2. Ibid. *Telugu Sanskrithi*, Telugu Bhasha Samithi, Vol.I, p.73
3. Umakanta, Pandita, Op.cit., p.26
4. Umakanta, Pandita, Ibid.

the year 1404 A.D. Besides *Palnāti Vāera Charitra*, Srinatha's prolific output included *Maruttarāt Charitra, Śālivāhana Saptasati, Kātama Rāju Katha, Sriṅgāra Naishadhamu, Hara Vilāsamu, Bhīma Khandamu, Vīdhinātakamu and Chatuvulu.*

Nritta Ratnāvali: Nritta Ratnāvali of Jāyapa *Senapati* is a work of great importance to the students of *Nātya Śāstra* and cultural history of Andhra desa. Jayapa was a Commander-in-chief under Kakatiya Ganapatideva. He was probably a commander in charge of the elephant wing of the Kakatiya army. The work was composed in the year 1253-54 A.D. It is said that Jayapa Senani has also composed another work *Vādya Ratnāvali*[1] which at present is not available. The work is extremely useful for a study of *Desi* and *Mārga* forms of dance which were in currency in Andhra region in particular and India in general.

Some scholars[2] believe that the dance sculptures found in the famous Palampet temple were carved according to the text of Jayapa *Senapati*. It is controversial whether this view is correct, but it appears certain that the dance sculptures in the later day Kakatiya temples must have been inspired by his work to a large extent. The then *Sthapatis* must have followed the *agamas* for portraying the divine idols and various *Nātya Śāstras* particularly of *Bharata, Jayapa Senani, and Śilpa Prakāsa* etc. for modelling the secular forms. In fact, it is a common knowledge that every *sthapati* still preserves manuscripts handed down to him from generation to generation.

Raṅganātha Rāmāyana: There is an unending controversy regarding the authorship of this work, whether it was composed by *Ranganatha* the poet-laureate of Kona Buddha Reddy, who ruled over Dharanikota area of Guntur district or by the King Kona Buddha Reddy himself.[3] It is the opinion of many scholars that the author of *Ranganātha Rāmāyana* was a contemporary of Palkuri Somanatha who lived between 1282-1340 A.D.[4] Mallampalli Somasekhara Sarma argues that it was composed during the latter half of the 14th century A.D. The work is composed in *dvipada* metre (couplet) which was more popular among the commoners and which can also be sung as a ballad. It consists of six chapters starting with the performance of *Putrakāmesthi yāga* by King Dasaratha and ends with the beheading of Ravana at Laṅka. The work also provides glimpses of contemporary flora, fauna, arms,armoury, ornaments etc.

Simhasana Dvatrimsika: Composed by Koravi Goparaju, it consists of thirty two stories of Vikramarka narrated by a similar number of *Sālabhaṅjikas* to King Bhoja. The work is based upon *Kathāsarithsāgara,* a Sānskrit work. The author lived during the last quarter of the 14th century and early 15th

1. Raghavan, V., *Nṛutta Ratnāvali*, p.12
2. Raghavan, V., Ibid.
3. Ibid *Sri Ranganatha Ramayanam,* p.15
4. Ibid.

century A.D.[1] It mentions the Goddess Kākati; the town of Orugallu (Warangal); good and bad omens; the sixty four fine arts; kinds of food stuffs; silk weaving centres like Kamavaram, Kundavaram etc., different shades of clothing, of silks; and hunting, fishing,swimming; the festival of spring; various kinds of drums and trumpets; about the tribes like Chenchus and their life styles; about sacred pilgrim centres like Kalesvaram, Dharmapuri, Manthani; bad and good dreams, astrological configurations to prove that the author was an adept in astrology; about gambling and dicing,its ill effects; magic etc.

Though the present study is mainly based upon contemporary literature and sculpture; nonetheless some stone inscriptions also of the period have provided additional source of information. The inscription found at Kondaparti issued by Chaunda *Senapati* in connection with the installation of a Linga named as *Chaundesvara,* is important for a study of architecture.[2] The Dharmasagar inscription informs about a musical instrument, *Jalaja-karanda.*[3] The Chebrolu inscription of Jayapa gives an account of the donations made for the dancing girls and musicians, attached to the temples.[4] The training of the dancers is mentioned in some of the inscriptions published in Epigraphia Indica and South Indian Inscriptions. The inscription at Pillalamarri, of the 12th century gives information about painting.[5]

The Hanumakonda *Niroshtya Kāvya* epigraph[6] records the dressing of hair of the peasant women in the shape of spreadout plumes of the peacock. The same inscription informs about the gem-studded nose ornament[7] of the damsels resembling the stars in the sky.

1. Koravi Goparaju *Simhasana Dvatrimsika*, Part-I, p.1
2. Venkataramanayya, N., op.cit., p.131
3. Venkataramanayya, N., Ibid., p.226
4. Epigraphia Indica, vol.V, p.142
5. Annual Report, Hyderabad Archaeological Series, p.18
6. Epigraphia Indica, Vol.XXXVI, p.216
7. Ibid.

CHAPTER - II

THE POLITICAL BACKGROUND

The history of the Kakatiyas of Warangal is of paramount importance and interest in the annals of Deccan in particular and that of South India in general. They dominated the destinies of the Andhras for more than three centuries. The period of the Kakatiyas of Warangal started from about the 10th century and came to an abrupt end in the first quarter of the 14th century A.D. The Kakatiyas were the first to establish their sway over the entire Telugu speaking region after the fall of the Satavahanas and before the rise of the Vijayanagara empire. Their reign can very well be styled in the medieval history of Andhra desa as the "Age of the Kakatiyas of Warangal".

The Kakatiyas claimed that they were the descendants of one Durjaya.[1] Several feudatory families who ruled different regions of the *Andhra desa* in the medieval period, viz., Kotas, Kondapadamatis, Velanādu Cholas, Chāgis, etc., also claimed descent from Durjaya[2] who is generally believed to be a legendary person. But the Bayyāram tank inscription of Kakatiya Mailama clearly states that he was a historical person born in the line of Kshatriyas who sprang from the shoulders of Brahma.[3] However, it is not easy to establish relationship between the Kakatiyas and Durjaya.

The historians are not unanimous regarding the derivation of the family name, viz., 'Kakatiya'. The *Pratāparudriyam*[4] of Vidyanatha states that the family of these kings came to be known as 'Kakatiya' on account of their being the worshipers of the Goddess Durga in the name of Kākati. It is also stated that She was the *Kula-Devata* of the Kakatiyas. But it should be stated here that besides Goddess Durga in the name of Kākati, the Kakatiyas also worshipped the *Svayaṁbhūdeva* (Śiva) as their family deity.[5] Further, none of the numerous inscriptions issued by the members of this dynasty mentions Kakati as their family deity. Thus the derivation of the word *'Kakatiya'* from the Goddess Kakati cannot be accepted as final.[6] The

---

1. Epigraphia Indica, Vol.XII, p.168 and also Epigraphia Andhrica, Vol.I, p.72
2. Sastry, P.V.P., 1978 *The Kakatiyas of Warangal*, p.37 & *S.I.I.*, Vol.X, No.395
3. Epigraphia Andhrica, Vol.I, p.18
4. Kumarasvami, K.,(Ed.) 1954 *Vidyanatha's Prataparudriyam*, p.134
5. 1954 *Ibid.*, p.20, 32, 113, 130. 165 and 181.
6. Epigraphia Andhrica, Vol.I, p.8

Bayyaram tank inscription of Mailama gives us some interesting information in this connection. It states that Venna, the founder of the family, ruled from a town called Kakati and on account of this, his descendants came to be known 'Kakatiyas'. Rudradeva, the son of Prola II, is known to have had the title *'Kakati- Puravarādhīśvara.*[1] The Garavapadu inscription of Ganapatideva, dated in 1260 A.D. also refers to a place called Kākati and its association with the early members of the Kakatiya family.[2] A Warangal inscription refers to Ganapatideva,*'Śrimaṅ Mahāmaṅdaleśvara Kākatiyya-Puravarīśvara Ganapati'*.[3] An inscription found at Tripurantakam records that Kakati was the *kula-pura* or the family town of the Kakatiyas.[4] The *Pratāparudrīyaṁ* not only refers to the existence of the town called Kākatipura but also gives a very interesting description of the ladies of that town.[5] It is thus likely that Kākati was a *pura* and the family name Kakatiya might have been based on the original connection of the members of this family with that town. It is not easy to locate the region where the Kākatipura was situated. However, Parabrahma Sastri opines, "It is not impossible that the town Kakati is identical with Kandara village in the Nanded district, as the early Kakatiyas seem to have come from the Rashtrakūta kingdom."[6] Lakshminarayana Rao views that the word Kākati denotes a place which he identifies with the present village of that name situated about 12 miles north of Belgaum.[7]

The Kakatiyas of Warangal, as stated in the Bayyāraṁ tank inscription, originally belonged to some *Ratta* or *Rashtrakūta* family called *vrishni* or *vishti*.[8] But after acquiring considerable prestige they might have traced their origin from the well known Kshatriya races,viz., the solar or the lunar. This is what exactly reflected in the inscriptions of Ganapatideva and his successors where they are connected with either the solar or the lunar race. It should be noted here that the inscriptions of Ganapatideva issued after the conquest of the Velanandu Cholas refer to the solar or the lunar pedigree of the Kakatiyas.

The Garuda banner was the insignia of the Kakatiyas. *Pratāparudrīyaṁ*, the Ekamranath inscription and finally the name *Garudāṅka* Beta, unmistakably indicate that the Kakatiyas were originally having Garuda as their royal

1. H.A.S., No.13, p.97
2. Epigraphia Indica, Vol.XVIII, p.354
3. H.A.S., No.13, p.58
4. S.I.I., Vol.X, No.254
5. Kumarasvami, K., 1954 Op.cit., p.201, 223, 277 and 314
6. Epigraphia Andhrica, Vol.I, p.74
7. Sastry, P.V.P., 1978 *Op.cit.*, p.23 and also Karnataka Historical Review XIII-1, p.619
8. Epigraphia Andhrica, Vol.I, p.74

emblem.[1] Subsequently when they became subordinates of the later Chālukyas of Kalyana, they adopted *'Varāha'* as their royal emblem. About the significance of the Garuda banner of the Kakatiyas, Parabrahma Sastri observes,"It may not be out of place to consider the real cause behind their having the Garuda or eagle banner. The Polavasa chiefs were also having this symbol on their banner and they were undoubtedly the followers of Jaina persuasion. The Kakatiyas in spite of their having the Garuda symbol, seldom appear to be devotees of Vishnu. The Yaksha of Sānthinātha, the 16th Tīrthānkara is represented by the symbol of Garuda. We may not be far wrong in believing that these chiefs adopted Garuda as their family symbol, not out of their faith in the Vishnu cult, but according to their attachment to Jainism".[2]

Early Rulers:

Venna - Prola II:-

The Mangallu plates issued by the Eastern Chalukya King, Danarnava (956 A.D.) and the Bayyaram tank inscription of Kakati Mailama indicate revolutionary changes in the early history of the Kakatiyas of Warangal.[3] It is known from the latter lithic records that Venna was the founder of the Kakatiya dynasty. It is further stated that he ruled from the town called Kākatīpura on account of which his descendants came to be known as Kakatiyas. He might have flourished in 800-815 A.D. He was succeeded by Gunda I and later by Gunda II. We have no information about the political activities of these chiefs. They may be placed between 815-865 A.D. Gunda II was succeeded by Gunda III. It is known from the Mangallu plates that Gunda III accompanied his Rashtrakuta overlord, Krishna II and fought a battle against the Eastern Chalukya King, Bhima I and his son, Irimartiganda at Peruvanguru. Gunda fought with peerless ferocity and won a flashing victory. But he lost his life in the battle field. The Rashtrakuta Emperor rewarded Eriya, the son of Gunda III, with the governorship of the Koravi region for the meritorious services rendered by his father in the battle at Peruvanguru. Thus the Kakatiyas entered Andhra for the first time during the time of Gunda III as the commanders of the Rashtrakuta emperors in the 9th and 10th centuries A.D. and very soon established themselves as powerful chiefs in the *Kurravadi* region which can be safely identified with the modern Koravi region of the Warangal district. It is known from the Mangallu plates that Erra or Eriya was succeeded by Betiya, but is not mentioned in the Bayyaram tank inscription. It has been held by some that

1. Sastry, P.V.P., 1978 *Op.cit.*, p.25
2. 1978 *Ibid.*
3. 1978 Ibid., p.37.

due to reasons like disability or premature death, his name might have been omitted in the Bayyaram inscription which simply states that after Erra Pindi Gunda came to rule without stating how they were related to each other.[1]

Betiya was succeeded by Gunda IV. He is also known as Kakatya Gunda or Pindi Gunda (950-990 A.D.). It was during his time an internecine war broke out between Ammarāja-I and his step brother Dānārnava in the Eastern Chalukya Empire. The Rashtrakuta Emperor, Krishna III, not only accepted the request of Dānārnava for help but also immediately deputed his general Gunda IV already stationed in the Koravi: region to support Danarnava. With the active support extended by Guṅda IV, Dānārnava defeated Ammarāja and captured the throne of Vengi. Gunda continued to be a loyal subordinate of the Rashtrakutas till their sudden collapse in 973 A.D. The last quarter of the 10th century A.D. witnessed some remarkable changes in the political fortunes of the Deccan in general and that of Andhra in particular. The death of Dānārnava, the capture of Vengi by Jatāchöda Bhīma and the end of the Rashtrakuta domination were some of these changes. Taking the disturbed political set up into consideration, Guṅda IV availed himself of the opportunity by carving out a principality of his own at the expense of Mudigonda Chalukyas. But this did not make him an independent chief, for in 995 A.D, Chalukya Tailapa II became the overlord of the Telaṅgāṇa region. Thus the end of the Rashtrakuta subordination and the beginning of the Chalukyan domination over the Kakatiyas was witnessed by Guṅḍa IV.

Gunda IV was succeeded by Beta I. It is known from the Kazipat inscription that Beta churned the ocean of the army of the Chola King and obtained Lakshmi (victory).[2]

Beta I was succeeded by his son Prola I (1051-1076 A.D.). The Kazipet inscription of his grandson, Duggaraja, dated in 1097-98 A.D. is the main source of information for the political exploits of Prola II. It is stated that Prola set straight the affairs of Chakrakuta-*vishaya* by scoring a victory over a certain Bhadranga. He is also said to have scored a victory over the neighbouring chief Annayya, the son of Kadaparti Durga and also saw the end of the Purukuta chief by name Gonna.[3] All these military exploits were undertaken by Prola I on behalf of the Western Chalukya Emperor,

1. Epigraphia Andhrica, Vol.I, p.7
2. *H.A.S.*, No.13, p.25 Being a petty chief, Beta could not have undertaken this expedition against the Cholas independently. It is known that the Western Chalukya Āhavamalla Somāśvara-I fought a battle against the Chola king Rājādhirāja I. Beta and his general Recherla Brahma most probably participated in the war against the Cholas on behalf of their Chalukya overlord, Somesvara I. The Sanigaram epigraph, dated 1051 A.D. is the only record of this chief so far discovered.
3. Venkataramanayya, N., 1974 *Inscriptions of Andhra Pradesh, Warangal district*, p.46

Somesvara. Impressed by the meritorious services rendered by him the Emperor bestowed upon Prola I, the Anumakonda - *vishaya* as a hereditary fief.

Prola-I was succeeded by his son Beta_II. He is styled in the Hanumakonda inscription, *Śrīmaṅ Vikramachakri'* and, *Śrī Beta Maṅdalikōthama'*.[1] He was a subordinate of Tribhuvanamalla Vikramāditya-VI. Beta II was succeeded by his son Duggaraja. *Tribhuvanamalla and Chalamartigaṅda* were the titles assumed by this Chief. It is known from the Kothapalli epigraph that Prola-II managed to take over the power for himself by putting an end to Duggaraja.[2] It would thus appear that Prola II's accession to the Kakatiya throne was neither normal nor peaceful.

Prola II ruled from 1116 to 1157 A.D. The Hanumakonda inscription of Rudradeva, dated 1162-63 A.D. gives some interesting information regarding the military exploits of Prola II. It is stated that he made Chalukya Tailapadeva captive in war and afterwards set him free out of loyalty and compassion. He made Govindaraja also captive and after releasing him, Prola bestowed his Kingdom upon certain Udayāraja. It is also stated in the above epigraph that Prola-II beheaded certain Gunda, the lord of Mantrakuta. He made Edaraja flee from the battle-field in the very presence of his overlord. He also inflicted a crushing defeat upon Jagaddeva who attacked Hanumakonda.[3] The phrase *'nripeśvarapurātah'*, found in the Hanumakonda inscription, clearly shows that Prola-II achieved all the above referred victories right in the presence of his overlord, the Western Chalukya Emperor Jagademamalla II.[4]

Rudradeva (1158-1195 A.D.):

Rudradeva, the son and successor of Prola-II, was one of the greatest early chiefs of the Kakatiya dynasty. It was during his able and energetic rule the Kakatiyas asserted independence and thereby opened a new chapter in the annals of medieval Andhra. His Hanumakonda inscription of 1162-3, a legnthy document of great historical value, gives a graphic description of his military exploits. It states that he vanquished Dommarāja and conquered his town Nagara. He humbled the pride of Medarāja and also shattered to pieces the confederacy of the rival kings. He suppressed the pride of Mailigideva. He also invaded the town Vardhamānapura of Bhima, who proclaimed himself the king after the death of Tailapa. He is said to have burnt the town of Chōdoḍaya and married his daughter, Padma. Parabrahma Sastri made an extensive study of the Hanumakonda inscription of

1. Venkataramanayya, N., 1974 Ibid., No.13
2. Sastry, P.V.P., 1978 *Op.cit.*, p.46
3. Sastry, P.V.P., 1975 "Anumakonda Inscription of Kakati Rudradeva - A Review", *J.A.H.R.S.*,
4. *Ibid.*

Rudradeva and successfully indentified the various chiefs with whom Rudradeva came into conflict.[1]

Rudradeva after scoring victories over the above chiefs appears to have concentrated his attention on the conquest of the coastal Andhra region which lay between his kingdom and the sea. Some scholars are of the opinion that Rudradeva established his control over the coastal Andhra region.[2] It should be noted here that the Hanumakonda inscription which gives a graphic account about the military campaigns of Rudradeva does not make a reference to his conquest of the coastal Andhra region.[3] If at all he conquered the coastal Andhra region, it can be only after the date of this inscription.

Rudradeva was a great patron of arts and letters. The famous Thousand Pillared temple situated at the centre of the modern city of Hanumakonda was constructed during his reign. In one of the Draksharama inscriptions he is styled *vinayavibhūshana*'.[4] The authorship of the work on *Rājanīti* entitled *Nītisāra* is ascribed to him on the authority of an apocryphal verse found in one of the manuscripts of Baddena's *Nītisāramuktāvali*, but this ascription is doubtful.

Mahādeva (1195-99 A.D.):

Rudra was issueless and hence he was succeeded by his younger brother Mahādeva. We have only two inscriptions of this king, one from Sundela, dated 1197 A.D. and another a broken and undated record in the Warangal fort. Mahādevā's reign was neither glorious nor eventful. The only remarkable political event of his reign was his war with the Yādavās of Devagiri. In this encounter, Mahādeva not only suffered a crushing defeat at the hands of the Yadava king but also lost his life. The Khandavalli copper plate grant states figuratively that while plundering the enemies camp Mahadeva "slept on the two temples of the elephant stained with blood as if smeared with the red sandal of the breasts of the Goddess of Victory".[5] The Garavapadu and the Yanamadala inscriptions of Ganapatideva and the tradition preserved in the *Siddheśvaracharita* and the *Pratāpacharitra* also allude to this.[6] The death of Mahādeva and the success of the Yadavas are referred to in the Pātna inscription of Singhana II (1200-1247 A.D.) and the Paithan grant of the Yādava Rāmachandradeva.[7] But it is not clear in the present

1. *Ibid.*, p.16
2. Yazdani, G., 1960 *Op.cit.*, p.191
3. *J.O.I.*, Vol.XX, p.450
4. *S.I.I.*, Vol.IV, No.1155
5. Epigraphia Andhrica, Vol.IV, p.114
6. Epigraphia Indica, Vol.I, p.344
7. Epigraphia Indica, Vol.III, p.101 and p.341

state of our knowledge that under what circumstances Mahādeva declared war on the Yadavas of Devagiri. However, it is certain that the Yadava king did not entertain any enemity with the Kakatiyas, for it is evident from the Bahal inscription of Singhana that Jaitugi, an ocean of compassion and affection rescued Ganapatideva and made him the lord of the Andhra country.[1] The Seuna inscription, no doubt, attribute his regaining of freedom due to the compassion felt for him by the Yadava Monarch, Jaitrapāla, Sympathy and generosity may indeed have played their part, but political compulsions must have weighed with the Yadavas in setting the youthful captive at liberty. He probably desired to secure himself against an attack from the east in the event of a conflict with the Hoysalas in the South. The aggressive policy of Ballāla-II, who had already wrested from him a large part of the northern Karnataka must have made him apprehensive regarding the safety of his southern frontier.[2]

Mahādeva and Bayyāṁbika have one son called Ganapatideva, and two daughters, Melāmbika or Mailambika and Kuṅdāmbika.Mailāmbika was given in marriage to Rudra, the chief of the Natavāda family. Kundambika was given in marriage to another Rudra, most probably the son of Natavadi Buddha. Dhruvesvara *pandita* was the spritual *guru* of Mahādeva.

GANAPATIDEVA (1199-1263 A.D.)

Ganapatideva was the greatest ruler of the Kākatiya dynasty. It was during his reign that the sway of the Kākatiyās extended upto Kañchi. However, the beginning of his reign was not peaceful. The defeat and death of his father at the hands of Jaitugi and the capture of himself at Devagiri paved the way for disorders in the Kakatiya kingdom. It is known from the Palampet Pillar inscription dated 1213 A.D. that the recalcitrant nobles and the refractory subordinates rose in revolt. But Recherla Rudra *senāni*, the loyal subordinate of Ganapatideva successfully quelled the revolts and restored peace and tranquility in the realm.[3]

Ganapatideva after consolidating his position turned his attention first to the coastal Andhra region. The Kakatiya army led by Malyala Chaunda *senāni* proceeded to the island of Divi and captured it. This fact is attested by the Kondaparti inscription of Chaunda (1203 A.D.).[4] After the occupation of Divi, the Kākatiya forces penetrated deep into the Vengi region which was under the control of the Velanādu Chola Chief, Prithvīsvara. In this enterprise the Kakatiya King was supported by Tikkabhupala, the ruler of Vikramasimhapura and a certain *Mahāmandaleśvara* Bollaya of Kammanadu.[5]

---

1. Ritti, S.H., 1972 *The Seunas of Devagiri*, p.70 and also Y.Gopala Reddy, 'The Kakatiya Ganapatideva and the Yadavas of Devagiri', *J.A.H.R.S.*,Vol.XXX,P.64
2. Yazdani, G., 1960 *Op.cit.*, p.600
3. Venkataramanayya, N., 1974 *Op.cit.*, p.138 and p.199
4. Sastry, P.V.P., 1965 *Select Epigraphs of Andhra Pradesh*, p.62
5. Yazdani, G., 1960 *Op.cit.*, p.103

It appears that Prithviśvara not only faced defeat but also lost his life in the hands of Ganapatideva. In some of the inscriptions, Ganapatideva is praised as *'Prithvisvara-sirah- kanduka-krida-vinoda.'*[1] the player of the ball that is the head of Prithviśvara. Thus the coastal Andhra region, during the time of Ganapatideva became part and parcel of the Kākatiya empire.

The other important event that was witnessed in the reign of Ganapatideva was the restoration of the Teluga Choda kingdom of Vikramasimhapura to Manumasidhhi-II

Ganapatideva after establishing his authority over the coastal region naturally desired to bring Kalinga kingdom under his control. The available epigraphical evidence clearly shows that Ganapati attacked Kalinga more than once. Rajinayaka, Indulūri Sömaya and Jāyapa *senāni* played a very signifiant role in these struggles. The Upparapalli inscription[2] of 1236 A.D. states that Rājināyaka scored victories at Bokkera, killed the chief bearing the title *Godhumarati,* captured Udayagiri and put to flight certain Padiraya. Ganapatideva's expedition against Kalinga was no doubt a brilliant demonstration of his military strength exhibited by his generals like Somamantri, Rajināyaka and Jāyapa but it produced no material results. The Eastern Gangas with whom Ganapatideva must have come into conflict during the expedition soon asserted their authority and shook off all traces of his expedition in the Kaliṅga region.[3]

Ganapatideva subjugated the Kolanu chiefs.[4] He maintained cordial relations with the Yadavas of Devagiri. He even went to the extent of giving asylum to a Yadava prince by name Paramadhideva, the son of Singhana.[5]

Jatāvarman Sundara Pāṅdya, the greatest representative of the Pāṅdya dynasty, led an expedition against Manumasiddhi-II. The latter immediately appealed to Kākatīya Ganapatideva for help. Accordingly the Kākatiyas, Yadavas and a certain Bāṇa chief extended their fullest support and cooperation to Manumasiddhi II. A battle was fought at Muttukuru in 1263 A.D. In that battle Jatāvarman Sundara Pāṅdya I scored a brilliant victory over the Kakatiyas, Yadavas, the Bānās and the Telugu Chöda chief of Vikramasimhapuri. As a mark of this great victory, Jatavarman Sundara Pandya celebrated *Virabhisheka* at Nellore and Kāñchi and also issued special coins bearing the symbol of the Kakatiya boar on the obverse and the Pāṅdyan emblem of Fish on the reverse.[6] This military rebuff virtually saw the end of the active political career of Ganapatideva.

1. Sastry, P.V.P., 1978 *Op.cit.*, p.113
2. Venkataramanayya N.1974 op. cit Ins No.30
3. Itihas, Vol.III, No.2, p.19
4. Sastry, P.V.P., 1978 *Op.cit.*, p.111
5. Venkataramanayya,N., 1974 *Perur Inscriptions,* Ins.No.12
6. Sastry, P.V.P., 1978 *Op.cit.*, p.115

Ganapatideva's reign may be considered as one of the glorious periods in the history of the Kakatiyas of Warangal. His reign witnessed the rise of Pāsupata Saivism. The credit of changing the capital from Hanumakonda to Warangal also goes to him. He had no male issues and hence he nominated his daughter Rudramadevi as his heir to the Kakatiya throne.

Rudramadevi (1262-1289 A.D.):

Rudramadevi is known to history under different names,viz., Rudradevi, Rudrāṁba, Rudradeva-*mahārāja*, Rudrayyadeva-*mahārāja*, Tribhuvanādhipati- Kākatiya-Rudradeva etc.[1] The accession of Rudramadevi to the Kākatīya throne was a remarkable event in the annals of South India, for she is the first woman who ruled the Telugu speaking region under a male name. She was very fortunate to witness the excellent administrative arrangements and brilliant military conquests of her illustrious father as a co-regent from 1259 to 1260 A.D. Ganapatideva's last years, as stated above, were not peaceful. Nellore region was under the control of Vira Gandagopala, a Pāṅdyan subordinate. Bhujabala Vīranārāyana Someswara *Mahārāja* was ruling *Mulikinādu* and other adjacent regions with Valluripattana as his capital. The Kākatiya sway over the Veṅgi region also received a rebuff. Apart from these internal troubles, if the information furnished by the *Pratāpacharitra* is correct, Rudramadevi also faced a challenge from Harihara and Murārideva, the sons of Ganapatideva by his other queens. Rudramadevi, however, consolidated her position by checking the revolting nobles. She was actively assisted in this work by Jannigadeva and his brother Tripurāri,the Velama chief Prāsāditya, etc. Rudramadevi having thus proved herself a worthy daughter of a great father appropriated for herself the title enjoyed by her illustrious father, viz., *'Rāya Gaja Kesari'*.

Rudramadevi, before going to streamline the administration of the realm, faced an invasion from the Yadava king Mahādeva. But Rudramaevi fought with matchless ferocity, destroyed the Yadava army and even chased Mahadeva upto the walls of the Devagiri fort. The account of this great victory scored by Rundramadevi is supported by epigraphical evidence. The Bidar inscription[2] states that a subordinate of the Queen by name Bhairava of the Sinda family is said to have accompanied Rudramadevi in her expedition aganist the Yadava King. The existence of this record in the southern part of the Yadava empire clearly shows that not only Rudramadevi secured a victory but also annexed the Bidar region into her empire. It is likely that Mahadeva after tasting defeat might have concluded peace with the Kakatiya Queen. It may not be out of place here to state that some of the Yadava princes by name Ṣarangapanideva and Yellanadeva were ruling

1. *H.A.S.*, No.13, p.82 and p.142 and *S.I.I.*, Vol.X. No.428
2. Sastry, P.V.P., 1965 *Op.cit.*, Ins.No.21

as the subordinates of Queen Rudramadevi in the Kakatiya Kingdom. Rudramdevi also offered one of the her daughters in marriage to Yellanadeva.[1]

Rudramadevi's victory over the Yadavas of Devagiri did not restore tranquility in the Kakatiya Kingdom, for she was immediately forced to divert her attention to a revolt staged by Ambadeva - the greatest member of the Kayastha family of the Kurnool-Cuddapah regions. The Kayasthas became the subordinates of the Kakatiyas right from the time of Gangayasahini. Jannigadeva and Tripurari were some of the loyal subordinates of Ganapatideva and Rudramadevi. After Tripurari, his brother Ambadeva defied the authority of the Kakatiyas. The Tripurantakam inscription of 1250 A.D. gives a mine of information regarding the daring military exploits of Ambadeva.[2] It is stated that Ambadeva got substantial assistance from the Pandyas and Yadavas - the traditional enemies of the Kakatiyas. He become the overlord of Mulikinadu,Renadu, Pedakallu, Sakali, Eruva and Pottapinadu. He made Valluripattana his capital. Then he challenged the authority of the Kakatiya Queen, Rudramadevi who observed carefully the activities of Ambadeva decided to have a trial of strength personally with the Kayastha chief. The Chandupatla inscription, dated 1289 A.D. records the gift of land to the God Somanathadeva by a *bantu* or warrior for the merit of Rudramadevi and her general, Mallikarjuna Nayaka, both of them having attained *Sivaloka,* which indicates thier death.[3] Thus it is clear that Rudramadevi and her general along with their army fought a battle against Ambadeva and died in the battle-field. About the significance of this event, Sastry observes: "The only political disturbance perceivable in the kingdom at this time was that of Ambadeva", as can be understood from the language of the Tripurantakam record. It is quite possible that Rudramadevi in spite of her old age, led the armies against Ambadeva and met with a fatal end along with her General, Mallikarjuna Nayaka. Though not explicit, the boastful praise of Ambadeva in the inscription, *'Sarvan Andhra mahipatin rana-mukhe- jata-yaso-labdhavan'*, significantly indicates that he conquered all the kings of Andhra including the Queen.[4]

Thus the glorious reign of Rudramadevi came to an end.

Rudramadevi was married to a Chalukya prince by name Virabhadra, son of Indusekhara of the Nidadavolu branch of the Chalukyas. She had three daughters, viz., Mummadamma, Rudrama and Ruyyamma. The eldest was given in marriage to a Kakatiya prince by name Mahadeva. The second daughter was offered in marriage to the Yadava prince by name Yellanadeva

1. Epigraphia Indica, vol.III, p.101
2. *S.I.I.*, Vol.X, p.334
3. Sastry, P.V.P., 1978 *Op.cit.*, p.125
4. 1978 *Ibid.*

and the last one to Induluri Annayya.[1] Rudramadevi was succeeeded by her grandson Prataparudradeva, the son of Mahadeva and Mummadamma.

Prataparudradeva (1289-1323 A.D.):

Prataparudradeva was considered to be one of the most romantic personalities in the history of south India. He was the last great representative of the Kakatiya dynasty. He was a valiant fighter, sound administrator, and a great patron of arts. and letters. But his reign started at a very crucial and critical time, for it began immediately after the sad and sudden demise of his grand-mother, Rudramadevi in the battle-field.

Prataparudradeva, though called upon to guide the ship of the state at a very young age, set himself the task of reorganising the army, administration and fortifications. Then he turned his attention to supress the Kayastha chief Ambadeva. Knowing fully well that Ambadeva was in league with the Yadavas and the Pandyas, Prataparudradeva proceeded very cautiously to crush him. In this task he organised a three pronged attack against Ambadeva. In the first instance, he despatched to the Tripurantakam region an army under the command of Manuma Gannayya, son of Kolanu Somamantri, and his cousin Annayyadeva, son of Induluri Pedagannayya Mantri. Though we do not posess the details of the campaign, it is certain that the Kakatiya forces were successful in that quarter. The Telugu Choda Kingdom of Nellore which was under the control of Manuma Gandagopala became the target of his second expedition. The Kakatiya army under the command of Adidam Mallu defeated and killed Manuma Gandagopala and in his place a certain Madhurantaka Pottapi Choda Ranganatha was installed on the throne of the Telugu Choda Kingdom as a subordinate of the Kakatiyas. The third expedition was despatched by Prataparudradeva against the Yadavas who supported the cause of Ambadeva. The Raichur fort inscription of 1294 A.D. states that Gona Vithala, a feudatory of Prataparudradeva, captured the forts of Adavani, Tumbalam, Manuva and Haluva in the Raichur Doab. It is obvious from this epigraphical evidence that the Kakatiyas must have wrested the Krishna-Tungabhadra doab region from the Yadavas of Devagiri.

Prataparudradeva, though succeeded in defeating the Kayastha Ambadeva and his allies, could not enjoy peace for long. He was immediately forced to face the most potent external threat from the Sultans of Delhi, and as a consequence he spent the rest of his life fighting against the Muslims.

The first Muslim invasion over the Telangana was led by Allauddin Khilji in 1303 A.D. This resulted in a failure. But Allauddin Khilji in order to take revenge and to restore his fallen prestige despatched a large army

1. Ramesan, N., 1962 *Copper Plate Inscriptions of Andhra Pradesh*, Vol.I, p.109

under the command of Malik Naib Kafur. In this encounter the Muslims scored a decisive victory over the Kakatiyas. Prataparudradeva concluded peace with the deputy of Allauddin Khilji and surrendered much of his wealth and prestige. After the death of Allauddin chaotic conditions prevailed in the Delhi Sultanate. Malik Naib Kafur placed the younger son of Allauddin by name Shihabuddin on the throne of Delhi and started ruling the Kingdom as a regent on his behalf. But Malik Naib Kafur did not enjoy that status for long, and he was ultimately murdered by Qutubuddin Mubarak Shah, another son of Allauddin. Taking these conditions into consideration Prataparudradeva asserted his independence in the Kakatiya kingdom and defied the authority of Delhi. It was during this phase another expedition was sent against the Kakatiya kingdom under the command of Khusrau Khan. Prataparudradeva without offering any resistance concluded peace and finally paid the annual tribute in the form of elephants, horses, gold and precious stones.

The death of Qutbuddin Mubarak Shah saw virtually the end of the Khilji domination over the Delhi Sultanate. The Tughluqs captured power. During the period of transition Prataparudra asserted his independence and refused to pay the annual tribute. Ghiyasuddin Tughluq after consolidating his position at Delhi, sent an expendition against Warangal under the command of Ulugh Khan in 1323 A.D. This expedition was a failure. But Ghiyasuddin, being a man of strong will and determination, without wasting any time, sent another expedition against Warangal. Prataparudradeva fought like a lion against the Muslim forces with the intention of preserving the independence, integrity and honour of his subjects, people and the realm, but in vain. He became captive in the hands of the victorious Muslims who immediately decided to send him along with his family to Delhi. It is known from the Vilasa grant[1] of Prolaya Nayaka that Prataparudradeva lost his life on the banks of the river Somodbhava, i.e., river Narmada. Warangal, the capital of the Kakatiyas was occupied by the Muslims and it was renamed as Sultanpur. The Kakatiya empire became a part and parcel of the Delhi Sultanate. Thus the glory and grandeur of the Kakatiyas sunk unceremoniously in the sea of Islam.

1. Epigraphia Indica, vol.XXXII, p.248

CHAPTER-III

ARCHITECTURE

The Kakatiyas of Warangal who dominated the destinies of Andhra from the tenth to the first quarter of the fourteenth century A.D., were great builders. Rudradeva (1158-1195 A.D.) Ganapatideva (1199-1262 A.D.), Rudramdevi (1262-1289 A.D.) and Prataparudradeva (1289- 1323 A.D.), not only evinced keen interest in expansion and consolidation of the kingdom but also in the erection of secular and sacerdotal edifices. In fact, the age of the Kakatiyas of Warangal witnessed hectic building activity.

The Kakatiya temples are found at Bayyaram, Vakkalli, Bejjanki, Burugugadda, Garla, Ghanapur, Kothapalli, Katakshapur, Kondaparti, Kolanupaka, Nidikonda, Pillalamarri, Hanumakonda, Warangal, etc., and distributed throughout the length and breadth of the present Telangana region of Andhra Pradesh.

The Kakatiya temples provide a fruitful and fertile field for a student of architecture and art, not only for a critical and analytical study of the evolution of the Kakatiya architecture but also afford an opportunity to note how and where the Kakatiya architects deviated from the Late Chalukya art traditions. It should be noted here that the Kakatiya polity, society, economy, religion, architecture, art, etc., were very much influenced by the Later Chalukya ideals and institutions. In this chapter, an attempt is made to reconstruct the Kakatiya architecture and art by taking the sculptural representations into consideration.

Lethby states that "Architecture is the matrix of civilization". To such a definition, it may be added that viewed historically architecture remains as the principle, visible and material record through the ages of man's intellectual evolution. Each great cultural movement has made its own particular contribution to the art of building so that the aspirations of the people and even their way of life stand revealed in substantial form for all to see. In the medieval history of Andhra desa the ideals of man, one of the secular and sacerdotal, have found expression in numerous noble, impressive and imposing monuments. To the student the value of these monumental productions needs no emphasis, for from such achievements it is possible to reconstruct much of the past and to visualise the social, political, religious and economic conditions of the country or the region as phase succeeded phase, and one period merged into another. It may be mentioned in this connection that the outstanding quality of the Indian architecture is the spiritual content. It is thus evident that the fundamental purpose of the building art was to represent, in concrete form, the prevailing religious consciousness and the the aesthetic sentiments of the people. It is the mind materialised in terms of brick, rock or stone. The Kakatiya monuments are no excepation to this rule. Hence in the following pages a careful and analytical study of the Kakatiya sculptures is attempted with a view to reconstruct the organisation of a temple, the alignment of its various architectural adjuncts like pillared mandapas, pillars and brackets, cornices *kapotas, vimanas* or the superstructure, etc. Several scholars attempted to study the monuments as a whole but no stress was given to the sculptural representation of the monuments.[1] Thus this study, based on architectural and sculptural representation of the Kakatiyas, is the first of its kind.

Temple and Its Organisation:

Though there are countless Kakatiya temples strewn throughout the length and breadth of the present Andhra Pradesh, the sculptural representations of the same are extremely rare. But a solitary linear representation of a Kakatiya temple on the top of a pillar inscription found at a place known as Pusulur is of extreme importance. The pillar on which the above linear sketch of a Kakatiya temple (Fig.3a) is carved, contains an inscription issued by Cheraku Bollaya Reddi a subordinate of the Kakatiya Queen Rudramadevi. It is dated 1288 A.D.

The linear sketch represents the cross-section of a Kaktiya temple. It contains two chambers, i.e. *garbhagriha* and *mandapa*. Gracefully modelled *linga* and a pleasingly designed *panavatta* are noticed in the centre of the *garbhagriha*.

Nandi, in a couchant position and looking at the *linga*,is in the centre of the *mandapa*. A stepped *sikhara* with a bulbous finial is shown on the top of the *garbhagriha*. The presence of a linga on a *panavatta* and the couchant *Nandi* show that it is a Siva temple.

The Kakatiya temples, exactly tallying with the above referred linear representation, are found in plenty. The best examples of this type are noticed in the centre of the Warangal fort, Panugal (Chayasomesvara temple), Ghanpur, Dharmasagar, Kanapur, Nagunur, Madikonda, Matedu, Kondaparti, Upparapalli and Palampet, distributed in Warangal, Nalgonda, Karimnagar and other districts of the present Andhra Pradesh.[2]

1. Sharma, M.R.K., 1972 Temples of Telingana: The Architecture, Iconography and Sculpture of Chalukya and Kakatiya Temples.
2. Gopala Reddy, Y., 1980 "The exterior architectural and Artistic embellishment of the Kakatiya Temples" *Itihas, Vol.III*, No.1,Pl.VIII, Fig.16

It may be not out of place here to mention the other types of Kakatiya temples. It will also help us to have a comprehensive idea about the organisation of the temples, its various component parts and finally the type of ground plans adopted by the architects of the period under consideration.

The Kakatiya temples are of medium size, except the Rudresvara temple at Palampet.[1] They are devoid of excessive ornamentation, both on the interior and exterior. The following are the principal types of the Kakatiya temples.

Type I : A temple of this type has *garbhagriha* and *maṇḍapa* only.Examples of this type are found at Palampet, Panugal, Ghanpur, Warangal fort etc. The liner sketch found on the top of the Pusulur Pillar inscription also falls under this type.

Type II : It is just like the above, but in front of the *aṅtarāla* a *sabhā-manḍapa* or pillared hall is additionally attached.

Examples: The Vishṇu temple, the Jaṅgamesvaraguḍi, the Rāma-gudi and the Vīrabhadreśvara temple in the Warangal fort. The Śiva and Vishṇu temples at Madikonda and Matedu are also included under this type.

Type III : Trikūtālaya or triple-shrined: These are the most popular and common type noticed in the temples of our period. In this type, three shrines of similar dimension having *garbhagriha* and *antarāla* are arranged round a common *navaranga*. The temples of this type are found at Warangal, Katakshapur, Kondaparti, Kothapalli, Manthani, Garla, etc.

Type IV : A temple of this type has cruciform ground plan. The important feature of this temple is that the *sabhā- mandapa* is provided with three entrances. These entrances are normally in the form of projected porches having long flights of steps. Excellent examples of this type are noticed at Pālampet, Jakaram and Ghanpur.[2]

Type V: *Pañchāyatana* type. The structural scheme of temple of this type is very interesting. It has five shrines and they are arranged two each on the eastern and western ends and one on the north side respectively. They are all connected to a common *navaranga*. Only one temple of this type is noticed so far and it is found at Ramanujapuram in the Mulugu taluk of Warangal district.

The Kākatiya architects took very keen interest in the spatial distribution of the various architectural adjuncts in and around the main temple and within the *prākāra* wall. The temples,in most of the cases, are provided with the *prākāra* walls. These *prākāras* are adorned with ordinary and pillared entrances. Subsidiary shrines of various dimensions and sizes

---

1. Sharma, M.R.K., 1972 *Op.cit.*,PL.22
2. Rama Rao, M., 1966 *Select Kakatiya Temples*, Pl.XXXIII, Fig.1 and XXXIX, Fig.1

are judiciously distributed round the main temple complex. The temples that are found at Palampet, Pȧnugal, Ghanpur and Manthani are the best examples of this type. But the sculptural representation illustrating all the above temple types are yet to be discovered.

Pillared Mandapas:

Erecting pillared *maṇḍapas* very near to the main temple complex and also within the *prākāra* wall was started by the Ikshvākus in the Trans-Kṛishṇa valley.[1] This tradition was not only followed but also perfected by the Pallavas, Cholas, later Chālukya, the Kākatiyās and the Vijayanagara rulers.These pillared pavilions were used as *kalyāṇa-maṇḍapas* to celebrate the marriage of the divine couple once in a year. It is probable that the kings might have also used these huge pillared pavilions for purposes of public use. However, they become architectural adjuncts and ornamental appendages of the imposing temples.

The Kākatiya architects also showed interest in erecting impressive pillared *mandapas*. The classic examples of this type are found very near to the main temple complexes at Hanumakonda, Ainole, Palampet and Ghanpur.[2] The architects of this period, in this connection, were very much influenced by the Later Chalukya art tradition. The Kalleśvara temple at Bagali and the Mahādeva temple at Ittagi are having pillared halls.[3] The Kakatiya pillared-halls, like the Later Chālukya ones, are peristylar in exterior and possess intricately designed ceilings.

The sculptural representations of the pillared-halls are extremely scarce. But the sculptured panel unearthed in the excavations conducted in the neighbourhood of the Sāmbhuni-gudi in the Warangal fort is of inestimable value in this connection (Fig.36). It represents a multi-storeyed pillared-hall. The celling of each storey is supported by a row of pillars, exquisitely designed. The surmounting part of the pillared-hall is adorned by a bulbous member with *kalasa* or finial. Beautiful representation of dancing girls are shown in the centre of each storey and on the pillars. Another representation of multi-storeyed mantapa with three *tala* is noticed from the same place. (P1.I).

Another extremely interesting three storeyed pillared *maṇḍapa* is found carved on one of the pillars supporting a *maṇḍapa* at Dharmapuri (Fig.3c). In this case the *Kapöta* or the cornice is shown projecting considerably and it has a curved termination. This type of cornice is conspicuously absent in the first example. Another peculiar feature of this example is the presence

1. Sarma, I.K., 1982 *The Development of Early Saiva Art and Architecture*, p.104
2. Rama Rao, M., 1966 *Op.cit.*, Pl.VII, Fig.2
3. Rea, A., 1896 *The Chalukyan Architecture* and also Brown, P., 1956, *Indian Architecture (Buddhist and Hindu)*, p.154

of lateral brackets under the massive eaves. A detailed discussion regarding these brackets is attempted elsewhere in this chapter. Multi- armed Siva is sculputured in the centre of the lower storey. On either side of the outer periphery of the pillared hall, are carved human figures in various postures and positions.

A careful comparative study of the extant examples of the pillared halls with that of the sculptural representations of the same, will enable us to state that there is sharp a difference between these two. The extant examples that are noticed at Ainole, Ghanpur and Palampet are devoid of storeyed arrangements. They are further provided with flat roofs. It is not too difficult to find the reasons for the absence of the multi-storeyed pillared-halls. It is possible that they might have been destroyed by the Muslims in the course of their invasion. It is known that between 1303 A.D. to 1323, the Muslims invaded the Kakatiya kingdom not less than five times. However, a solitary storeyed pillared *maṇḍapa* is standing very near to the *Śaṁbhuni-guḍi* in the centre of the Warangal fort. The value of these sculptural representations of the pillared-halls should not be undermined, for it is with the help of these sculptural representations, we are in a position to state that the Kākatīya architects constructed not only imposing temples but also impressive multi-storeyed pillared- halls.

Pillars and Brackets:

The pillar is the regulator of the whole composition of a building. James Fergusson rightly observes: "If any one wished to select one feature of Indian architecture, which would illustrate its rise and progress, as well as its perfection and weakness, there are probably no objects more suited for this purpose than these *stambhas* or the free-standing pillars".[1] Percy Brown also opines: "The proportions of the buildings were determined by a unit, this unit being the height of the monolithic shaft of the pillar in the interior, which in its turn, depended on the greatest length of stone which was economically possible to extract from the quarry. As all parts of the temple were proportioned strictly according to rule, each member being fixed in relation to all the others, the pillar shaft served as a standard for the purpose of measurement, and the entire composition was therefore executed to that scale".[2]

It is thus evident that a pillar or *stambha* is one of the most important architectural and ornamental members of a temple. The height, grandeur and the loftiness of a temple mainly depends upon its pillars, *upapiṭha, adhishṭhāna*, etc. The pillars support the superstructure of the *ardhamandapa, sabhā-manḍapa* and the pillared pavilions of single or multistoried ones, placed

---

1. Fergusson, J., 1891 *The History of Indian and Eastern Architecture*, p.277.
2. Brown, P., 1956 *Indian Architecture* (Buddhist and Hindu), p.154

inside and outside the *prākāra* walls of a temple. They are the principal features of the temple interior. They will give not only depth to the interior of temple itself, but also provide suitable place and ample opportunity for the sculptor to exhibit his skill and imagination in carving decorative motifs and figure sculptures. One of the prettiest parts of a temple is the *Bhuvaneśvari* which envelops the central bay of the *sabhā-maṇḍapa*. The shape. size, organisation and the decorative scheme of it depends very much upon the style of the inter-columnation of the pillars .

The sculptural representation of pillars are overwhelming. They are found in differnet places mainly serving ornamental purposes. They are shown supporting the superstructure of the ornamental niches.[1] Sometimes, sculptors used them judiciously for the distribution of the figurative space. In this connection they are employed to separate the floral and figurative sculptures.[2] Both plain and ornamental pillars are found used in plenty on the sculptured panels under consideration. The pillars represented in the sculptured panels are technically called 'Pilasters'. However, they will give a lot of information regarding shape, composition and decoration of the pillars that were used in the temple proper.

The sculptural representation of pillars (pilasters) are normally attached ones, whereas the free-standing pillars are detached. In style, technique, composition and in general shape both display close resemblance. Base, shaft, circulr or wheel-like moulding, *abacus* and the four-square bracket are the principal component parts of a pillar. The shaft is the most important part of the pillar. It is this part that normally determines the height of the pillar, which in its turn decides the very height of the roof, the *ardha-mandpa,* sabhā- maṇḍapa), etc. The shaft has four principal parts, viz., the lower rectangular prism-like section, octagonal portion, central square block and finally the circular portion with a tapering top. It is generally on the base, the lower rectangular section and square block of the shaft, and on the circular wheel-like moulding the sculptors exhibited their skill in carving geometrical, floral and figural motifs.

In workmanship and artistic effect, the Kakatāya pilasters and pillars far surpass the pilasters and pillars of both north and south India, probably with the exception of those of the Höyasāla temples. They possess beautiful lustrous polish and exhibit the greatest possible exuberance of varied designs and motifs boldly designed and finely executed to the minutest detail. It may not be out of place to state here that Alexander Rea, Colonel Meadows Taylor and Percy Brown are of the opinion that these pillars were actually turned on a lathe. But this view has been rejected by G. Yazdani who states: "Some authorities are of the opinion that the pillars were actually

1. Rama Rao, M., 1966 *Op.cit.*, Pl.III, Fig.1, Pl.IV, Fig.1 and Pl.XVII, Fig.2
2. 1966 Ibid.

turned on a lathe in order to secure this polished surface. This may be true, but the pillars of the main hall of the rock-hewn shrine, Kailasa, which shine like a mirror, cannot have been turned on a lathe, the temple being monolithic. The fact is that the craftsmen of the Deccan had acquired consummate skill both in carving and polishing stone from the early centuries of the Christian era onwards. The sculptures on some pillars are sharp and crisp as if they were only finished yesterday".[1] It is to be noted in this connection that the miniature replicas of the main pillar types used as ornamental pilaster motifs profusely on the exterior of the *kakshāsana*, are arranged on the half walls of the *sabhā- maṇḍapa* of the Kakatiya temples. Further the structural ornamental pilasters *(kudya-stambhas)* employed to enhance the decorative effect of the *garbhagṛiha* and *aṇtarāla* doorways, are simply the true reproductions of the free-standing pillars that are supporting the roofs of the *ardha-maṇḍapas* and *sabhā- maṇḍapas*. The *kakshāsana* slabs and the door-jambs, being massive, monolithic and heavy, cannot have been turned on a lathe. Hence, it is reasonable to assume that the Later Chalukya, the Hoysāla and the Kakatiya pillars were the products of a long, continuous and hard earned consumate skill of the Deccan architects in cutting, carving and polishing noticed right from the early centuries of the Christian era.[2] Yazdani speaks of the polish which can be achieved by differnt process other than lathe turning. But by turnning on lathes, geometrical precision is obtained to the various decorative motifs like the moulding etc. of the pillar.

The other important feature closely ralated to the pillars and pilasters is the brackets. A careful examination of the pilasters represented in the sculptured panels, show that they are invariably provided with the brackets. They serve, only in sculptured panels, as ornamental appendages. Two types of brackets are noticed in the sculptural representations. The first type represents the decorated architectural pieces (lateral brackets) and the second type represents the figural representations in the form of human, animal of mythical animal (vyala). A sculptural representation of a bracket adorned with vyāla figures can be noticed on a slab in the Warangal fort sculptures (Fig.3d). These brackets are not only found in the sculptural representations but also in the temples and *tōraṇāas*.

The decorated architectural bracket which looks like a *cyma recta* in section is not the invention of the Kakatīya architects. The early Chalukya architects were the first to use it. It is found on the top inner edges, supporting the massive coping stone of a gateway located in front of the Konti-gudi group of temples at Aihole.[3] The Later Chalukya architects also

---

1. Yazdani, G., 1952 *History of the Deccan, Fine Arts,* Vol. I, p.23
2. *Itihas,* Vol.II, No.1, p.132
3. *Ibid.*

used these brackets to support the massive architraves of the gateways. An excellent example of this type is found at Kolanupaka. This is in the form of a lion bracket.[1] From the Later Chālukyās, the Kākatīyās inherited the tradition of constructing gateways and adorning the same with lateral lion brackets. For the Kakatiya gateways that are found at Indresam, Ainole and Warangal[2] these brackets are arranged on the outer side and are shown springing from the shoulders of the pillars. The lower end of the bracket is fixed to the pillar whereas the upper end is fixed to the architrave. These brackets not only increase the beauty of the tōranās but also give the required architectural stability to the whole conception, As the toranas are top heavy, the architects might have thought it better to introduce these lateral brackets to provide additional support to the vertical uprights (pl.2).

The human or animal *vyāla* brackets are not only found in the miniature sculptural representations[3] but also in the temple proper. They are normally arranged under the massive eaves of the *sabhā-maṇḍapa*. They are meant to serve both ornamental and architectural purposes. As the roofs of the *sabhā-maṇḍapa* are massive and projecting considerably, they require additional support to keep them intact. In this case the *Vyāla*-brackets served an architectural purpose. Further these brackets are gracefully designed and beautifully modelled to provide added elegance to the exterior of the temple. The main temple at Ghanpur, the Rudresvara temple at Palampet and the Svayambhu temple at Warangal are adorned with these *Vyāla* bracket figures. It is of considerable interest to state here that in some cases, besides lateral and *Vyāla* brackets, the human figures in various postures and positions are also used to serve the purpose of brackets. These female figures, known as *Madanikas,* like the *Vyāla* figures, are arranged under the massive roofs of the *sabhā-maṇḍapas* and spring from the shoulders of the pillars arranged on the dwarf wall. Excellent examples of this type are found at Palampet and Ghanpur.[4] It appears that Kakatiya architects, in this connection, drew inspiration and guidance from the Later Chalukya architects.[5]

In Indian architecture, the temples are divided into different styles like Nagara, Dravida and Vesara with a number of sub-types like Bhūmija etc. In dividing the temples into various types, the shape of the Vimana viz., parts of the sanctum from the *ahishtāna* to the kalasa are taken into consideration. The portion above the roof of the sanctum forming the

1. Sarma, M.R.K. 1972 *Op.cit.,* p.178 and also *Itihas,* Vol.II, No.1, p.154
2. Murthy, S.G.K., 1964 *The Sculpture of the Kakatiyas,* Figs.42, & 43 and also Sharma,M.R.K.,*Op.cit.,* Pl.61
3. Murthy, S.G.K.,1964 *Op.cit.,* Figs.45b and 45c
4. Sharma, M.R.K., 1972 *Op.cit.,* Pl.55 and also Gopala Reddy, Y., "The Madanikas of Palampet", *J.O.I.,* 1974, p.219
5. Gopala Reddy, Y., 1974 "The Madanikas of Palampet", J.O.I., p.219

superstructure is known as sikhara. Often the shape of the sikhara is taken as the criterion in the identification of the style of the temple as Nagara, Dravida, Vesara etc.

Sikhara or the Superstructure :

The sikhara is that portion of the temple which is normally found on the top of the *garbhagriha*. It is generally square on plan and diminishing in size as it goes up. Sculptural representations depicting various types of sikharas are found on the exterior and interior walls, on the pillars, *kakshāsana* slabs and in individual panels. These miniature sikhara models are valuable guides for us to know the various types of Kakatiya sikharas and the nature of their composition and organisation. The following are the representative types of the Kakatiya sikharas.

Nagara Vimana:

In this variety, a *Nagara vimāna* of five, seven, or nine *talas* is represented. It contains a conical central offset surmounted by an *amalasārika* and *kalasa* or finial. It is observed that in some cases the conical central band is decorated with creeper designs. It appears that the Kākatiya artists preferred to present a single spire or mono- spire, known in the *Vāstuśāstra* as *Latina* on the top of a *stambhika* in the *salilantaras* of the exterior walls of the temples.[1] The *venu-kosa* of the *vimanas* is decorated with wedge-shaped *mālās*. This type of *Vimāna* is noticed on top of the ornamental niches of the Thousand Pillared temple at Hanumakonda.[2]

Bhūmija Vimāna:

This variety represents the Kakatiya version of Bhumija vimana.[3] It has been suggested that a "*Bhūmija sikhara* consists of a storied arrangement of (Latina shaped) *kūtas* or *sringas* placed over miniature *stambhas,* arranged in rows, creating an illusion of vertically thrown necklaces of gigantic beads (*śringānāṁ mālika kramah*). There is no *venukosa* of the *Nagara* form but the *madhyalata* receives a strong central emphasis in the shape of a *mala*".[4] A miniature model of this type is represented on the top of a niche located on the left side of the *antarāla* of the Gautamisvara temple at Manthani.[5] It is a three-storied *Bhūmija vimāna*. The *urah- śringās* are shown on either side of the *mula- sringa,* which contains two ornamental *stambhikas* canopied by a *saurasena* arch with a *kirtimukha* at the apex. A human figure standing

1. *Itihas,* Vol.VIII, NO.1, p.14
2. Rama Rao, M., 1966 *Op.cit.*, Pl.XXXIV, Fig.1
3. *Itihas,* Vol.VIII, No.1, p.17, Fig.21
4. Dhaky, M.A., 1977 *The Indian Temples in Karnataka Inscriptions and Architecture,* p.18
5. *Itihas,* Vol.VIII, No.1, Fig.21

in *samapada-sthanaka* posture is shown in the centre of the niche. This *Bhūmija* model departs from the normal type in one respect, i.e., the *kūta-stambhas* or the *sringa- stambhas* which are conspicuous by their absence. But this type of *vimāna* is somewhat akin to the *Bhūmija vimāna* that is found on the top of the *garbhagriha* of the Mūlasankareśwara temple at Turuvekere which was constructed in the 13th century A.D.[1]

Dravida Vimana:

Miniature models of *Dravida vimāna* (storeyed pyramidal *vimanas*) are found represented on the projections and in the *salilantarās* of the exterior walls of the temples, on the exterior of the *kakshāsana* slabs and on the top of the *deva-koshthas*.[2] A very interesting model is represented on the top of a niche in the Thousand-Pillared temple at Hanumakonda.[3] It represents an *eka-tala* type of Dravidian Vimāna. It has a shorter *griva* surmounted by a cupola formed sikhara. The cupola is adorned with prominent *cyma reversa* mouldings. The recesses on either side of the *grīva* contain short pilasters.

Excellent miniature models of this type are also found on the exterior walls of the Kakatiya temples found at Palampet and Nagulapadu. *Dvitala Dravida vimāna* with a prominent *grīva* is noticed at Nagulapadu. It contains a *kapōta* ornamented with *kudu* arches. It may be stated here that the convention of decorating the exterior walls of the temples with the *Dravida vimana* models is also followed by the later Chalukya architects. This is very well illustrated by the Kalideva temple at Bagali, Tārakeśvara temple at Hangal, Siddheśvara temple at Haveri, Mallesvara temple at Kikkeri, Tripurāantakeśvara temple at Baligamve and the Chennakesava temple at Marale.[4]

Vesara Vimana:

This is a very interesting model wherein the *Nagara* and *Dravida* vimana models are harmoniously blended. An excellent example of this type is represented on the central offset of the east wall of the Surya shrine in the Thousand Pillared temple at Hanumakonda.[5] In this example the lower section represents a meticulously modelled *eka-tala Dravida vimāna*. The first *tala* has a row of pilasters with lotus designs in the recesses and a projecting *kapota*. There is a wide *grīva* crowned by a combination of three *ayatasra Dravida sikharas* with a row of three *kalasas*. The central facing side of the cupola is very gracefully decorated with *simha-lalata* gable. The

1. Dhaky, M.A., 1977 *Op.cit.*, Fig.32
2. Sharma, M.R.K., 1972 *Op.cit.*, Pl.20 and also *Itihas*, Vol.VIII, No.1, Fig.18
3. *Itihas*, Vol.VIII, NO.1, p.17
4. Dhaky, M.A., 1977 *Op.cit.*, Figs.2,3,4,6,8,15,22, & 23
5. *Itihas*, Vol.VIII, No.1, Fig.28

venu-kosa of this part of superstructure is adorned with wedge-shaped *mala* - the characteristic feature of the *Nagara vimana.* Above this section are shown again three *vimana* models standing on pilasters. The central one which is the replica of the lower composite model stands on double pilasters. The *vimana* models which are shown on either side of the central one represents a cirular *Nagara vimana* of the Latina type. In this *vimana* model the Kakatiya architects ingeniously combined the *Nagara* and *Dravida vimana* types. The whole composition is canopied by an over-hanging cornice, the lower edge of which is decorated with semi-circular and triangular elevations. Over the whole range of the Kakatiya *vimanas* this occupies a unique place for its composite nature. A *vimana* of a *misraka* class, showing the combination of vertical and horizontal *Dravida* and *Nagara kutas* are represented on the walls of the Kalesvara temple at Hirehadagalli.[1] It is a crisply carved model of a three storied *Dravida vimana* with the usual *Dravida karna-kutas* and the *bhadra-sālās,* but the *kuṭas* flanking the *salas* are of the *Nagara* class.

Stepped Pyramidal Vimana:

This type of *vimāna* deviates from the *Nagara* and *Dravida* vimānas. An excellent linear sketch of this is found on the top of the beginning of an inscription found at Pusuluru. In this case the *vimana* has four stepped bands, diminishing in size as they go up. There is a deep recess in between these bands. Every band has a slanting termination. The surmounting portion of the *vimāna* is occupied by a bulbous dome and a *kalasa.*

Another interesting variety of this type is found represented on the exterior of an *āsanapattika* in a temple located very near to the main temple-complex at Palampet.[2] In this case the *vimana* is composed of six stepped pyramidal tiers. The lower edges of these tiers are decorated with graceful triangular projections. The *vimana* is surmounted by an *amalasārika* and a *kalasa*). The most interesting part of this *vimana* is a central conical band which runs vertically from bottom to top. The Kakatiya architects maintained a judicious balance between the horizontal and vertical patterns. The *amalasārikas* and the central vertical band which are prominently shown in this example are conspicuously absent in the above example.

It is thus evident from the above discussion that the sculptural representations of the miniature models of the *vimānās* are varied in nature, composition and in general lay-out. It appears that the Kakatiya architects showed insatiable curiosity and interest in adapting various types of *vimānās.* The *Dravida, Nagara* and the stepped pyramidal are of the principle types that are found in the sculptural representations.

---

1. Dhaky, M.A., 1977 *Op.cit.*, Fig.48
2. *Itihas,* Vol.VIII, No.1, Fig.28

We may now proceed to examine the structural representations of the *vimānās* of the Kākatiya temples that are found above the *garbhagrihas*.

The *Dravida* or the pyramidal *vimāna* type is noticed on top of the temples found at Palampet, Ghanpur, Warangal, etc.[1]

The Palampet example is the most massive and imposing one. Each *tala* is composed of *kūtas* standing on a row of *stambhikas*. It is constructed with bricks and fine mortar, apparently to reduce the weight of the *vimana*. The Ghanpur and Warangal examples are constructed with finely dressed stone slabs, but not with bricks. As the size of these *vimānas* are very small and intended to adorn the *garbhagriha* of the subsidiary shrines, stone was used. All these *vimanas* are surmounted by bulbous dome-like members, but the *kalasas* are missing.

The *Nagara* and *Bhumija* structural examples are also found in the Kakatiya temples. Excellent examples of this type are found at Ghanpur, Warangal, Pillalamarri, Nizamabad etc. Vertical arrangement of the *urah-sringas*, strong central conical band, i.e., *rah-paga*, and the flattened *amalasārika* on top are some of the principal features of these *vimānās*.[2] It is very interesting to note that in all these cases a miniature ornamental niche is arranged at the base of the central offset. Inside these niches are carved miniature *Nagara vimana* standing on a slender *stambhika* and dancing human figures in various postures and positions.

The stepped *vimanas* are found on the temples that are located at Nagunur, Warangal, Panugal, Palampet and Rāmānujapuram. In the sculptural representations and in the actual structural examples, two types of this variety are noticed. In the first type the *vimana* is simply composed of stepped pyramidal tiers, surmounted by a bulbous dome with a *kalasa*. Examples of this type are noticed at Nagunur, Warangal, Panugal, Ramanujapuram, etc.[3] The presence of a strong central conical band and *amalasārika* with a *kalasa* are noticed in the second type. These are absent in the first type. Examples of this type are found at Palampet and Nizamabad.

The composite type, a combination of *Nagara and Dravida vimanas*, is found only in the sculptural representations but not in actual specimens.

Kapota or Cornice:

The *kapota* or cornice normally represents that particular part of the roof which projects beyond the walls of the *ardhamandapa*, *sabhā-mandapa*, *garbhagriha* and *antarāla* walls.

1. Rama Rao, M., 1966 *Op.cit.*, Pl.XVI, XXXV, Fig.2 and XXXVI, Fig.1
2. 1966 *Ibid*, Pls.XXXVII, XLI
3. 1966 *Ibid*, Pls.VIII, Fig.1, XIII, Fig.2, XXXVIII and also *Itihas*, Vol.VIII, No.1, Fig.16

The sculptural representations of the *kapota* are extremely rare and those that are represented are not in a position to give the correct idea of the same. Both short and projected *kapotas* are noticed. In the first case it has foliating edges and decorated with narrow chanelled grooves. A slight variation of this type is noticed in some other representations. In this case the facing edge of the *kapota* is decorated with graceful drop designs whereas its underside is decked with a series of lotus pendants.[1] The second type of *kapota* is a projected one. An excellent example of this type is noticed in the miniature pillared-mandapa represented on one of the pillars at Dharmapuri. In this case the *kapota* is shown not only projecting considerably from the pillars supporting it but also is curved in section (cyma recta). But the patterns used to decorate its underside are not clear.

A close examination of the actual temples enable us to state that the *kapotas* of the *ardha-mandapas* and *mandapas* received special emphasis in the hands of the Kakatiya architects. They are shown projecting considerably from the body of the temple. In some cases they are shown projecting more than four feet from the temple. It contains as many projections as there are on the *adhishthāna* below. Its underside is divided into various compartments by introducing horizontal and vertical rafters. The underside of the rafters and the edges of the cornice are decorated with rows of hanging lotus buds. In some cases, it appears, the underside is also painted. According to some writers, traces of paintings are still intact in the temples at Ghanpur and Palampet.[2] But after all, they may not be actual paintings but the traces of natural colour of the sand- stone and the action of the water on it.

It is thus evident from the above discussion that the sculptural representations are of immense value for the reconstruction of architectural styles of a given period. This further supplements the information gathered from the actual monuments. Sometimes we way get even new information which the actual monuments fail to supply. For example the composite *vimana* models (combination of *Dravida* and *Nagara* specimens) represented on the top of the ornamental niches, are not found in the actual monuments.

---

1. Murthy, S.G.K., 1964 *Op.cit.*, Figs. 45b and 45c
2. Rama Rao, M., 1966 *Op.cit.*, Pls.XVI, XVII, XXXV and also Sharma, M.R.K., 1972, *Op.cit.*, Pl.55

CHAPTER-IV

ART

From the beginnigs of the Indian art, a close association between religion and art is clearly noticeable. Grunwedel observes "The most important basis for the development of an independent art among any people lies in its religion."[1] The religious character, so deeply rooted in the national life of the Indian races, has also continued to be the guiding principle in their art."[2]

Unless one is unbiased and has a clear vision of Indian thought, religion, culture and tradition, a proper appreciation of Indian art is difficult. Vincent Smith,[3] an outstanding historian in his charcteristic style, while commenting on the image of Natarāṛa from Ceylon remarked "If it could be freed from the horrible deformity of the extra arms, it might receive almost unqualified praise, but the monstrosity of the second left arm drawn across the breast and calling for the surgeon's amputating knife to remove the diseased growth, spoils an otherwise elegant and admirable work."[4] It is apparent that he had only a superficial knowledge of religion and most importantly the Indian culture. The highest cultural achievement among the races of the world is the Indian dance and its varied forms. Right from the Harappan times they have imprinted this form of culture on any mallaeble media on which their hands could be laid. The so-called 'monstrous' form of Natarāja is nothing but their inherent predilection of depicting a dance pose. This may be the reason why this particular form of Siva was popularly known as "The king of the dancers". In order to show the swirling and swaying movements and conventionalised dance gestures, this is the most ingenious invention of any Indian artist. If the artist intended to depict each pose separately, he had to model not one, but several images of Nataraja. Here it may be mentioned that one of the favourite themes of the Indian or the Kakatiya artist is to carve out three or four dancers in one. The intention was to picturise the dramatic and rhythmic movements

---

1. Banerjea, J., 1956 *The Development of Hindu Iconography* (Second Edition), pp.2-3.
2. 1956 *Ibid.*
3. 1956 *Ibid.*
4. Gangoly, O.C., 1957 *Indian Arts Heritage*, p.8.

of the dancer, at the same time depicting as many *karanas* and *angaharas* as possible.

The ambition of the Indian aritst is to realise something beyond human perception which is eternal and infinite. His main endeavour is to suggest something sublime and subtle but never to glorify bodily curves and mundane perfections of physical forms.[1] Max Muller noticed "The idea of the beautiful in nature did not exist in the Hindu mind; they never excelled either in sculpture or painting."[2] The idea of Max Muller's beauty may be a three dimensional photograph of human body or the beautiful nature. Havel who was probably the first European to speak about Indian art with a proper insight observes that "the basic principle of Indian philosophy is to regard anything we see in nature as transitory and illusive phenomena", and declares that "the only reality is the divine essence or spirit."[3] Throughout the ages the Indian artist believed that the highest type of beauty must be to visualise in mind but not to picturise the human and natural forms that are before the physical eye.[4] According to Havell, the basic elements of the Indian art are idealism, mysticism, symbolism and finally transcendentalism.[5] Indian sculpture is a bridge between transcendental and phenomenal, between cosmic and human.[6] According to the Buddhist text *Saddharma Paundarika,* "...... the image as such is of no value. All depends on what he does who looks at it, what is expected of him (on looker) is an act of contemplation (*Yoga*) such that he sees before him .... the whole person of Buddha".[7]

This is regarding the divine images. Apart from these the Indian artist has shown as much enthusiasm and knowledge while depicting the secular figures. James Fergusson, an outstanding authority on Indian architecture wrote "When Hindu sculpture first dawns upon us in the rails of Bodhgaya and Bārhut, 250-200 B.C., it is thoroughly original, absolutely without a trace of foreign influence, but quite capable of expressing its ideas, and of telling its story with a distinctness that never was surpassed, at least in India.[8] Some animals, such as monkeys and deers are better represented there than any sculpture known in any part of the world".[9] A thorough knowledge of an artistic anatomy and the nature is no doubt the highest

1. Havell, E.B., 1908 *Indian Sculpture and Painting,* p.25.
2. Gangoly, O.C., 1957 *Op.cit.*, p.4.
3. Havell, E.B., 1908 *Op.cit.*, P.24.
4. 1908 *Ibid*, p.25.
5. 1908 *Ibid*.
6. 1908 *Ibid*.
7. Radhakamal Mukarjee, 1965 *Cosmic Art of India,* p.4.
8. Gangoly, O.C., 1957 *Op.cit.*, p.9.
9. 1957 *Ibid*.

accomplishment of all the good sculptors and painters.[1] The Indian artist's ideal of manly or womanly beauty set before himself was not represented by a Rajput warrior but by the divine Buddha, Krishna or Śiva. His ideal of female beauty was not seen in the most beautiful of the Indian women, but in the Goddess Lakshmi, Pārvati, Saraswati and the heavenly nymphs.[2]

Survey of Pre-Kakatiyan Sculpture:

Before discussing the art of the Kakatiyas, a survey of earlier periods is necessary to trace the evolutionary stages and also to evaluate the characteristics of Kakatiya Art. The Andhra Buddhist art of Amaravati - Nāgārjunakonda, of the early phase of Buddhism is mainly symbolic which slowly gives way to a narrative style in order to convey the message of the Buddha like the modern cinema. A scene is an episode depicted in a panel finds its continuation in the next panel. This becomes necessary for depicting the life story of Buddha or to narrate the important *jātaka* tales. The Buddhist artists understood that visualization of episodes created a lasting effect on the minds of the common folk. However, some important events in the life of the Buddha such as the Birth, Renunciation, Enlightenment, *Dharmachakra Pravartana,* and *Mahā Parinirvāna* are shown in disconnected panels. Whenever a particular episode is to be visualized, it is represented in a series of panels and when an event is to be portrayed it was shown in a single narrative panel. For instance, the *Māndhata, Champeya, Sibi, Kinnera Jāataka* tales have been depicted in serialised panels. Mention may be made of *Mahābhinishkramana* seen at Nāgājunakonda and Amarāvati. At Amarāvati, Yashodhara and Rahula are in deep sleep and Siddhārtha peeps through the window to have a last glance at his beloved wife Yasodhara and the child.[3] That the event occurred during midnight is indicated by a torch in the hands of an attender. This is one of the most magniifcient pathetic portraitures of snapping the bond of love. At Nāgārjunakonda we have a representation of the return of the horse, *Kaṅtaka,* to Suddhodhana's palace at Kapilavastu. The horse genuflects at the feet of Yasodhara to convey its helplessness, Yasodhara in a chastising mood and heart broken Suddhodhana restraining Chenna's further narration of the great departure are noteworthy.[4]

The caves at Moghalrajapuram, Akkanna-Madanna at Vijayawada and Ananthasayi cave at Undavalli are probably the earliest Hindu cave temples in Andhra Pradesh. In cave No 4 at Moghalrajapuram the narrative panels in the upper square portion of the pillars carry medallions depicting

1. Havell, E.B., 1908 *Op.cit.,* p.32.
2. Radhakamal Mukerjee, 1965 *Op.cit.,* p.7.
3. Sitapati, P., & Krishna Sastry,V.V., 1980 *New Satavahana Sculptures from Andhra Amaravati,* p.8,pl.3.
4. Ramachandra Rao, 1956 *The Art of Nagarjunakoṇḍa,* p.128. p.XLVII.

Gajendramöksha and *Puthana Samhara.*[1] In cave 5 at Moghalrajapuram, the projecting pilaster supporting the facade has the figure of a *Pūrnaghata* tied with garlands and foliage emanating from its mouth.[2] Almost similar *Pūrnaghatas* are found in the later cave temples at Ellora and Aurangabad and also in the early Brahmanic temples at Aihole. The *Malavahakas* found in these caves as also the *Hamsas* are the echoes of earliest Buddhist representation of Amaravati and Nārjunakoṇḍa. The architectural style of the cave temples of Vijayawada, with contiguous three-celled shrines is widely adopted in the later *Trikuta* shrines of Kakatiyas. The Kakatiyas have adopted Vishṇu, Śiva and Sūrya concepts, Siva gaining more emphasis by being enshrined in the central shrine flanked by Vishnu and Sūrya.

Now reverting to the later art styles, the narrative panelling of the early Buddhist art of Amaravati and Nagarjunakonda had percolated to the Vishnukūudin caves at Mogalrajapuram, Undavalli and Bhairavakonda, then to Badami where they become more numerous. The panels of *Gajāsura saṁhāra mūrthy, Kalayānasundara, Lingōdhbhava* etc., vividly recount the episodes of *Śiva purāna*. The Kakatiyas were staunch Śaivites yet were liberal enough to paṭronise Vishnu in the form of Vāsudeva-Krishna and Chennakeśava. While the former is enshrined in one of the *Trikutas*, the latter found place in exclusive separate shrines.

The sculptural wealth of the Kakatiyas as found in the temples may be classified into the following items : (1) Main fixed images or *Dhruva beras.* (2) Images to be installed in the *Devakoshtās*, (3) Images in the minor shrines, (4) Sculptural representations on the walls, pillars, lintels and ceilings. (5) Non-iconic human sculptures decorating the outer walls of the temples like the *Alasa kanyas, Mithunas,* Donors, *Yogis* and hero stones (6) Animals and birds. (7) Decorative freizes consisting of floral designs, *Kīrti mukhas, Gavākshās* or windows, *Poorna Kumbhas* etc.

Icons and Lingas permanently installed in the main shrines:

The Kākatīya sculptor mainly selected the black basalt stone, which is locally available in dykes for making the imagery. The mirror-like polish over the lingas and the pillars of the *mahā mantapa* is probably unparalleled. Among the lingas there are three varieties, one is the ordinary type with incised *Sōma Sūtra,* the second is *Chaturmukha liṅga,* the third type is *Sahasra liṅga.* The *Chaturmukha linga* has on the four sides four faces of Siva carved upto the bust in bold relief over the linga.[3] The simple *jata makutas,* the *sarpa latāta pattas* with hanging tassels and dissimilar *karnakundalas, nāgābharanṇas* around the neck suggest a strong Chalukyan influence. The *Chaturmukhas* represent Īsāna, Vāmadeva, Tatpurusha and Aghōra. The main

1. Soundara Rajan, K.V., 1965 *Architecture of Andhra Pradesh,* p.12.
2. 1965 *Ibid.*
3. Gopalakrishna Murthy,S., 1964 *The Sculpture of the Kakatiyas,* Fig.31 and 32.

body of linga represents Sadyojatha who is usually depicted as the crowning emanation.

Sahasra Lingas, (thousand miniature lingas on the body of the main linga) are noticed at Kolanupaka, Umāmaheśwaram, Śrīsailam etc., all assignable to the Kakatiya period.

Anthropomorphic forms of Siva: Virabhadra, a militant incarnation of Siva, worshipped by all the battle-going Hindu princes of the historical past, was also a favourite deity of the Kākatiyas. Mention may be made of the image that is found inside the Svayambhu temple. The ten-handed war god carries weaponry like the sword, trident, serrated mace, *Khatvāṅga* (hafted skull), an arrow in his right hand, a hafted battle axe in his hand held in (abhaya) hand, a curvaceous shield, *Khetaka,* firmly held, a *śaṅkha,* a serpent and a bow in the rear-most hand. He stands in *alidha* pose with his left foot kept forward in an attitude of plunging into the battle. This Kakatiya God of valour may be contrasted with that of the simple two handed early Chalukya image at Alampur, exhuming tranquility and compassion after a fierce battle. He carries a curved sword in the right hand while resting his left hand over the shield. The *Vīrabhadra* image of the Pratāpa Rudra period, 1288 A.D. as found at Umāmaheśwaraṁ[1] is massive, evoking of terror to shock the placid pilgrims.

Bhikshāṭana Mūrthy: Another terrific form of Śiva, *Bhikshātana Mūrthy* from Yeleswaram[2] of Nalgonda district is very interesting. He stands with his left leg slightly flexed, while the right one is firmly placed over the ground. The elaborate *Jatamakuta,* the garland of skulls in *upavita* fashion and the *sarpahāra* around his neck make the form more terrific. However, the inviting posture of the left leg and prominent genitals must have prompted thousands of childless devotees to offer obeisance. The double-coiled serpent on his right is symbolic of his virility and the benedictory power of this god of fertility. (Pl.3).

A figure of Bhikshāṭana Mūrthy from the Śiva temple of Umāmaheśwaram of the time of Pratāparudra is a masterpiece of the Kakatiya art. The nude God is in a posture of movement, as to entice the wifes of *Sapta Rishīs,* with curling halo-like *jaṭas* slightly twirling up. Though the sword, bowl of skull and trident in his hands instill terror among wrong-doers, the small hour glass type drum (*ḍamaru*), the jingling waistband of rattles aoove the nude figure beckon the believers. The emaciated figure of Chandi with drooping breasts, lolling tongue, bulbus eyes is on the right

1. The Image is now exhibited in the office of Director of Archaeology and Museums,A.P.,Hyderabad.
2. The Image is exhibited in the Khazana Building Museum, Golconda, Hyderabad, A.P.

in a squatting posture and drinks from the cup of blood. Another emaciated standing figure probably *Chāmuṇḍi* raises her hands upto the chin to drink drops of the liquid coming down from the bowl of the God.

Chennakesava: Chennakeśava was the most favoured incarnation of Vishnu. We find a series of temples of the period at different places. The figure of Chennakeśava from Kaṭākshapura[1] with four arms (all mutilated by vandals) is in *samapada sthanaka* pose with slender and graceful features. However, the youthful figure of the God with thin limbs appears slightly disproportionate to the broad frame on which the bas reliefs of the Kakatiya pillars are shown.

Among the figures of Vishṇu the one found at Sayampet Haveli[2] is probably one of the excellent specimens. Vishnu holds a serrated mace in his fore left hand, and a lotus, proper right hand *in abhaya, Saṅkha* in rear right, a *Chakra* in rear left gives the pacific figure a pronounced benignity. There are *Daśāvatāras* of the God over the triangular *Prabhāvali* (frame). The graceful trefoil design around the head, the vibrating *makara* and *chakra kuṇḍalas*, the *vanamāla* hanging down to the knees, reveal the extreme care of the sculptor in chiselling, thereby endowing this stolid yet pacific form a pronounced benignity (P1. 4).

The figure of Chennakeśava from Ryali,[3] East Godavari district, is an exact replica of the figure found at Sayampet, which represents the culmination of the Kakatiyan plastic art. In this unique composition, the most charming God in his exuberant youthful form casts a spell ȯver the devotees. The Kakatiya practice of providing a radiating coiffure at the rear side of the idol, the bulging buttocks with feminine tenderness makes the spectators presume that the rear side represents *Mōhini* who distributed nector churned out of milky ocean to the God. No wonder the extreme radiance of this magnificent sculpture is known as *Jaganmōhana* - Enchanter of the world.

Naṭarāja: One of the commonest sculptural delineation is the figure of Naṭarāja which is found in most of the temples as at Hanumakonda, Palampet, Ghanpur, Pillalamarri, Warangal fort and on the walls of Panugal temple in Nalgonda district. Unlike the massive figures as in the Chalukyan and Rashtrakuta temples, Naṭarāja is depicted in the Kakatiya temples on the architraves, above the door jambs and on the ceilings inside triangular panels. A variety of Naṭarāja figures are found on the ceiling of the Palampet temple built by Recherla Rudra, the Commander-in-chief of Gaṇapati deva. Here the ten handed dancing God in a delicate *tribhaṅga* posture raises his right foot while the left one slightly bends forward. The

1. Gopalakrishna Murtht,S., 1964 *Op.cit.*, Fig.28.
2. 1964 *Ibid.*,Fig.67.
3. Appa Rao, V., (Ed.) 1947 *Reddy Sanchika*, p.22.

rhythmic movement is well poised by dextrous carving. The supple swirling gait is indicated by the flying scarf over the knees. The array of weaponry held by the God creates a sense of awe and supplication. The dwarfish forms of the female and male devotees and the musicians enhances the cosmic form of the God (Pl-5).

The Pillalamarri inscription of Nami Reddy contains a verse referring to *Tāṇḍava* Śiva "I salute the two feet of Saṁbhu, which bestow all prosperity, and which are saluted by all the chief gods, demons and sages The dance of Siva shines rousing the joy of Śiva's attendants, dispelling the darkness of the twilight, making all the mountains beautiful and splendid like heavenly mountains, and tinging the quarters and the sky with a red lustre emanating from the gems on the hoods of the great serpents which form his ornaments and which spread out of great exultation.[1]

Annapūrna: Among the various images of the Goddesses, the figure of Annapūrṇa from Kasipet in Karimnagar district is extremely delicate. The two-handed Goddess takes out food from the vessel of plenitude. She is seated in *lalitāsana* and holds the ladle tenderly in her right hand, while the globular pot is held in position in her left hand. Profuse ornamentation like the torques, *hāras*, double-stringed necklaces and another beaded-*hāra* curving over her full breasts and passing across them and attached with a gem-studded pendant above her navel - all these features emphasize her opulent motherhood. The beautiful *karanda mukuta* and the halo-like hair dress at the back and her bulbous eyes are symbolic of her cosmic divinity (P1ate. 6).

This is an excellent specimen which exhibits the carver's dexterity and brings out the most pleasing blend of human and divine elements.

Madanikas: The *madanikas* or the bracket figures found over the outer pillars of the *sabha mantapa* supporting the cornices at the temples of Palampet and Ghanpur are the most remarkable examples of the Kakatiya art. When compared to the Sālabhañjikās from Sañchi, Mathura, Amaravati, or Nagarjunakonda, the Kakatiya *madanikas* do not display much refinement in the anatomical details yet these are the best examples of movement and youthfulness, as exhibited, by the delicate gestures of hands and postures of the body.

Among these *a figure of Nāgini* carries a snake in her lifted hands, another snake hanging like a garland over her shoulder. We see here an attempt of the sculptor to camouflage the stark nakedness of the feminine body with the serpent and to distract the inquisitive mind of the onlooker. In order to suggest her as belonging to the nether world of Nagas, two flying human dwarfish figures flank on either side while the nude colossal Nagini stands over a double coiled serpent. (P1. 7).

---

1. *H.A.S.*No.13, p.119.

The bracket figures are evidently *alasakanyas*, the indolent maidens. It is prescribed in *Silpaprakāsa* that without the figures of women (*alasakanyas*), the structure of the temple will be of inferior quality and bears no fruit.[1] It is further stated that the *gańdharvas*, the *yakshas*, *rākshasās*, *nāgās* and *kinnaras* become enchanted on seeing the graceful postures of women.[2] According to her different moods, she is given names as prescribed by the *śāstras*, such as *Alasa*, *Torana*, *Mugdha*, *Mainini*, *Dala-malika*, *Padmagańdha*, *Darpana*, *Vinyāsa*, *Ketaki-bharana*, *Mātrumūrthy*, *Chamara*, *Gunthana*, *Nartaki*, *Sukasārika*, *Nūpura-Padika*, *Mardala* (*Mrudanga mardini*). These are the sixteen improtant types of *alasakanyas*.[3] The same text also prescribes that these figures should be made beautiful with extreme care and should be erected over a rectangular background lest the movement of the *alasa* will not come out properly.[4]

The *Mardala* of Palampet in her *abhańga* posture has her legs flexed so as to indicate the fatigue she suffers due to incessant drumming. The flanking miniature figures with drums provide symphonic orchestra to the drumming maid.

The *Dala Malika* appears to have been lost in jungle, which she passed through wearing high healed shoes as a safeguard against thorny situations. The thin scarf wound around her body, caught up tightly in a bush of serpentine cactus, emphasizes her sensual sinuous curves.

Mānini is a modest girl, who is extremely sensitive of her femininity. The Manini of Palampet represents the lyrical imagination of the sculptor. Here the molester is a monkey, a personification of the urge and desire of the male. The echo of this imagination is found in a splendid verse in *Śivānańdalahari* supposed to have been composed by *Adi* Śańkara where he addresses the lord Śiva "You, the Omnipresent, are a beggar holding a bowl in hands. If you take a monkey in your begging rounds you get more alms. I have a monkey in the form of my heart (mind), which roams about the forest of family bondage and scaling the hills of feminine curves, and running into boughs of desires. This uncontrollable animal is tormenting me. O, Lord bind it with the rope of devotion to you".[5]

The slim figure of '*Mānini*' with a bronze-like finish attempts to cover her nudity caused by the little monkey pulling down her scanty robe, while she restrains the animal of desire with her lifted right hand (P1. 8).

The huntress or Amazon is another favourite theme of the Kakatiya sculptors. A huntress at Palampet portrayed in a jungle-setting gets the

1. Boner Alice, 1966 *Ramachandra Kaulachara Silpa Prakasika*, p.46.
2. 1966 *Ibid*, Sloka 394.
3. 1966 *Ibid*, Sloka 397.
4. 1966 *Ibid*, Sloka 402.
5. Sivananda lahari. Sloka 20 P.16 Jnana Vikas Publication. Hyderabad

thorn out of her left foot by a dwarfish male. The mounting agony of the amazon (due to the thorn) is characterized by the twinge in her facial expression.

A similar figure from Jakaram temple exhudes a posture of ease and elegance. The forest cover is absent. Sometimes the tribal huntresses are fancifully depicted, wearing shorts made of leaves.

Narrative scenes: Some selected episodes from Śiva Purānas, *Bhāgavata* and *Rāmāyaṇa* are carved on the cornices and lintels of the doorways to antechambers, architraves, *sabhamantapa* and also on the pillars.

There is a very interesting panel depicting the 'Penance of Parvati' at Palampet. In this narrative, *Tārakāsura,* seated on a high pedestal, is flanked on his right by two ladies, on his left by a coiled serpent, *Vāsuki,* over a tripod table illuminating the palace of *Tarakasura* with glittering gems studded over his hood. The guardian deities like the *Agni, Varuna,* and *Vāyu, Kubera,* are all are seated in *lalita* postures, in the service of the demon king. Towards the left is *Manmatha,* the God of love, standing in an expectant mood who had already released floral arrows of infatuation against Śiva in penance on the Himālayan mountains. By the side of Siva is Parvati in penance in a cave like frame, in *padmāsana* with hands in *Liṅga Mudra*. At the extreme right Parvati in a second sequence is shown in a jungle scene inside a *Sarvatobhadru* frame; beneath her is a figure of a tortoise to indicate *Kurmaprasthara*. Outside the four corners, animals like bear, deer, lion and a horse remind the description of *Kalidasa* in *Kumāra saṃbhava,* that all animals had forgotten their mutual enemity and lived like friends.[1] The last scene is the consummation of her desire.

This is a unique and dramatic picuturisation of Parvati's Penance as described by Kalidasa. *Nannechōda* who is supposed to have lived in 12th century A.D. composed the Telugu version of the same work as a beautiful mellifluent lyric. Śrīnātha, a later Telugu poet, took the cue both from *Kalidāsa* and *Nannechōḍa* and made the episode more popular through his effective versification so that they are memorised by many even to the present day.

The scene of *Aṅdhakāsura saṁhāra* episode is purposefully represented in a triangular frame of the ceiling. The colossus form of Śiva in *tāṇḍava,* after destroying the demon *Andhakāsura* with his forceful trident, thrust into the body of the demon, is greatefully worshipped by the diminutive forms of Brahma and Vishnu flanking either side and the still smaller figures of musicians attuned to the dance of victory. The carver's intention to project the triumphant Śiva as the greatest of all the gods is amply fulfiled. This is an excellent example of best utilization of a limited space to emphatically convey an idea to the viewers.

1. Ramaswamy Sastry, V., (Ed.). 1961 *Kumara Sambhavam by Nannechoda,* p.147.

The scene of *Tripurāsura Saṁhara Mūrthy* also at Palampet over a rectangular panel is a battle scene in action on a stage chiselled out of a deep cavity; the actors in the drama are vigorously brought forth. The presentation is not overcrowded to confuse the mind of the viewers. Śiva in *'alidha'* over a four-wheeled chariot drawn by a charioteer faces the viewer in a triumphant mood. The demons of the three cities *"Tripuras"* are shot and hang in the air at the top. The elephant headed lord, *Gaṇapati* also in battle mood with sword and shield, gives physical support to his father. Brahma and Vishnu stand at the flanks reverentially on either side of the fighting Śiva. A stark naked figure of a *Kāpālika* enticed by damsels is a stolid onlooker. This reminds us of a strong impact of the Kāpālika sect on the Kakatiya sculptors. The imaginative artist of this panel is solely engrossed in the battle that portrays Siva and Ganapati lose their physical identities and look more like muscle men with slim and well built frames. Ganapati with emaciated belly is a picture of youth and valour.

Among the *Rāmāyana* scenes, the *'Sapta tala'* or *Sala chedana, Tārāvilāāpa* and the battle between Rama and Ravaṇa are the frequently depicted scenes. In *Vālmīkī Rāmāyana,* Rama felled the seven sala trees with a single bow, but the Kakatiya sculptor must have adopted a different version of *Rāmāaṇa* to picturise his favourite theme.

In *Kishkindhakāṇḍa* of *Ranganātha Rāmāyana,* it is stated that Rama felled seven toddy trees (*Tala*) not seven *Sala* trees as found in the original work of *Vālmiki.*[1] *Sapta tala chedana* or cutting of seven trees is a commonly recurring theme in Hoysala sculpture as found at Halebid etc. In Kakatiya temples we find this representation repeated at Nagulapadu, Nidikonda, Pillalamarri and Warangal.

In Nagulapadu panel, Rama who is probably behind Sugrīva towards the left of the trees is still in battle action holding a widely drawn out bow in left hand and legs in *alidha*. The carcass of *Dundubhi* in petrified human form is on the extreme left. The tala trees are supporting the body of a serpent.

The most pathetic scene of *Taravilapa* is found on one of the lintels of Nidikonda temple constructed by Kundamāmba, sister of Kakatiya Ganapati Deva in 1219 A.D.

In *Vālmīki Rāmāyana,*[2] *Tāra* while lamenting the death of *Vāli* addresses Rāma thus "Oh Rāma, my beloved Vāli would be longing for me in the heavens just as you are longing now for your wife Sīta. You understand well, the pangs of separation from one's wife are unbearable. Do me the favour of killing me as well, so that you relieve Vāli from the grief of separation. You may be hesitant to commit the sin of killing a lady, but it

---

1. Ramaswamy Sastry, V., (Ed.) 1960 *Sri Ranganatha Ramayanam*, p.181.
2. Srinivasa Siromani, 1956 *Valmiki Ramayanam,* p.46.

is not so. Being the wife of Vāli I am only the physical reflection of his soul. By sending me back to my husband (who is dead) you will further be relieved of a great sin of killing a hero".[1]

In the Nidikonda panel the dying Vāli is nursed by Sugrīva who penitently holds the legs of his brother. Rama triumphantly stands at the back of Lakshmana beaming with a sense of fulfilment for having curbed *adharma*. Laskshmana holds the arrow, probably taken out of the body of Vāli. Aṅgada, son of Vāli flees for fear of meeting the same fate of his father. The youthful and sensual figure of Tara tending her husband on her knee rebukes Rama. This is one of the splendid compositions of the Kakatiya artist in which the varied human emotions of sorrow, penitance, contentment and fear are adroitly treated (PI.9).

Another notable narrative panel from *Bhagavata* is taken from the *Jalakrīdas* of Krishna,[2] who steals the garments of *Gōpis* taking bath in the river Yamuna and is carved on one of the pillars of Palampet temple. The eight nudes in the panel may represent *'Ashta Nāyikas'* who are *Swadhina Pathika. Vāsava Sajjika, Viraḥotkantika, Vīpralabdha, Khanditha, Kalahantarita, Proshita Bhatrika* and *Abhisārika. These eight nayikas* are considered to be sensuous and appear in different situations in literature and art. In this panel their voluptuosity is characterised by their heavy youthful curves, smooth and rounded bodies. The forward bend of their body contours is intended to keep off themselves from the view of omnipresent Krishna looking through the boughs of trees. Six of them are in beseeching attitudes with hands upraised in *anjail* and the remainning two nudes kneel down and entreat (PI.10).

Non-iconic human forms: There is a triangular piece in Surabhandesvara temple at Kondaparthi with a horse rider,probably Chaundeswara, the commander-in-chief of the Kakatiyas who constructed the temple of Siva and installed a *Linga* in his name as Chaundesvara in 1203 A.D.[3] Chaunda (Senapati) appears in the panel as slim figure holding the reigns of a galloping horse with his left hand and beckons his followers with his right hand to surge forward. The triangular space is fully stuffed with human figures. Soldiers who accompanied him carry swords and shields; ladies of the town, some with *Chāmaras,* some with upraised hands in *añjali*, some carrying garlands pay obeisance to their beloved chief returning home. The panel pulsates with movement within the limits of a triangular frame work. The diminutive figures cluster and adore the central figure of the commander (PI.11). The picturisation of a clivalrous theme with crowded but dynamic

1. *Ibid*, p.71.
2. *Sri Mahbhagavatam* by Bommera Pothana, pp.402-404.
3. Venkataramanayya, N., 1974 *Inscriptions of Andhra Pradesh, Warangal District*, P.131.

figures is highly poised. Undoubtedly this is one of the best compositions of the Kakatiya artist.

THE PAINTINGS :

The art of painting has a hoary past in Andhra desa; the origin may be traced to the prehistoric times when it is mostly rock art, drawn over flat surfaces in one or two colours such as red ocher or white pigment. The prehistoric paintings are noticed at Hassanabad,[1] Regonda[2] in Karimnagar district Kokapet in Medak district.[3] Bollaram[4] in Mahboobnagar District, Durgam and Ketavaram in Kurnool district[5] and Rajampet in Cuddapah district.[6] However, the paintings of the subsequent period if there were any, are not traceable. During the early historical period, palaces of kings and nobles and other important dignitaries seem to have had paintings. The excavation at Keesara in Rangareddy district revealed fragments of painted surfaces on lime plaster.[7] Similarly, the brick temples plastered with lime at Gollathagudi in Mahboobhagar district have traces of paintings.[8]

The paintings on the wall surfacees of the temples or residential houses of bricks have disappeared,in the debris of dilapidated structures. After the practice of constucting stone temples in the place of the brick ones came into vogue, the practice of painting on the wall surfaces was substituted to a great extent by carving of sculptures.

Some of the mural and ceiling paintings at Ajanta and Ellōra are made more out of necessity than love for colour display. The faulty surfaces of the carved icons and other religious imagery on Deccan trap had to be smeared with lime plaster and then painted. Such a need must not have arisen in the early Buddhist art of Andhra pradesh and in the later temple art, as the selcted roack was solid without natural faults.

---

1. Krishna Sastry.V.V., 1983 *Proto And Early Historical Cultures of Andhra Pradesh*, pp.46-48.
2. 1983 *Ibid p..109*.
3. 1983 *Ibid*.
4. Personal Communication from Krishna Sastry, V.V.,Director of Archaeology and Museums, Govt. of A.P.,Hyderabad.
5. Krishna Sastry, V.V., 1983 *Op.cit.*, p.48.
6. The Rock paintings at Bommavaram near Rajampet were noticed by some students of Deccan college and later by the A.P.State Department of Archaeology. Unfortunately none of the above have not made an attempt to publish. The name Bommavaram was known as such in view of the existence of rock paintings. Bomma in Telugu means a picture.
7. 1981-82 Annual Report of Dept of Archaeology and Musuems
8. 1985 Annual Report, Department of Archaeology and Museums, Hyderabad, A.P.(1971-71).

The Kakatiya artisans preferred black basalt, the hardest of all the avilable varieties of stone and chiselled out innumerable pieces of sculptures. The one major problem encountered by the sculptors was to select blocks of stone of required dimensions. The fine grained black basalt after chiselling would also not sustain colour painting.

Most of the Kakatiya temples do not have paintings. The ceilings of the *Sabhāmantapās* at Gollathagudi, Palampet, Ghanpur, Ramanujapuram, etc., are carved out of a fine variety of red sandstone. The ceilings have exquisite carvings of lotus medallions, floral designs, geometric patterns etc. The colour of the sandstone is so skilfully utilised for the decorations that the viewers mistake them for painted surfaces.

However, there are numerous references to painting of pictures in the contemporary literature. In the Telugu version of *Kumāara Sāmbhava, Nannechōḍa* records that Pārvati painted beautiful pictures of Siva as a substitute of his physical presence to relieve herself from the pangs of separation.[1] In *Krīḍābhirāmam* a late Kakatiya work, we find a vivid description of the painted gallery of Machala devi, the famous courtesan of the Kakatiya King Prataparudra deva.[2] The gallery consisted of paintings of such themes as Siva in *Daruka* forest enticing the wives of the seven *Rishis*, Vishnu and Lakshmi over a bedstead; Krishna encircled by the Gopikas on the sandy beaches of the river Yamuna, Indra enticing Ahalya, wife of Gautama, Chandra enjoying the company of Tara, wife of Brihaspati, Matsyagandhi with Parāsara and Menaka with Visvāmitra.

The fresco paintings in the Kakatiya temple at Pillalamarri executed on the architrave of the corridor between the *mantapa* and anti-chamber shows the churning of ocean by the *devas* and *asuras*. Yazdani, while describing the paintings felt that "the art is highly conventional and of a decadent type, but it is interesting to note that the sculptures of this temple are are of quite high order............. 'It may be inferred that the skill in the paintings is alomst decayed".[3] Yazdani and many other scholars have mistaken these paintings as pertaining to the Kakatiya period. But a close examination would reveal that the frieze was added at a much later period.

1. Ed. Ramaswamy Sastry, V., 1961 *Op.cit.*, pp.99,119,114 & 120.
2. Ed. Prabhakara Sastry,V., 1960 *Kridabhiramam by Srinatha*, p.60.
3. 1927-28 *Ann.Rep.Hyd.Arch.Dept., p.20.*

CHAPTER-V

MUSIC

Indian music has a long history and distinguished tradition in the world. Its origin may be traced from the chanting of the lyrical poetry of the Sāmavēda. Like all other arts, music has had much to do with religious fervour which has always been one of the principal sources of artistic inspiration and has provided the creative force for artisitic productivity[1], all over the world.

Fine arts like music and dance have reached glorious heights during the period of the Kākatīya rulers. The wide spectrum of music and dance in the Kakatiya period is attested to by the triple testimony of epigraphy, literature and sculpture. The Pillalamarri inscription of Recheruvula Nami Reddy[2] records the gift of houses to musicians, drummers and dancers attached to the temples. The Chebrolu inscription of Jayapa[3] speaks of houses being granted to sixteen dancers, musicians, etc. The Pāngal inscription of Mailamba[4] memtions similar endowments for music and dancing. The Dharmasagara inscription[5] issued during the reign of the king, Kakatiya Gaṇapatideva records that the land granted to the God was apportioned among temple servants, singers, dancers, drummers, flutists, *'Jalaja Karanda'*[6] *vādakās* etc.

The Malkapuram inscription of Rudramadevi[7] records the grant made by her to ten dancing girls, eight drummers, two pipers, one Kashmirian singer and fourteen songstresses etc., who were attached to the service of the temple of Viseswara Śiva.

The Pithapur inscription[8] records that Mallideva and Manmaya Satya of the Kona Haihaya family made provisions for singing, dancing and music

---

1. Gosvami, O., 1961 *The Story of Indian Music,* p.1 where he referred to *The Primitive Art* by Adams, L.
2. Corpus of Inscription, No.37
3. Epigraphia Indica, Vol.6, p.38
4. Corpus of Inscriptions, No.36
5. *S.I.I.*, X, p.395
6. A type of musical instrument probably akin to *'Jala Tarangini'*.
7. Venkataramanayya, N., 1974 *Inscriptions of Andhra Pradesh, Warangal district,* p.226
8. Epigraphia Indica, Vol.5, p.145

in the temple of Kuntimādhava. Likewise many other inscriptions throw light on music and liberal patronage extended for its development, by the rulers, nobles and private individuals or by temple authorities.

The work *Palnātivira Charitra*[1] refers to the court of Nalagāma and Mallideva at Gurijala as having attached importance to music and dance. The court of Velnatichoda is said to be resplendent with singers, musicians, and dancers. Nannechoda, who was himself a king makes mention in his work *Kumāra Saṁbhava,* of different styles of music. Jayapa, the commander-in-chief of King Kākatīya Gaṇapatidēva was a famous scholor and highly proficient in music as also in the arts of dance.

The array of musical instruments and dancing figures carved on the temple walls and the pillars are testimonials of creative genius of music and dance.

Music may be broadly divided into two classes, viz., Vocal, *gita* and instrumental *Vādya.*

The music culture of the people reflects the customs and traditions of a particular society. During the period under review music was distinguished into two forms, namely *Dēsi* and *Mārga* styles. Dēsi style of musical form can be defined as an indigenous emanation of songs and styles sung by common folk in their day- to-day life.

Desi:

The earliest reference to the *Dēsi* style of music is found in Nannechōda's *Kumāra Saṁbhava*. While describing the marriage ceremony of Lord Śiva, the author states that songs were sung in the *rāgās Ahiri, Phalamañjari, Andoli, Bhairavi* and *Nata*. The ladies sung *Althi(maṅgala hāratis)* and wedding songs in the rāgās mentioned above.[2] The other known wedding songs of our period are *Ānandagitams, Śankaragitams* and *Jatigitams.*[3] Nannechoda also mentions the songs of tribal people known as *Gauda-geetamulu* sung by the dames of Himalayan tribes while drinking toddy and dancing to the lilting lyrics.[4] Other *rāgās* were sung by *Sabaras* while pounding rice, plucking flowers and tappers while tapping toddy.[5] Other folk songs were *ōoyala Pāṭalu* (singing while swinging). It is said that Pārvati before her marriage with Śiva learnt different aspects of dance in which *'Aṅkamālika'*[6] was one. *Aṅkamālika* was a kind of opera accompanied by devotional songs.

---

1. Umakantha Pandita, (Ed.) 1969 *Palnātivira Charitra,* pp.17-19
2. Ramaswamy Sastry,V., 1961 *Kumārasaṁbhavaṁ* by Nannechoda, p.134 and p.269
3. Subrahmanyam, G.V., (Ed.) 1969 *Basava Purānam by Pālakurki Somanatha,* p.39
4. Ramaswamy Sastry, V., 1961 (Ed.) *Op.cit.,* 145
5. J.A.H.R.S., VI, p.34
6. Ramaswamy Sastry,V., 1961 *Op.cit.,* p.61

Besides these, there was an other popular folk music called as *Padas* (*Padamulu*) in Telugu. These are metrical compositions set to both devotional and folk styles. The contemporary work *Paṅditārādhya Charitra* enumerates a large number of *Padas* of *Desi* style. Mention may be made of *Tummeda Padamulu* which are romantic lyrics depicting the expression of love by a maiden addressed to a black bee. Even now the peasantry sing these padams, as the *Prabhāta Padamulu,* the lyrics sung in the early hours of the day. *Parvata Padamulu* are lyrics about sacred hills or songs of the hill tribes. *Nivali Padamulu* were sung while burning incense in a temple. *Gobbi Padamulu* were sung by the village maidens, who observe *Gobbinomu.* The celebrations of *Gobbinomu* takes place in the month of *Dhanurmāsa* when the Sun traverses the sign of Sagittarius. In the early morning the girls collect cowdung and make it into round balls and decorate them with flowers of varied hues and turmeric powder. The decorated dung balls are kept in the midst of a circle of maidens who move in a rotary motion singing in praise of the Mother Goddess. It is also common that the encircling girls make sounds with small sticks in perfect harmony with the songs. *Vennela Padamulu* were sung under full moon. *Saṅdhyā Varṇana Padamulu* describe the beauty of setting Sun with the saffron hues spreading over the indolent clouds while the horizon is engulfed by the demon of darkness. *Guṅavarnana Padamulu* were the lyrics[1] sung in praise of the Gaṇās of Śiva.

Dvipada metre of Telugu poetry was intended to propagate devotional music in *Desi* style. It was popularised by the authors like Pālkurki Somanātha, Ranganātha etc. Their works were composed in a simple language to make them more acceptable and accessible. It was also used to compose lyrics to be sung while attending daily chores and other activities by the common people. Palkurki Somanatha states that he was inspired to use the metre suited to the simple Telugu language used by common folk[2] *Jāna-Telugu.* He further states that his work *Basavapurāṇa* was based on the traditional and devotional songs sung in praise of Bhaktas. In his other work '*Paṇditārādhya Charitra*' he mentions that he heard people reciting the Basavapurāṇa and other ancient ballads while engaged in their day-to-day work.[3] Similarly the author of *Ranganātha Rāmāyaṇa,* mentions that he was inspired by the *Dvipada* metre and composed *Rāmāyaṇa,* in a simple language to popularise the cult among the commoners and for adaptation for puppet shows.[4]

In *Kṛīdābhirāmaṁ* we find a reference to *Palnati Veerula Katha* sung by the folk singers with musical accompaniments, such as *Viragumphita*[5]

1. Narayana Rao, Ch., (Ed.) 1974 *Op.cit.*, p.118
2. Subrahmanyam, G.V., 1969 *Op.cit.*, p.7
3. Subrahmanyam, G.V.,(Ed.) 1969 *Ibid.*, pp.16-17
4. Ramaswamy Sastry,V.,(Ed.) 1960 *Śrī Ranganatha Ramayanam,* p.16
5. *Veera Gumphita* is a small drum used by folk singers.

etc., who also performed different feats while singing. In the same work it is said that people sung the story of Parasurama[1] and *Akkalapata*[2] a song about the Seven Sisters or *Saptamātrikas*. *Akkalapata* refers to Kāmeśvari (the Goddess who fulfills all desires). Kāmeśvari is believed to be the last of the seven sisters and was specially worshipped by a sect of brāhmins when marriages are performed. These lyrics were also sung to keep the devotees awake during the whole night of a festival day. They were also sung by the folk singers known as *'Bavanidu'*[3] *'Jakkula* ladies'[4] and *'Gadidu'*[5] etc., accompanied by different musical instruments. There were also other folk singers known as *'Pichuka Kunties'*[6] *'Jangamas'*[7] *Vīramushtis*[8] *'Suddoos'*[9] etc. The above categories of people sing traditional and devoltional songs on religious themes, while going on rounds for alms.

The other popular folk music was *Yakshagana* which is also included under the *Desi* style of music. Sri Pandita Umakantha in his preface to the work *Palnativira Charitra* classifies the work under the *'Vira gita'*. According to him the 'yakshagana is a special branch of Telugu literature generally sung during moonlit nights in the presence of a large crowd with accompaniments and gestures in a semi-dramatic manner. In *Panditārādhya Charitra* there is a remote reference to *Yakshagaṇa*.[10] The song and dance were performed in imitation of the semi-divine beings during the celebrations of *Śivarātri* festival at Śrīsailaṁ.

The other style of songs called *Jadara*[11] being sung at Daksharama is mentioned in *Bhimesvara Purana*, propably of the *Desi* style. Perhaps Jadara type of song originated from this and is referred to many a time in the works of the later Vijayanagar period. Even now, particularly in the Telangana region, the village folk sing *Jadara* while ṭṛansplanting or harvesting crop.

Marga was the classical, more sophisticated and systematised style of music. Palkurki Somanatha exhaustively deals with this style in his works such as *Panditārādhya Charitra*, *Basavapuranam*, etc. After him Sāraṅgadeva made a great contribution to the Indian music in his work *Saṅgīta Ratnākara*.

1. Prabhakara Sastry,V., 1960 *Krīḍābhirāmaṁ*, p.42
2. 1960 *Ibid.*
3. 1960 *Ibid.*
4. 1960 *Ibid.*, p.45
5. 1960 *Ibid.*, p.72
6. Narayana Rao, Ch., (Ed.) 1974 *Op.cit.*, p.236
7. 1974 *Ibid.*, p.228
8. 1974 *Ibid.*
9. Rama Rao, M., 1935 *Kakatiya Sanchika*, p.234
10. Narayana Rao, Ch., (Ed.) 1974 *Op.cit.*, p.256
11. 1958 *Bhimeswara Puranam*, Verse 103. Jadara in Telugu means sandal powder. The songs sung while sprinkling sandal power during the ferstival of Vasant (basant) or. spring are known as Jadara songs

He was patronised by the Yadava king Singhana, who was a contemporary of Kakatiya Ganapatideva. The work, *Saṅgīta Ratnākara* is considered as an authoritative treatise on ancient Indian music both in the north and south.

For a study of classical music Palkurki Somanatha's *Paṇḍitārādhya Charitra* is veritable mine of information. The author who was proficient in Telugu, Sanskrit, Kannada and Tamil languages exhibits encyclopaedic knowledge of *Rāgās, Talas, Srutis, Gamakas,* etc. No other contemporary work provides us with such a deep insight into the knowledge of music. It is quite likely that he himself might have been a proficient musician and musicologist. Venkataramanayya confirms that he lived between 1280 to 1340 A.D.

Palkurki Somanatha classifies *'Talas'*[1] under four categories viz., *Pradhama, Suddha, Vibhangavinuta, Bhamgabhamga.* The seven *Pradhama* or primary *talas* are *Chenchuputa, Gachchaputa, Shadgita, Utputa, Mochita, Samatala* and *Satracheda.*

The Sudha Talas are 27 in number viz., *Yōga, Bombada, Yeda, Vada, Garu,Hadaka, Bandhakarana, Badakarana, Kraunchapada, Sarakarana, Asthānamandapa, Phala, Chakravala, Kalahaṁsa, Arya, Lalita, Sarala, Virala, Umamandira, Matthamātaṁga, Rathya-Matthe, Mudava, Bandha-Matthe, Vara rūpaka, Ekatala, Matthe and Suddha.*

The Vibhanga Vinuta and Bhangabhanga Talas are: "Khandita tara, Yava khanda, Kankala, Khandita, Chandaki, Khanda-varna, Ghurnita, Kutila-ghurnita, Ava ghurnita, Ghosthi, Yarna, Kacchana, Yana, Adimatrika, Tarakshana-putri, Udvikshana, Uchchavati, Akshyolika, Chatika, Yasthika, Purva kankala, Manimisra kankala, Khanda kankala, Kavya-kankala, Pañchala, Bhinnaka, Kokilapriya, Niravadya, Kuñjara, Phanirāja, Chatusra-dhara, Kritti, Achchavidyadhara, Raktadhāra, Uttamameru, Tambulayana, Malapu, Utpullaka, Maātanṅga arthakalika, Saraswati, Kaṅthabharaṅa, Simha vikridita, Simhanāda, Simhānaṅdaka, Lakshmi sthana, Mukta-tala, Pañcha brahma, Dasa vriddha, Pañcha-tala, Chayana, Paritala, Prasakta, Khura, Visara khura, Uttara, Punchavana, Harina, Mayaakhana, Adikamkhana, Chaturasra khanjara, Krishna khanjara, Asamana khanjara, Tala, Lankavati, Dhruva, Laya, Tanubhadra, Lankhaniyana, Vilambita, Adi, Matthe, Vali, Dhruvamatthe, Jhampe matthe, Munutega maana matthe".

He enumerates eighten types of sounds known as *vasanadas or Vamsanadas.* They are *Jaativasa, Vijaativasa, Kumaravasa, Pakshavasa, Bhuvanavasa, Svetavasa, Bhaskaravasa, Vara Rudravasa, Harivasa, Nidhivasa, Ashtadigvasa, Rushivasa, Kartikavasa, Jananutaghoravasa, Brahmavasa, Tripuravasa, Sivabhaktivasa and Bhuvanadhipathivasa".*

The twenty two varieties of *Gatis are: "Alapa, Helana, Vyapti, Bedamgu, Chalana, Sulikeyu, Jara, Impu, Sompu, Anuvu, Tiviru, Jaya, Ajunaya, Komku,*

1. Narayana Rao, Ch., (Ed.) 1974 *Op.cit.*, p.260

Vunavuna, Vali, Bhajavana, Pamvu, Sevana, Vahani, Savyamgula-Vahani, Adhara Vahani".

There are seven type of *ālāpas* or melodies, namely *Arohi, Avarohi, Sakravala, Sampada, Pravyakta, Suvyakta* and *Laalita*. The seven notes are *Sa, Ri, Ga, Ma, Pa, Da, Ni*. There is a list of twenty two srutis such as:-

Notes and Srutis

Sa *Sahdjama Sakala, Guda, Nishkala* and *Samhruta*.

Ri *Rishabha Naavali, Madhura, Ekakshari*

Ga *Gandhara Brumgijaati, Parengita, Samgati*.

Ma *Madhyama Purva Vaasaramjaka, Alamkarini*.

Pa *Panchama Renuka, Prastavaasi, Lalita, Svaravaasi*.

Da *Daivata Bhashagni, Nartaki, Purna*.

Ni *Nishadha Prachchanna, Sarvavyapti*.

There are twenty two kinds of *gamakas*, namely *Dirgha, Lalita, Dirghikadirgha, Dirghollasita, Dirghakampita, Ullasita, Samollasita, Uchcarita,Spurita, Moordhnikshipta, Komala, Akshipta, Bramita, Mahata, Lalitottama, Lalita, Prastuta, Gumphita, Sukshmanta, Kunchita, Karasthita, Naaradakruti*, etc. and also there is a list of seven special *Gamakas* namely, *Dharu Kampita, Spurita, Leena, Tribhinnottara, Saptadha, Amdolitaahata* and *Suktakalana*.[1]

Palkuri Somanatha further gives us a long list of one hundred and eight *Rāgās*. They are as follows:-

"Sriraga, Andoli, Sitrangi, Lalita, Soura, Gauli, Sankarabharana, Gandhari, Madhyama gandhari, Raktagandhari, Panchamagandhari, Devagupta, Srikasikagupta, Gandharigupta, Sadharanagupta, Kannadiga, Desi, Kumbhaka, Dhannasi, Kambhodi, Desakshi, Madhukari, Divi, Megharanji, Rangavarali, Tarangini, Bahuli, Bangala, Mahuri, Brahmani, Suddha-vahini, Brihati, Devapriya,Rupa, Sohari, Saindhavi, Suddhavarali, Sourastra saindhavi, Paurani, Bhinna paurani, Utpali, Pada panjara, Nagavarali, Karnata varali, Nagadivikuranji, Nata, Trinetri, Malava gaula, Ramakriya, Saya gaula, Dravida gaula, Karnata gaula, Saurastra gaula, Desala gaula, Bhairavi, Saranga bhairavi, Nandayanthi, Nadottari, Anya saindhavi, Vasantha, Meghachchavi, Saundari, Takkara, Jauhari, Rakkasi, Soma, Masara varali, Ballatakalindi, Dhaivati, Ghantarava, Vyalindi, Deshali, Abhrapanchama, Gandhikamodhi, Srikantha, Kāmbhoji, Sindhu varali, Kausiki, Purna, Naata, Gujjari, Saurastra-gujjari, Dravilagujjari, Malahari, Kolahala, Malavi, Kaulika, Madhya, Vibhinna, Salaganaata, Bhupala, Saya, Todi, Sauvira, Hindola, Turakatodi, Divyavati, Tundakriya, Nata Narayani, Rishabhi, Nartaki, Suddha hira, Kaitaki, Vyabhichari, Karmari, Velavuli, Chitravelavuli, Mālava, and *Srimadhumalati*. Even today most of these *Rāgās* are rendered by the classical musicians of South

1. 1974 *Ibid.*, p.262

India. Somanātha divides these *rāgās* into three genders viz., Female, Male and Neuter.

Four types of suitable human voices are mentioned by Palkurki Somanatha. They are *Bambala, Arata, Misra* and *Kavula*. There are twelve *Anuvachakas namely Hayi, Suhayi, Gunayi, Godhayi, Vayi, Denayi, Bahulayi, Dhruti Badiyayi, Ghananibidayi, Chokshayi* and *Dikshayi*.

Krīdābhirāmam mentions some of the *Rāgās* like *'Nagasindhu Prabhedha'; Nanavarata; 'Gandharvalahari'; Sankarabhharana* as recited by snake charmers while playing Nagaswara. *In Palnātivira charitra* there is reference to *'Murchana'*[1] which means ascending and descending note of a *raga* in a particular movement.

Vādya Saṅgīta or Instrumental music :-

The musical instruments of India have a history as old as the music. References in ancient writings, representation on seals, and on temple walls testify to the creative genius of the ancient Indians in the art of fabricating and utilising musical instruments.

Traditionally the musical instruments have been classified under four categories, namely 1) *Tata* - stringed instruments like the flute and conch; 2) *Sushira* - wind instruments like the flute and conch; 3) *Anaddha* or Anabadhva which comprises percussion instruments and 4) *Ghana* which includes cymbal-like resonators.

We find mention of the *Vīṇa* and *Mridaṅga* in Vedas. It is thus believed that Mṛidaṅga was used as a rhythmic accompaniment even at such an early period. In contrast to *Vīṇa* the *Venu* is rarely mentioned in the Vedas. Goswami is of the opinion that this is perhaps due to the Aryans not wishing to associate themselves with a pastoral instrument like the *Venu*. Lord Krishna who hails from the Yadava community is conceived as always associated with *Venu*.

In the *Riksamhita*, one of the earliest literary works of India, we find the names of the *Vinas* and their sizes. The *Vīnās* were named variously according to their shape and size, namely *Shoni, Picchola, Aghati, Ghatalika, Nadi, Vanaspati, Audumburi, Khandavina, Vana or Satatantri, Karkari, Pinga, Apaghatalika, Aisiki* and *Kāśyapi* or *Kacchapi*.[2]

All the above varieties have been in vogue during the period under review. In most of the Kakatiya temples we find exquisitely carved panels showing music concerts and vibrating dance postures which reflect the aesthetic sense of the contemporary society.

---

1. Umakantha Pandita, (Ed.) 1955 *Op.cit.*, p.17
2. Gosvami, O., 1961 *The Story of Indian Music*, p.293

(1) Stringed Instruments :- The *Vīṇa* is a very ancient instrument dating back, in a less developed form, to Vedic times. It is associated traditionally with the Goddess Saraswati as also Dakshiṇā Murthi, a form of Lord Śiva. Saraswati otherwise known as *Vāk-devi* is a bestower of learning and fine arts. *Vīṇa* is used in South India both as an accompaniment and for playing melodies independently. It possesses a gourd shaped bowl carved out of wood with another small gourd on the upper side. It has twenty four movable frets fixed to the base, over which pass seven strings, four for playing and three for rhythm.

The science of music seems to have received great impetus during the Kakatiya tiems. In the work *Panditaradhya Charitra,* Somanatha mentins thirty two varieties of *Vinas, namely Anivani, Ambuja, Aakasa, Adumbari, Kasyapa, Kinnera, Kurma, Kailasa, Kolashti, Kaumara, Gananatha, Gandharva, Gauri, Ghoshavati, Tantri-Sagara, Tivari, Pināka, Manoratha, Mallari, Molla, Rāvana, Varavadi, Vinottama, Sara Sarala, Saraswati, Sāārañga and Svayaṁbhu.*[1]

It is now difficult to explain the meaning , significance and exact time of use of these several kinds, or their decorative features of shapes or of the deity with whom they were associated. The meanings of some of the names may probably indicate the Gods or Goddesses or the king or the place at or with which the particular type was popular. The word *Ambuja* means born of water, probably an epithet of Srilakshmi. *Audambari Vīna* might have been made of *Udumbara* wood. *Kinnera* was probably carried by the semi-divine beings known as *Kinnaras*. *Kurma* means a tortoise. The base of the *Vīṇa* might bave been shaped like a tortoise. Similarly Gandharvās are a group of semi-divine beings or *Gaṇas* reputed for their songs and music. *Kumāra, Gananātha, Pinaka, Brahma, Rāvana, Saraswati, Svayaṁbhu* are perhaps the instruments carried by the respective Gods or mythological personalities. *Ghoshavati* may either mean a town of that name or a peculiar sound which the instrument emitted. *Tivari* might have originated in Tevar. It is not improbable that some may denote the brand names or the names given by the manufacturers or *Vinakaras*. Some instruments may have been derived from the *Ragas* like *Manōratha, Mallari, Sara, Sarada, Sārañga etc.*

Palkurki Somanatha provides us the names of five series of strings used in them viz., *'Ubhayanuga, Geetanuga, Drutanuga, Pramanavininyoga and Mukha vinanuga'*.[2]

There are plenty of sculptural representations of *Vīṇas*. It was perhaps the most favourite instrument of the period. Inside the Svayambhu temple in Warargal fort there is a loosely kept *Prabhavali* of Jaina origin brought from elsewhere inside the fort. On either side of *Nāga Prabhāmaṇḍala* is a frieze containing garland bearers and two seated figures in *Padmāsana* playing

1. Narayana Rao, Ch., (Ed.) 1974 *Op.cit.*, pp.259-260
2. 1974 *Ibid.*

Viṇas. The insturment is kept across the body and the gourd-shaped bowl rests over his left shoulder.

The instrument can also be seen at Bejjanki carved on the base of pillars of the *Mukha-mantapa.* On one pillar, a standing nude lady is shown playing *Vina* with a small gourd shaped head. The second nude lady is shown dancing to the tune in ecstasy. On another pillar, the instrument is being played by a half-dressed lady and the other lady is shown dancing.

The architrave above the antarala in Ramanujapuram temple, near Ghanpur consists of a band of Vina-players. The instrument is a simple one with the upper sides shaped like peacock. Perhaps this may be the *Mayūra Vina.*

Another representation of *Viṇādhāri* or a beautiful *madanika* shown seated in *sukhāsana* posture and carrying the instument across her body is depicted on a wall at Panchala Somesvara temple (Panugal). The instrument is simple with its lower side shaped like a pumpkin.

Sushira Vādyas:- Sushira means that which is having a tube or channel or perforated. It also means air or hollowness.

Nādaswara, is a sister insturment of *Sheḥnāi* but much larger. It is sometimes made of silver but more often of wood, the *nādaswaram* has twelve holes, six of which are intended for playing and six to regulate the pitch. The *ninkrina* is a smaller type of *nādaswaram.* The *pongi* is another instrument which is used to give the drone accompaniment during a *nādaswara* recital. The *nādaswara* is played in a high pitch often making a shrill, piercing sound and is meant to be heard from a distance. It is known in Telugu as *Sannāi* which is a derivation of *Shehnāi.*

The sculptural representations of *Nādaswara* may be seen on the door-jambs of the Thousand Pillared temple at Hanumakonda. Often the musicians are shown playing nādaswara with the pipe end of the instrument kept in the mouth and their hands on the holes of the instrument, which signifies the recital of the *nādaswaram.* Another scene of *nādaswara* recital is carved on the maṇḍapa wall facing the south eastern side at Ramappa temple. In another panel a man is shown playing the instrument held in his left hand while the right hand rested on the waist.

Bansuri or *Basuri* is one of the most ancient Indian instruments with a pastoral association. It was used as a drone by the Aryans even before they adapted the *tambura* from the indigenous population. *Bans* literally means a bamboo; any flute made of bamboo is called *bansuri.* Nowadays flutes made of metal have become common. A south Indian flute with one end closed and having eight finger holes is known as *Veṇu* (which also means bamboo).

We have numerous references to the flute in literature and as well as plastic representation. It appears to be the commonest and the most popular during the Kakatiya period.

On a pillar in the *Rangamantapa* at Rāmappa temple, the instrument is being played by Lord Krishna, carved in shallow relief. He is shown standing in *tribhanga* and holds the flute with his two hands. It seems to be made of long hollow bamboo at the end of which are found tassels hanging down as decoration **(Fig. 4a and 4b).**

The *Śaṅkha* or coṅch is another accompaniment specially used in the Hindu rituals. It can also be classified under the wind instruments. The *Sankha* is shown being blown by folk singers at the Thousand Pillared temple on a door-jamb panel, which shows a man blowing the conch held tightly in his two hands.

The other often mentioned wind instrument in the literature is '*Nāgasoramu*' (or *Nāgaswara*) which was commonly used by snake charmers. The other names used for the instrument in Telugu are 'Buralu, Potudharalu, Kahalavankini, Kalikommulu.'[1]

3)Anaddha Vadyas : Anaddha means bound on, tied, or covered. Avanaddha is that which is covered or tied with leather like the Mṛidanga. As stated earlier the *mṛidaṅgaṁ* is also an ancient musical instrument. It was used for both indicating time and rhythm and continued to be used as such in the South India as the tabla in the North.

Mridanga is 'earthern bodied', otherwise known as *Pucca Awāj,* or pure sound in the North Inidan. It is shaped like a barrel with its left head being tied with a goat skin, shorn of its hair. The skin is tightly fixed with the help of rings through which plaited straps of leather pass. The middle portion of the parchment on the left is pasted with a mixture of iron filing, block soot and gum in the form of a roundel. On the right face some dough is pasted to suppress the tone as desired which also adds to resonance.

Some specimens of *mridanga* commonly occur in the Kakatiya sculptures. In the main temple of Ramappa, on either side of the entrance, the *jalis* are decorated with dancing figures in trefoil cusps. Each dancer is shown flanked by *mridaṅga* players on either side. They are carrying two types of *mṛdaṅgas*. One is longer than the other. The longer one is in the shape of a barrel and the wooden or leather ribs are clearly seen **(Fig.4g & h).**

Another representation from the same temple is that of a bracket figure shown as a drummer playing on a well decorated *mridaṅga* with her right hand; her left hand is simply resting on the drum. The *mridaṅga* is carved on the ceiling of the *mukha mandaṇdapa* at Nidikonda. To the right

1. Umakantha Pandita, 1955 *Op.cit.*, p.4

of Nataraja are two *mridanga* players beating the instrument. Another man is shown in a standing posture by balancing his two legs on the waists of drummers, and doing *abhinaya* with his hands and head. At the same time the two drummers are exhibiting foot work in accordance with the rhythm produced by the instrument (Fig. 4,e). Another *anaddha vadya* is carved on *asanapattika* in Pachchala Somesvara temple at Panugal. The instrument appears to be a *tabla,* being played by a person seated cross legged. The person is shown with four hands. The back hands carry some flowers. The body of the *vādya* tapers to the mouth. The musician probably a *gandharva* is playing with his two front hands. His expression shows that he is deeply inmersed in the music. The tabla is kept over his left thigh **(FIG.4i).**

The third class of bifacial *anaddha vadyas* are the waisted ones, also called the hour-glass or the damaru-shaped drums. This form has a hoary past. Generally it is played in religious ceremonies.

The other type of the dimunitive *ḍamaru* is known as *Budbudke* in Telugu. Particularly it was carried by men who brings monkeys for begging rounds.

Damaru is a very small drum sometimes measuring a few centimeters in length. The body is waisted of wood and bears two parchments, one on each end and are held together by moderately thick cotton threads. At the waist there are two strings with knots at their ends. On twirling or shaking, these knots beat on the skins and produce a rattling sound.

In the Kakatiya sculptural art, the very commonly found instrument is *Damaru*. It is often associated with Lord Siva and with *jangamas* (Śaivite mendicants). In the temple of Surabhandesvara, at Kondaparti the ceiling panel represents a band of musicians playing different varieties of instruments. Some of them are playing *Damaru* **(FIG.4F).**

The instruments like drums were not only used as accompaniment for music, but also used during times of war. War musicians escorted the marching army beating specially made drums like "*Damayee, Muraja, Bheri, Dolli, Tamatammas, Viranas,* and other musical instruments such as *Buralu* (bugles), *Potudharas, Kahalavamkinis* (ling pipes), *Kalikommulu* (Pipes), *Saṅkhas* (Coñches), *sannāyi* (Clarions), *Muralis* (flutes), *Naragalu, Tappetalu* (Solid-instruments), *Chiru ghamṭalu (Mañjīras)* etc."[1] The sound produced by the war-drums, are evidenced by an epigraph of the period. The Mamillapalli inscription records: "As a result of the force of the rising state of confusion born by the great noise of his (Rudradeva) expediton of victory, multitudes of clouds fall, worlds shake, mountains whirl round, the tortoise struggles, the serpent *Adisesha* faints and the quarter elephants become lame".[2] The

1. 1969 *Ibid.*
2. *H.A.S.,* No.13, p.18

Kotagiri plates[1] of Rudramadevi state that the enemy kings become scattered with fear on hearing the terrible great noise of war drums, resembling the wild drum of Hara (Lord Siva) beaten sportively at the end of the *Kalpa*.

The other drums mentioned in the literature are 'Viragumpita, Gummeta' etc., especially used by the folk singers of the society.

4)Ghana vadyas:- The specimens of *ghana vadyas* are commonly noticed in the reliefs of musical instruments. They are temple bells, gongs, cymbals, rattles etc. These instruments were used in the temple rituals in the *bhajans* and in dance performance.

Gongs: A panel in Thousand Pillared temple shows a man beating a gong with a (wooden) rod in his right hand held by the thread, which was tied to it. The gong appears to be in the form of a thick metal disc with rim **(FIG.5A).**

Cymbals: The cymbals have a great antiquity in India. They appear in the sculptures of 'Bharhut'[2] Nāgajunakonda[3] and in the paintings of Ajanta.[4]

In the Kakatiya art, the representations of cymbals appear in almost every temple relief. Two varieties of cymbals are noted; one is samller and tulip-shaped, while the other is bigger and dome-shaped possibly made of brass or bronze **(FIG.5B & FIG. 5C).**

The other known solid instruments known form the literature are *'kanaka-tappeta'* (probably gold coated gongs), *chegantalu* (hand-bells), *chirughantalu* (small bells), *Kaimudi'*.[5]

Kaimudi was a kind of instrument, used for keeping time in the dance performances.

The other intersting instrument referred to in the Dharmasagara inscription of Kakatiya times, is *'Jalaja Karanda'*.

The word *Karanda*[6] in Sānskṛit is explained as a "basket or covered box of bamboo wicker work or a piece of wood'. *Jalaja* means that which originated from water. *Jalatarangini* a musical organ consisting of metallic cups filled up to the required levels with water for emanation of the seven notes *(Shadjama)* when gently beaten with sticks, might be a later evolution. If Jalaja Karanda was a slang for Jala Karanka, then it means a conch which is commonly used in temples for blowing at the time of worship and represented as repeatedly in sculpture. Jayapa suggesta that a *desi* type of

1. H.A.S., No.6, p.8
2. Cunningham, A.P., 1962 *The Stupa of Bharhut*, p.126
3. Krishna Murthy, K., 1977 *Nagarjunakonda-A Cultural Study*, pp.188- 189
4. Dhavalikar, M.K., 1973 *Ajanta - A Cultural Study*, p.122
5. Umakantha Pandita (Ed.) 1955 *Op.cit.*, p.4, and S.I.I., X,No.474
6. Sir Monier Monier Williams 1979 *Sanskrit-English Dictionary*, p.254

dance should be accompanied by *desi* type of instruments. The drama Sivapriya (a desi form play) is to be accompanied by an instrument known as *Sivapriya* (a *Desi* form of play), is to be accompanied by an instrument known as *'Kirikitti'*;[1] a reference of which is also found in Saragadeva's *Sangītaratnākara*. Sarangadeva describes it as a large metal shell three inches broad and two and a half cubits long, looking on the whole like a Serpent. with deep lines of furrows. It was rubbed with a horn-like piece, *'Kona'* to produce rhythmic sounds.[2]

The *Kirikitti* or its varieties is one of the most primitive instruments we have. This is referred to in English as the scraper, rasp or stridulator. Unfortunately none of the sepcimens carved in the Kakatiya sculpture are good, but excellent sculptures of Kirikitti players can be seen in a number of Hoysala temples of Karnataka of about the 12th-13th Centuries A.D. Similar rasps are found in the earlier periods which are datable between the 5th and 7th Centuries A.D.

In a *Desi* type of dance, known as Ghatisa-stri, an instument *Huddukka* (a sort of drum) is prominently played as also the other drum called *'Karttal'*[3] In another dance form Jāyapa refers to 'Ghargharas'[4] The way of sounding Ghargharas could be with or without *tala*. In the dance form of *Prenkhana* he refers to the instrument *Jhankara* and *Ghallana*,[5] probably made of metal.

---

1. *Nṛuttarathnāvali*, Raghavan, V., (Ed.) 1965 *p.147*
2. 1965 *Ibid*.
3. 1965 *Ibid*., p.151 Karttal may also refer to making rhythnic sounds with hands (Kar+Tala)
4. 1965 *Ibid*., p.139
5. 1965 *Ibid*., p.141 Ghallana may be stringed rattles made into a bundle. Jhankara is the sound produced by a black-bee. An instrument which produced similar sound might be known as Jhankara

CHAPTER-VI

DANCE AND DRAMA

Dance in India is an ancient art. In Harappan culture, dancing was perhaps a part of the ritual. It also might have had a secular import. A small bronze figure of a nude dancing girl was discovered at Mohenjo-daro.[1]

In the *Kausitaki Brahmana,* dance, song and instrumental music are mentioned.[2] In the *Jataka* tales there are many episodes connected with dancing. It is stated that a king named *Kalubu,* who was intoxicated due to, a strong drink, went to a garden with a troupe of dancing girls.[3] In another episode Patala, a male dancer is said to have lived near Banaras.[4]

In the *Arthaśāstra,*[5] Kautilya prescribes that dancers, singers, instrumentalists and prostitutes will have the same rules and they should be under the Superintendent of Prostitutes. The sons of prostitutes should be trained to be the chief actors on the stage. Vātsyāyana in his *Kamasutras*[6] describes dancing as one of the sixty four fine arts and states that a princess or a daughter of a high born official, as long as she cultivates these sixty-four arts, will certainly enjoy her husband's favour in spite of his having a thousand wives in his harem.

The history and antiquity of dancing in Andhra goes back to very early times. The dancers in Amarāvati, Nāgārjunakoḍa sculptures are the testimonials to the *'Pindibandhas'* or a group dance. The dancing figure of Nataraja at Mogalrajapuram near Vijayawada is probably one of earliest representations in South India.[7] The forms of *nṛitya* or *nritta* can at least be dated to 3rd cent. A.D. The early Chalukyan temples at Alampur, Satyavolu and Kalyana Chalukya temples at Nandikandi represent the great heritage of the dancing God Nataraja.

---

1. Mahajan, V.D., 1968 *Ancient India,* p.45
2. 1968 *Ibid.,* p.42
3. Ramesan, N., 1961 *Glimpses of Buddhism,* p.66
4. Rukmini Devi, 1959 "Indian Dance: The background", *Indian Inheritance,* vol.II, (Arts, History and Culture), p.28
5. Shyama Sastry, R., 1915 *Arthasastra,* p.155
6. *Vatsyayana's Kamasutra,* Upadhyaya, S.C., 1963 *p.80*
7. Soundara Rajan, K.V., 1965 *Early Hindu Temples of Andhra Pradesh,* Pl.4.

Besides the above sculptural representations, the early literary works like *Gāthā Saptasati* of Hala, a Satavahana king refers, many a time, to the art of dancing. In one verse it is said:"It is pleasant to spend the night with a gazelle-eyed damsel who is tired after a dance performance.[1]

One important early work on dance, Abhinaya Darpana, by Nandikesvara which can be dated to 5th century A.D., deals with an elaborate description of *Hasta*, music and drama with a number of actors.

Betweeen 6th and 10th centuries A.D., not a single treatise on dance has survived. In the Virāta Parva of Āndhra Mahā Bhārata by Tikkana there is a reference to some dance forms, like *Dandarasaka, Kundalini, Prenkhana, Perana* as practised by Arjuna during his childhood days.[2] In another context Arjuna mentions to King Virata thus : "I can teach your daughter the art of dancing. I am an expert in the dance forms of *Dandalasaka* (or *Dandarasaka*), *Kundali*, *Prekkana* (or *Prenkhana*) and *Perani*. I can paly several musical instruments, I know songs, *Srutis, Gatis* and *Abhinaya*."[3]

There are exclusive and exhaustive treatises that deal with the art of dance during the Kākatiya period. In fact the period between the twelth and thirteenth centuries may be considered as the golden age in the history of dance, drama and music. The writers who referred more or less elaborately with the subject of dance are Palkurki Somanatha, Jayapa, Srinatha, etc.

In *Basava Purāna* and *Panditāradhya Charitra* of Palkurki Somanatha there are references to music, dance and drama. In the story of *Mugdha Sangayya* who was an innocent devotee, he visits the house of a dancing girl, also a devotee who entertains him with a variety of dances performed by her maids. Another devotee called *Natya Namuttanda* misconstrues the dance posture of Nataraja to be a deformity of the limbs of the lord and tries to straighten them in vain, He then prays to the lord who teaches him the *Tanḍava* form of dance.[4] Somantha in the same work refers to dance forms of *Kolatta, Dandarasaka, Patra* of which we hear for the first time.[5] *Panditaradhya Charitra* refers to popular *desi* type of folk dances which were played on *Śivaraātri* day at Śrīsailam temple. The more popular *Desi* dances described in this work are *'Vadayata'*, *Kodangiyata, Perini, Bahurupa, Veddaṅga* which is full of *Karanas* and varied gatis in imitation of celestial and semi-celestial damsels, 'bird dance', dance on top of bamboos, shadow plays showing Bharata and other episodes, puppet shows and fancy dress. Lastly

1. Ramachandra, T., 1983 *Gathasaptasathilo Telugu Padalu,* p.39
2. *Sri Andhra Mahabharatam,* Ramanujayya, B., (Ed.) 1939 p.23
3. 1939 *Ibid.*
4. 1969 *Ibid.*
5. 1969 *Ibid.*, p.38

Somanatha has a very interesting list of gaits in imitation of different birds and animals like swan, peacock, elephant, bull, monkey, goat and serpent.[1]

In *Palanāṭivira charitra*[2] there are references to these *desi* dances. The author gives a detailed description as to how the musicians and dancers in the royal court of Palnad entertained the rulers. The description is as follows :

The musicians held the *vinas* and the strings are tuned up for the singing concert and ready for the *ārāoha* and *avaröha* (crescendo and decrescendo) and to play several melodies and tunes (*murchanas*). Then the players entered the scene after making obeisance to the king, Nalagama. The drummer took his place to the right of the stage and the musician to the left to keep time-beats *Kaimudi*. The player of *mukha-vina* stood then and the accompanying singers at the rear end. The lotus eyed *prima donna* entered majestically like the Queen of Cupid. She had a sweet voice and was an expert in Bharata's *Naṭya Śāstra*. She wore strapsof anklet bells, Ghungharu and dressed in colourful costumes. Timing was tuned to the beat of the drum. She stood in Samapada Sthanaka (Firm foot placement) and glanced at the *Sabhahati* (the lord presiding). She prayed to the Gods and offered flowers in obeisance. The chorus girls began singing from behind, then the dancer commenced the nine *Bhuchari* movements (ground moves), then the sixteen *Akasa charis* (Moves above ground) followed. In succession *anga haras* (limb movements) were displayed, *Bhramara* rounds were pirouetted, attitudes in cadences of hands and feet flowed out. She exhibited dance varieties of *Perini, Desi, Prenkhana, Suddhadandaka, Kundalini, Bahuchari* and the seven kinds of vigorous *Tandava* dance. She posed the patterned single and double hands communicating a variety of meanings combined with the actions of the hand, glances, cheeks, eye-brows, teeth, neck, chin, face and chest. Six actions of the limbs, six of the sub-limbs and other subsidiary limbs were cogently practised to heighten the excellence of the dance play.

A more detailed account of all dance forms is found in *Nṛutta Ratnāvali* of Jāyapa, Commander-in- chief under Kākātiya Ganapatideva. He was well versed in Sansakrit, music and dance. He mentined that he had composed two other treatises on music entitled *Geeta-Ratnavali* and *Vādya Ratnāvali*, the texts of which are now extinct.

'Nrutta ratnavali'[3] the work of Jayapa contains eight chapters. Chapter one gives the definition of *Natya* and its four constituents, the four *Abhinayas, Nritya* and *Nrutta, Marga* (classical) and *Desi* and *Tandava* and *Lasya*. The

---

1. Narayana Rao, Ch., (Ed.) 1974 *Sri Panditaradhya Charitra,*
2. Palnati Vira Charitra of Sreenatha, Description of dance scene referred by N.S. Krishna Murthy in Andhra Dance Sculpture 1975. Hyderabad
3. Raghavan, V., (Ed.) 1965 *Nruttaratnavali,* pp.34-36

four Important *Abhinayas* are dealt with in the Second Chapter which included the *Angikabhinaya (Angas, pratyangas* and *upangas), Hastabhinaya* (single, double, *pratyangas* and *Upangas* ; Chapter three takes up the initial movements of the legs called *caris,* the poses of the legs called *sthānas* (postures which include different sitting and reclining postures). Then folows the description of sequences of *charis* called *Mandalas.* Chapter four describes the hundred and eight poses of the feet and hands called *karanas,* the *angaharas* which are composed of two or more *karanas,* and the movements of feet, hand called *rechakas* which are involved in those *karanas.* Chapter five is devoted to those *Desi* varieties of *sthanas, karanas* and *bhramaras* or wheeling movements, Chapter six describes the *Desi Lasyangas* in which are included finer and technical points and elements of grace of the dance. The chapter ends with the subject of *gatis* or different varieties of gait. Chapter seven deals with such general topics, times suitable for beginning lessons in dance, the stage, preliminary practice, excercises, costumes etc. The second part of the same chapter gives a description of several interesting popular dance-forms, *Desi-nrittas* as follows : *Perini, Prenkhana, Suddha- nartana, Rasaka, Charchari, Natya Rasaka, Siva Priya, Chintu, Kandukanartana, Bhandika-nritta, Ghatisani, Charana-nrutta, Bahurupa, Kolatta and Gondali.* The concluding part of this chapter describes the theatre and its types. In Chapter eight, the remaining general suggestions such as the time for presentation of a dance recital, arrival of the chief guest etc., are dealt with.

The basic and foremost authority on whom Jāyapa bases himself is Bharata. Next to him, he cited Kohala, Matanga, Bhatta, Tandu, Kirtidharacharya, Sankuka, Abhinava Gupta, and Somesvara as authorities on Natya Sastra.

As already pointed, *Nruttaratnavali* is noteworthy for its mentioning several regional forms of dance. In the first four chapters the work deals with the classical forms as handed down from Bharata. In Chapter five Jayapa describes the *Desi* forms as prevalent in his time, viz., *Perini, Prenkhana, Rasaka, Charchari, Danda-rasaka, Siva priya, Kanduka nritta, Bhandika nritta, Ghatisa Stri nritta, Charana nritta, Bahurupa, Gondali* and *Kolatta nartana.*[1]

Gondali :-*Gondali* may be identified with *Kundali nritya* played in both *marga* and *desi* styles by young women and girls moving in circles.[2]

The earliest reference to this type is found in *Manasollasa* of Somesvara. In a festival, king Somesvara witnessed a huntress, singing and dancing. Being captivated by her preformance he organised it into a regular dance sequence. Later it became popular as *Gondali Vidhi.*[3]

---

1. 1965 *Ibid.*, p.134-183
2. 1965 *Ibid.*, p.134
3. 1965 *Ibid.*

Perani :- The dance form *Perini* has a Saivite religious origin. The name *Perani* is also known as *Prerani.* The Perani dancer is most striking by equipment, as well as by dress. Jayapa describes *Perini* dancer as a man of attractive personality, of good pedigree, a man of taste, master of music and the instruments, endowed with excellent voice, adept in language, ready-witted and eloquent and acquainted with both *Tandava* and *Lasya.* Jayapa suggests that the dancer should wear a replica of the serpent hood over his head and bear in one hand a staff and a fly-whisk in the other. Before the main *Perani* dancer enters, four, six or eight associate dancers in the same make-up shall enter one after the other or in pairs and they shall stand on all sides of the main dancer in the centre.

The main constituents of Perani dance are five viz., *Nṛutta, Kaivara, Gharghara, Vikata* and *Gita.*

Nritta[1] is the opening dance, *Kaivara;* is extolling the chivalrous qualities of historical emperors and kings and eulogising the sabhapati as having similar traits The third item called *Gharghara* which is a *vadya* with or without *Tala.* The fourth item called *Vikata* or *Vahada,* putting on the make-up of monkeys, goblins, etc., in imitation of their gaits and grotesque grimaces, of the face, of the abdomen, of the arms etc.

Prenkhana[2] : *Prenkhana* is mentioned along with Perana by Jayapa. He describes the general nature of the dance *prenkhana.* It consists of *Utpluti-karanas, Bhramaris,* and *Charis* and *Mandalas. Prenkhana* seems to be a forceful dance specialising in jumps and wheeling movements.

Rasaka[3] : This is a group dance of ladies numbering sixteen, twelve or eight, presenting different patterns woven by the members of the group. These patterns are called *Pindibandhas* which came down from the time of Bharata.

Pindi might have been derived from *Pindana.* It is also known as *Srinkhalika* (chain like formation). Jayapa speaks of expert male dancers and dress of dancers such as saree, shorts, cotton wear of the body, hair in a bunch or plait, or dress according to the region.

The method of the entry of the dancers is described thus: As the instruments are being played, the dancers, executing the same charis, enter in pairs from either side. In *Rasaka* the dancing ladies are compared to *Gopis* thereby indicating a relation to the *Rasa* dance of the *Gopis* with Krishna.

1. 1965 *Ibid.,* p.137
2. 1965 *Ibid.,* p.141
3. 1965 *Ibid.,* p.142

Charchari[1] : When the dancers enter singing *charchari* songs, it becomes *charchari*. *Charchari* songs comprise of *Sringara* or *Vira rasa*, describing the seasons and the qualities of the patron-kings.

Natya Rasaka: *Natya Rasaka* was described as *charchari* by the previous authorities. Jayapa gave it a *Desi* form different from *Rasaka* and *Charchari*. The season for this too is *Vasanta*. The style of dance is *Padartha-abhinaya* and he mentioned songs that should be sung in *Hindola Rāga*[2] .

Danda Rasaka[3] : This is the next dance described by Jāyapa in the *Rasaka*-series. This should be played with short sticks in the hands which the dancers strike to keep rhythm. The sticks or *dandas* used are short coloured ones made of *Arjuna* wood. Instead of two *daṇḍas*, a fly-whisk or a dagger along with one stick was used. On the mode of entry, eight of the dancers may first enter and gradually by the addition of batches of four, the number may raise to sixty-four, formed in two rows.

Śiva Priya[4] :- This dance was performed by Śaivite devotees during the festivals. Trumpets, drums, cymbals and the *kirikiti* are usually played in it. The *kirikiti* instruments, looking like serpents with spread-out hoods are held by the dancers in one hand with the playing *konas* on the other. The dancers are dressed like Saivite devotees with holy ash and *Rudrākṣās* and comprise of men and women. The songs are in praise of Siva and the movements are in two rows facing each other or in a circle.

Cintu (Chindu) : *Chintu* is a south Indian mode of play, *Chindu* being a type of song. A noteworthy characteristic of *Chindu* is the rhythmic swaying by the dancing women of thier breasts, arms, and hips which is the *Desi Lasyanga* called *Kittu*. *Chindu* is practised till recent times in Andhra Desa by village communites as part of the festivals *Jātras* of village deities.[5]

Kanduka Nrutta[6] : The ball-game has been systematised into a dance. In this the ball was sent up in every direction and while doing so, the dancer moved about in a variety of poses of legs, hands *(karanas)* which are pleasing to look at. Because of the speed at which the ball was being hit on all sides, the female dancer had to spin fast, round and round, executing *maṇḍalas* appearing to create a cage round her. The other technical terms used for her movements are *Pañchabindu, Prasruta* and *Gomutrika*. According to Jayapa the *Kanduka Nrutta* is a group dance performed by several ladies. The balls might be of metal or wood with samll round pieces inside to make them resonant like rattles during play. The throwing and

1. 1965 *Ibid.*, p.145
2. 1965 *Ibid.*, p.146
3. 1965 Ibid pp 146-147
4. 1965 *Ibid.*, p.147
5. 1965 *Ibid.*, p.148
6. 1965 *Ibid.*, pp.149- 150

the catching of the balls involve movements and while moving, the *charis, gatis* and the *lasyangas* are to be displayed and it is this that lifts up the game of the ball into a dance.

Bhandika Nṛitta[1] :- This is a dance of clowns or *Bhandas* who shout and cry and make ail sorts of noises of birds and animals, like ass, dog, etc., and execute movements immitative of the lame, in their movements and themselves laugh. As the instruments are played, they keep the rhythm by uttering the rhythmic syllables by mouth or by clap of palms. This dance is intended to be comic and divert the king from monotony.

Ghatisa-Stri Nṛitta[2] : The next is a *desi* dance described by Jayapa as *Ghatisani. Ghatisani* or *Ghatisi* may mean the women with *Ghatisa.* The woman who is the dancer here is a Chandali and a sweet voiced singer, reciting songs of philosophical import. The subject of the songs is the God of the Hunters-Siva in the form of a *Kirata.* She herself carries on her shoulder the *Hudukka* which she keeps on playing and is surrounded by male and female singers, flutists, drummers and beaters of cymbals. Here the drum is known as *kartal.* The dance movements should be soft and graceful. While this is mainly a female dance, a male may also perform it[3].

Charana Nritta[4] :- This is a dance mode from Gujarat, which men and women of the ministrel class perform. The main characteristic is the circular movement, *mandalavritti.* Women throw over their heads the ends of their garments like a veil. The characteristic song of this dance is *Dohaka* derived from *Dohaka* metre. Besides the group going in a circle, there is also to be individual *Bhramaris,* along with hand movements ; steppings are to be forceful, though on the whole the style should be *lalitoddhatta,* partly soft and partly forceful.

Bahurupa[5] :- This dance is described in several works. It derives its name from the fact that it depicts a variety of characters of the world. The main *Bahurupa* player is to be quick, versatile, and capable of speaking different languages. The *Bahurupa* troupes are prone to present lower types involving unbecoming actions and speeches.

Kolatta Nartana[6] :- This is an acrobatic feat which involves walking on a high rope poising, singing or wheeling around on a high pole, escaping unhurt through sharp swards brandished about, lifting heavy weights and

1. 1965 *Ibid.,* pp.150-151
2. 1965 Ibid pp. 151-152
3. Ghatisa is a form of Hudukka, as the dancer carries it on her shoulder she is known as Ghatisa stri
4. 1965 *Ibid.,* p.152
5. 1965 *Ibid.,* p.153
6. 1965 ibid p. 154 paras 135,136,137,138 of chapter 7.

executing high jumps. These feats are accompanied by a large variety of drums, trumpets and cymbals. These acrobatic dances with swords etc., used to be exhibited till recently in South India. The dance on pole and rope is still practised by *Dommaras* who are particularly adepts in such type of feats.

According to Jayapa, it appears that before the actual dance starts the dancer stands on a raised platform with a canopy above, on the stage. In front of the dancer thus standing, there are to be three curtains or sometimes more. These curtains should be richly embroidered and measure eight cubits by four in dimensions. They are held at their ends by pairs of beautiful ladies. The dancer is to wear a close *ardhoruka* or half- drawer so that the thighs are to be seen for the correctness of the poses in *charis*, *karanas* etc. The *ardhoruka* is covered by a transparent apparel. The close pyjama and the sari worn over it down to a little below the knees is intended to provide a clear view of leg poses, which later developed as the traditional costume of the *nautch* dancers. Pearl garlands and other ornaments which do not closely attach to the limbs should not be used, as these would interfere with the free movement of the limbs[1]. The sculptural representations at the Ramappa temple at Palampet illustrate this aspect clearly.

The disposition of the orchestra : On the right of the dancer, the *Mukhari* is to sit in the foreground. On his left are to be the players on the *mridanga* (drum), next to them the other players on *hudukka*, conch, *desipatha* and karata. Next to them are blowers of kahala and beaters of cymbals. At their back the *Pratimukhari* and his supporting musicians are to be on the left. At the back of the dancer are to be the two chief lady singers and on either side of them those with cymbals and the other supporting lady singers.[2]

The chief court-dancer was a highly respected person, and she was entitled to come to the hall on a gilded palanquin attended by women who carry parasol, fly-whisks etc.[3]

The king's entry :- As the king or patron enters the hall, ladies with lamps lit inside golden vessels in their hands receive him and then the king enters into the dance-hall.[4]

The occasion for dance performance :- Dance performance was presented for the sake of one's prosperity and welfare, on the occasion of marriage celebration, the birth of a son, performance of *vratas*, prilgrimage, entry into a new city or a house, anointment, *Mahadana*, victory etc.[5]

1. 1965 *Ibid.*, p.154
2. 1965 *Ibid.*, p.159
3. 1965 *Ibid.*, p.161
4. 1965 *Ibid.*
5. Manmohan Ghosh, (Ed.) 1934 *Nandikeswara's Abhinaya Darpana*, vers.12-14

The exquisite sculptures in the temples at Palampet, Ghanpur, Nagulapad, Nidikonda, Pillalamarri, Bejjanki, Dharmapuri, Kothapalli and the sculptured fragments laying in the Warangal fort and other temples at Warangal, which contain delicately carved statues in charming and graceful dance poses amply testify the great level to which the art of dance had reached during the Kakatiya age.

The beautiful representations of *Nartaki* or dancer carved on brackets at the main Palampet temple is very important in this connection. These figures are said to be carved according to the poses mentioned in the *Nrittaratnavalli* and the dance poses depicted in the sculpture of the main temple need a careful study. At the beginning of the work *Nritta Ratnavali* there is an eulogy on the author and the patron which states that King Ganapati, noting his intelligence, devotion and loyalty took Jayapa, the author, even as the latter was a boy, and placed him under minister Gunda to be educated and trained. Jayapa gives the actual date at the beginning of chapter V of the work as Kali 4322 cyclic year Ananda, i.e. 1253-4 A.D.[1] The Palampet inscription, during the reign of Kakatiya Rudradeva records that Recherla Rudra, the loyal general in Ganpati's service, constructed the temple in 1213 A.D. Thus it is an ananchronism to suppose that the dance sculptures in the Palampet temple constructed in 1213 A.D. are carved according to the text *Nritta Ratanavali* written much latter. The specimens that we have are meagre and disclose no effort comparable to the ones represented in Chidambaram or Tanjore. But the representations of Palampet are popularised and practised by the dancers of Andhra Pradesh till recently, believing to be the poses reproduced from the work of *Nrittaratnavali* of Jayapa.

There are large sized bracket figures of dancers in the Ramappa temple. By examining them in the light of the texts and the illustrations relating to the *karanas* reviewed above, it becomes clear that they do not illustrate the *karanas* or even the *desi karanas*. The *charis*, mandalas or the gestures, may approximate to those in some *karanas* but the pose as a whole may not represent any specific *karana*.

The Kakatiya dance sculptures can be broadly classified into three varieties, namely i) Dancers, ii) Gods and Goddesses in dancing postures, and iii) Miscellaneous figures in *Desi* form of dance.

Dancers- We find many reliefs of dancers in almost all the temple sculptures and in the fort sculptures. In the Warangal fort, we come across beautiful damsels that appear in different postures. Many dancing women are represented inside beautifully and exquisitely carved *makara toranas* which may be indicative of the figures being court or temple dancers.

---

1. Raghavan, V.,(Ed.) 1965 *Op.cit.*, p.158

Dancer in Jayassi pose: With reference to this mode of dance a panel on a bråcket at the Palampet temple having a figure of dancer may be cited. It can be seen that her head is gracefully bent in *Nata,* the waist is in split *chinna* and the right hand is elegantly raised with the palm being in a *tripataka* pose. (Fig 6.B, Plate 8)

Her right hip is curved and the right leg is in *Udghatita* or firmly placed on the ground. The left knee is in *Swastika* crossed while the toes are in *Agratala Sanchara* or pointing to the ground. The left hand is curved over and the palm is placed on the waist in *Ardha Chandra* (crescent moon). The other two small dancing figures are carved relatively in tiny proportions moving round the main dancer. Scholars feel that these illustrations might be the reproduction of the text in *Nritta Ratnavali* by Jayapa senani. The particular attitude is named after the writer.[1]

A Dancer[2] : Another figure of a dancer is represented on bracket in the temple at Ghanpur. The forearms are mutilated but the palms of the figure are intact. The head is in *Unnata* pose (raised) as if questioning, the chest is in *Prakampita* (lifted up); the side is in *Vivarta* (slanting) in a graceful manner. The belly is emaciated; *Kati* (the waist) is in *chinna* pose (split and aslant); the right high is in *Valana* (twisted inwards), the left is slant and in *Stambhana mudra,* at rest and firmly fixed; the right knee is bent inward. The right foot is in *Agratala Sanchara,* while the left is steadily fixed. The aesthetic effect of the attitude of the figure is well preserved in spite of iconoclastic damage of the arms. The right palm (sticking to the ceiling) is in *Hamsasya mudra* (swan- faced). The left palm is in *Bhramara* pose (bee). The idea communicated cannot be made out because this is a still pose. Now this figure is shifted to the Warangal fort.

Nagini and other dancer: These two figures are represented on a dooor-jamb at Palampet temple. The third figure is that of a *nagini.* She is shown holding a serpent in her left hand. The left foot is well set on the ground. The waist is gracefully bent to the right. The hands are raised over the head.

The central figure and first one on the right are well costumed and their forearms are damaged. The figure stands firmly but the left hip is raised to give grace to the feminine standing posture. The right hand is raised above the head while the left is bent at the elbow. The forearms cover the belly. In the first figure the same posture is sculptured, but the right knee is bent to cross over the left foreleg which is damaged **(Fig. 6a).**

Gesture in rhythm : A dancer is represented on a pillar at Palampet temple. She is shown flanked by female drummers. The drummers are shown at the same time following the movements rythmically. The head

1. 1965 *Ibid.,* p.87 & p.115
2. Krishna Murthy N.S. 1975, Andhra Dance Sculpture P. 279-80

of the dancer is looking side ways. The left hand may indicate *Kataka Hasta*. The right hand is raised and is in *Vyavartita mudra* in the reverse. The right lefg is bent while the left is also bent but outwards and the foot is firmly placed.

A Dancer : Another figure of a dancer is found on a bracket in the Ghanpur temple. Her forearms are mutilated. The head is in *viddhuta* pose. The neck is in *tryasra mudra* (slightly aslant). The cheeks are in full bloom. The chest is raised and the waist is in *udvahita* pose (bent and slightly raised). The left leg is stretched out with a slight bend at the knee. The right leg is well set with the foot firmly planted on the ground **(Fig. 6d).**

Gesture in alignment: A bracket figure of a dancer found in the Palampet temple has her head in *adhootam* posture (slant) indicating inner desire. The eyes are fully open not out of fear or excitement but of fullness of amiable feelings. The chin is in *samabhanga* (normal). The mouth is in *udvaha* pose (closed lips). The neck is in *tryasra mudra* (side movement). The left hand is in *arala* pose (curved). The right hand is in *uttana mudra* (lifting up). The left palm is *kartari mukha* (scissor faced). The right palm is in *tryasra mudra* (triangular). The right knee is in *avartita* (circling) in the *nata* (bent) and in *parivaruta* poses (roundings). The left knee is normal but straightened. The right foot is in *agratala sanchara* (moving on the tips of the foot). The left foot is in samabhanga pose. (levelled). **(p1.12).**

Another figure of a lady is shown in standing in *tribhanga* posture by poising her entire weight on the right leg while the left one is raised and bent at the knee. Her arms are lifted up above her head and palms are in *hamsasya mudra*. Her supple waist and delicate neck are gracefully bent to the proper right. The half opened mouth suggests that the lady is singing. The graceful folds on the stomach, the amazing expresssion in her fully opened eyes are very attractive. Two drummers are shown in miniature sizes on either side of the central figure **(P1.13).**

Another figure of a lady is shown standing and exhibiting *abhinaya*. Her hands are raised above her head, but forearms are badly damaged. Her slender waist is bent to right. Her fully opened eyes are looking slightly upwords. On either side bottom of the central figure are shown drummers in rhythmic movements. **(P1.14).**

Another panel represents a *nartaki* in *bhujangatrasa* pose, poising her weight on her left leg while the right one is raised and bent at the knee point. Her proper right hand is raised above the head with palm turned downwards . The half open mouth and wide open eyes are suggesting the song and expression of an artist while doing a dance performance on the stage.

Dancers in different poses : The perforated window in fornt of the vestibule in the main temple at Palampet, depicts a lady dancer in different postures. The whole depiction is seen in six rows. The dancer is shown flanked by male and female drummers. They are also seen dancing in tune with the rhythm while playing the drums. In the first row the dancer is seen bending her right leg at the knee point. Her left palm is in *suchi mudra* (pointed upward) and *arala mudra* is depicted by the raised right hand. In the second, she is shown standing in the *abhanga* pose and right palm in *varada* and left in *mriga hasta mudra*. In the third row, she is seen bending right leg at knee point and raised her two hands upwards with the right palm stretched to a side while the left is in *suchi mudra*. in the fifth row she has her right leg bent at knee point raising the hands upwards. The right palm is stretched to a side while the left is in *mriga hasta*. In the sixth, she kept her right hand to a side and the left in *mukulita mudra* **(P1.15).**

The dancing Figures of Gods and Goddesses:

Siva the celestial dancer: The most exquisite dance form of Nataraja Siva is found on a wall sculpture in the temple of *Pacchala* Somesvara at Panugal.

The dance is the maifestation of primal rhythmic energy. Anand Kumaraswamy mentions about three forms of Siva's dance. The first is the evening dance or *Pradhosha*. The second is the *Tandava*. The third is *Nadanta*.[1] The dance represents his five activities, namely *Sristhi* (creation), *Sthiti* (preservation), *Samhara* (destruction), *Tirobhava* (illusion) and *Anugraha* (salvation or grace). According to *Umai Vilakkam* (verse 36) as quoted by Kumaraswamy the dance represents "creation arising from the drum, protection proceeding from the hand of hope, destruction from the fire and release from the foot held aloft"[2] In short, the dance symbolises the conquest of evil, as represented by the trampled figure of *Apasmara purusha* under the holy feet of the Lord and protection to those who believe in him.

The cosmic theme of Siva's dance is supperbly protrayed in a small creeper framed panel on the walls of the temple of Pacchala Somesvara at Pangal. The head of Nataraja is aslant with the curls of hair flowing sideways. There are the rhythmic movements of the set of four right hands. Among them two are bent upwards holding weapons - trident and *kapala*. Of the lower ones, one holds a tiny drum *damaru* symbolising the time of the movement. The other is in *abhaya*. The left set of hands are similarly poised. The uppermost is in *tripataka* and the other one just lower down holds the flame. The lower third on the hands is gracefully crossed over the chest in *Karihasta* and poised underneath the *abhaya* right palm. The *kati* (waist) is twisted and serves the pivot of the motion of whirlings. The left thigh is bent and poised with uplifted foot and the right one is touching it. The stamping foot is shown here resting on the personified Evil underneath.**(Pl. 16)**

1. Coomaraswamy,A.K., 1948 *Dance of Shiva*, p.84
2. 1948 *Ibid.*, p.87

Another panel representing Nataraja is found on the architrave of the Svayambhu temple in the Warangal fort. Siva is seen dancing in the centre, his bull sitting under his right leg. Vishnu is seen dancing to his left and Brahma to his right. Their *vahanas* (vehicles) *Garuda* and *Hamsa* are depicted in smaller sizes. The *dikpalakas* are depicted at the top corner. The drummers are also seen on both sides of the central figure. Siva is seen with his right leg raised in South Indian tradition unlike in the earlier sculptures as found at Alampur and Panugal. The Alampur mode of dance pose is *chatura* and *Lalita* but in the later examples at Nandikandi, Hanumakonda and Panugal, Siva is seen in half-bent leg posture.

An interesting Nataraja panel can be noticed on a pillar at Dharmapuri *mantapa*. Under the beautifully carved *prabhavali* the eight-handed Nataraja is seen dancing. The head is in *akampita* posture and standing on *Apasmara purusha* with left leg while the right is half-bent in the South India tradition. The lower two hands rest on his thighs. The drummers are seen on both the sides. Probably this panel indicates the evening Pradosha dance of Lord Siva.

Dancing Ganesha in group movement: Dancing Ganesa is carved on a pillar in the temple at Palampet. The panel represents a dance concert of Ganesa with other instrumentalists. Ganesa is seen with drummers on either side. Two more dancers are at either end.

On the lower panel round the top of the pillar is depicted another dance in motion. The figures though exquisitely executed remain undecipherable. They are playing on different musical instruments with dancers in between. We find many representations of dancing Ganesa in the sculptures of the Kakatiya period. The figure of dancing Ganesa on a pillar at Dharmapuri (mantapa) has eight hands, the front two held in *abhaya* and *varada* poses while the second pair is not clear. The third pair carry a *parasu* or battle-axe and *ankusa* with the fourth pair holding a serpent over the head. His right leg is raised a little above the ground and is seen flanked by drummers. The figure of the right drummer is very interesting. He is seen with a twisted waist looking upwards meeting the eyes of Ganesa. The second one raises his hand and left leg is in rhythm.

Harihara : This is another panel on a triangular frieze of a *mantapa* now reconstructed at the State Museum, Hyderebad. The cental figure is Harihara holding in his eight hands, several weapons like *trident*, conch etc. The figure is standing firmly with a slight slant to the right. The two figures of dancers on either side are in dance attitudes. In their uplifted hands they held *chauries*. The rest are also in dancing attitudes. The presence of the fawn looking up confirms the presence of *Hari* and *Siva*. The whole sequence is given an aesthetic finale in this lithic representation.

Narasimha in dancing posture : On one of the architraves of the Hanumakonda temple the theme of the dance of Narasimha is depicted. He is seen with his left leg bent in the South Indian tradition. His vehicle

Garuda is shown sitting beside his feet, while the *chauri* beares, musicians and drummers are seen moving around the main deity. Siva and vishnu are seen seated with their consorts on the backs of the *makaras*. The ten incarnations of Lord Vishnu are depicted in roundels above the cusps of the *makara torana*. (P1.17).

Venugopala : A figure of Venugopala on a wall sculpture at Palampet temple is seen standing in *vyatyastapada* pose playing flute in blissful concentration. There is a rare expression of divine musical rapture on his face, inviting the devotes to the enthralled world.

Saraswati in dancing posture : A dilapidatd *mantapa* from Warangal fort has been reconstructed in the State Archaeological Museum in Hyderabad, A.P. The ceiling of the *mantapa* is fully carved with figures of dancers and Goddesses. In a triangulaar piece, the Goddess Saraswati is shown mounted on her vehicle *Hamsa* (swan). The four sets of hands are seen holding a series of weapons besides a *Vina*. The figure is standing on the outstretched left leg, while the right is bent inwards at the knee. The right foot is in a *agratala sanchara* posture, the big toe pointing to the ground. The waist is beautifully bent towards the right, the *Vina* is now broken.(P1.18).

Vaishnavi : This is another panel from the same place mentioned above occuring in another triangular frame. The cental figure, that of *Vaishnavi* is standing cross-legged, which is popularly known as *vyatyastapada*. On either side there are two figures in dance poses.

Miscellaneous Figures of Dancers :

One as three ; We find four panels of "one as three" dancers carved on the pillars of *Navarangamantapa* and *Ranga mantapa* at the Palampet temple. These panels are indetified as *Perini a desi* dance form of Jayapa. The central figure of the main dancer appears legless, but a close observation reveals that the legs of the cental figure are the left leg of the figure to the right and the right leg of the figure to the left. The central figure is to be taken as standing knee to knee, while the side figures are bent and appear shorter than the cental figure (Fig.7a). The telescoping of attitudes is superbly achieved in the sculpture. Sometimes, the main dancers are shown in *anjali mudra* (P1.19) or stretching their hands like a bird (P1.20). The co-dancers are seen carrying *chamaras or rāsadandas* (small sticks). The danccrs are surrounded by drummers, instrumentalists and cymbal players. This is probably an attempt in still picturisation to show change of movements and attitudes of the dancers.

Kolattam : This means playing with sticks (Kolu = stick atta = play). This type of *desi* dance is described by Jayapa as Danda Rasaka in his *Nritta Rathnavali*. In the Kakatiya sculptures we find many reliefs of the above performance. On a pillar in the Palampet temple is represented *Kolattam* players in which a number of ladies are seen playing with sticks in a circular movement **(Fig.7 b & c)**.

Another panel representing three ladies playing with sticks is seen on a pillar of the *ranga mantapa* at Palampet. In this the central figure is standing with half bent left leg flanked by co-dancers. The co-dancers are turned to side and strike the sticks rhythmically **(Fig.7d)**.

Bhandika Nritta : We find this *desi* form more than once in the reliefs of the Kakatiya period in which a *vidushaka* or clown is the central figure. Jayapa described the dance of clowns as *Bhandika Nritta.*[1] *Bhāndas* are clowns who were experts in mimicry, shout or cry and make all sorts of sounds of birds, animals and execute movemnts imitative of the lame, the stunted and children and also animals like monkeys. They dwarf their limbs in their movements and were accompained by instrumentalists. This description is aptly applicable to a panel found on the exterior wall of the temple at Nagulapadu where a dwarfish clown is surrounded by drummers. This panel shows a clown in the centre with dwarfed legs and feet pointing sidewards.

Drama : The Kakatiya sculptor must have received inspiration from some of the dramatic themes current in the Kakatiya society. In the *Natyasastra* of Bharata the theme of chruning the milky ocean by the *Devas and Rakshasas* was woven into a type of play known as *'Dima'* in which the Gods and demons play dramatic roles.[2] Accordingly, we find narrative panels like the *Samudra mathana, Sivaparavati Kalyanam, Tara-vilapam* dramatically picturised and packed with various *rasas*. The theme of *Tara vilapam* found in one of the panels at Nidikonda temple is already described in the Chapter undr Art. The other two imprtant themes which require to be narrated are the *Samudra mathana* and *Sivaparvati-kalyanam*.

Samudra Mathana : On a ceiling in the temple at Nagulapadu is found the panel representing *Samudramathana* scene. On the left side demons are seen holding the head portion of the king of the Serpents, *Adisesha,* whose tail or the end is held by the Gods. In the centre is seen the *Mandara* mountain.

Siva Parvati Kalyanam : From the same place mentioned above, there is another panel representing the wedding scene of Siva and Parvati. The figures of Siva and Parvati and Himavan respectively are centred and flanked by eight other figures. These figures include Brahma, Vishnu and other Gods on the right and *Rishis* on the left chanting the Vedic hymns. They are accompanied by *paricharikas* (maids) carrying presentations in jewel boxes. Another panel depicting dancers and drummers is seen as continuation of the above.

---

1. Raghavan, V.,(Ed.) 1965 *Op.cit.*, p.150
2. Krishna Moorthy,N.S., 1975 *Andhra Dance sculpture,* p.253

CHAPTER-VII

COSTUMES, HEAD DRESSES AND FOOT-WEAR

Costumes are the notable characteristic of any society, whether it be civilised or uncivilised. It is not easy to answer as to why the primitive man had left his natural state of nakedness and started wearing cloths. As Pupul Jayakar[1] remarked, the inspiration and significanece of the vast field of Indian fabric should be seen against the social and historical background. The hypothesis that clothing originated due to inherent decorative impulse of man may not be true. The primitive man covered himself with whatever that has been offered to him by the Mother Nature. It was a need, rather than any instinct or impulse for decoration. He consumed flesh of the wild animals moving around him in the forests and covered himself with the hides of those animals killed by him. The custom of wearing deer hide had become ritualistic and survived till the present day, the reminiscence of which is seen in the *Upanayana* or the investiture ceremony prescribed for the Hindu upper castes. The drapery of Lord Siva consisted of the hides of the elephant and the tiger. By the time the tiger's skin was adopted, the society had already become familiar with the decorative impulse by selecting a beautiful hide as that of a tiger than those of an elephat or any other animal.

The word *Ajinavasin*,[2] meaning one who wears the skin of gazelle or goat is found in Satapatha Brahmana. In Rigveda the *Maruts* are said to be wearing deer skins.[3] Even the ascetics of the later Rigvedic period were clad in skins. *Soma* (an intoxicating drink) was sieved out of sheep wool and it was repeatedly mentioned as *Avi, Mesi, Avya* or *Avyaya* etc.[4] The main purpose of rearing sheep was for their wool and milk. In the later Rigvedic verses *Pusan*[5] is said to weave raiment from the wool of sheep. The sheep from Gandhara were famous for the their wool.[6] The process of weaving with a shuttle is mentioned as *Tasara*[7] and it appears that the work of weaving was the job of women from the Vedic times. An

1. Jayakar, Pupul, *Textiles and Ornaments of India*, p.15. 1956
2. Mac donell & Keith, 1958 *Vedic Index of Names and Subjects*, Vol.I, p.14.
3. *Ibid*, Vol.II, p.291.
4. *Ibid*, Vol.I, p.41
5. *Ibid*, Vol.II,p.291,Vol.I,p.41.
6. *Ibid*, Vol.I.p.41.
7. *Ibid*, Vol.I, p.302.

inferior variety of coarse silk and the cloth made of it are still known as *Tussore*.

Tarpya in *Atharvana Veda* and later Samhitas denote a garment probably made of linen or silk. It is likely that the linen might have been made of *Triparna* (three leaved) plant. The need for clothing was realised by the Vedic people as can be inferred from various other references to clothing as *Vasa, Suvasa* (splended garment), *Dursa, Arjuna vasa*[1], and *Sukravasa*.[2] It appears that two types of garments were worn by the vedic Indians, namely, *Neevi*[3] an under garment, *Adhivasa*,[4] an upper garment, presumably a mantle or a shawl. Similarly, the literature of the later period is replete with references to various items of clothing as the traditions, customs and manners were handed down from generation to generation in the society.

A popular and flourishing industry in the Kakatiya period was the textile industry. Many literary works in Telugu throw abundant light on the costumes and contain numerous references to dyed clothes and prints. Clothes were printed with different kinds of borders like the peacock tails, horses, birds, floral designs and various scenes from Hindu mythology. *Simhasana Dvatrimsika*[5] mentions about *Bommanchulu* (borders of pictures), *Hamsavalulu* (rows of swans), *Nagabandhamulu* (entwined serpents), *Gajavalulu* (rows of elephants), *Harinavalulu* (rows of deer), *Turangavalulu* (rows of horses), *Muyyanchulu* (triple bordered) and *Chiluka Chāllu* (rows of parrots). It appears that some of the auspicious scenes were borrowed from the *Puranas* like the *Droupadi Swayamvara, Lakshmi vilasa* (probably Gajalakshmi), *Madana vilasa, Vasantha vilasa* (the advent of spring), *Ratna kalita* (probably imprinted with diamond shaped decorations), *Raya Sringara, Kanaka danda (gold bars), Kachchilam, Karpura Gandhi, Sri topu* (dark brown), *Srirama topu, Srikrishna vilasa*. The same work also mentions different kinds of silks like the *Velipattu, Hompattu, Puligorupattu, Udayaragapattu, Netrapattu, Vajrapattu* etc.

Several varieties of costumes made of silk are mentioned in another work, *Basavapuranam*, by Palakuriki Somanatha,[6] such as *Venjavali, Jayaranji, Manchupunjemu, Manipattu, Bhutilaka, Srivanniya, Mahachini* (probably imported from China), *Chini* (also from China), *Bhavaja tilaka* (probably a colour), *Pachcha pattu* (yellow silk), *Rayasekhara, Raja vallabha, Vayu Megha* (silk dyed with the colour of clouds), *Gajaavali, Gandavada, Saripattu, Hamsapadi,*

1. Subba Rao, M., 1974 Rigveda Aryulu, p.158.
2. 1974 *Ibid*.
3. 1974 *Ibid*.
4. 1974 *Ibid*.
5. Koravi Goparaju, 1960 *Simhasana Dvatrimsika*, Part-I, pp.129-130.
6. Palakuriki Somanatha's Basavapuranam Ed. Sulrahmanyan. G. V 1969 pp 81-82

Veenavali, Varanasi (silk from Banaras), *Gouri ganaya, Kshirodaka* (varieties of silk), *Ratna pattu* (white and shining like diamond), *Sankupattu* (as white as conch), *Marakata Pattu* (green), *Velipattu* (wite), *Netrapattu, Pompattu* (also gold coloured or gold brocaded, (*Nerapattu, Indra Neela*) (blue), *Chandra tapa* (like moon shine), *Sandhya Raga* (the colour of dawn), *Mahendra Bhushana* (golden), *Sarath Megha* (colour of clouds during autumn season), *Rudrakshavanne* (colour of Rudraksha seeds), *Kambhoji* (imported from Kambhoja), *Puligorupattu* (colour of tiger claw), *Rudratilaka* (probably red colour), *Saripattu Gujarastra pattu* (silk woven in Gujarat) etc.[1] In another context, it is said that Basavesvara gave away a sari of his wife made of gold sequin which took 12 years to weave to a *Jangama* (Saivite mendicant)[2]

The use of bedsheets made of fur and fine shawls decorated with brocade seems to be popular.[3] The velvet cloth *makmal* was used as pillow covers and for covering furnitures in the royal palaces.[4]

Marcopolo visited Motupalli in the year 1291 A.D. when Rudramadevi was still ruling Andhra from Warangal. Among the items that were manufactured in the Kingdom of *Mutfilli* or Motupalli, the best and most delicate buckrams and those of highest price which looked like tissues of spiders' web. He further states that "there is no king nor queen in the world who might not be glad to wear them.[5] The buckram as mentioned by Marcopolo was evidently made of cotton. Masulipatnam and Motupalli were long famous for muslins and coloured chintzes.[6] Chintze is a cloth printed with various designs by the use of block painting. The modern Indian equivalent for the same is *Kalamkari*.

In the Motupalli inscription[7] of Kakatiya Ganapatideva, dated 1240 A.D., the tax on the silk yarn to be exported was fixed at a reasonable rate so that the local rapacious officials would not make unlawful extractions. In another Motupalli inscription of Devaraya[8] the taxes on *Ratna kambalas* (shawls) white cloth, saris, silken yarn etc., were regularised.

The products of the important centres of textile industries were named after the centres. Suravaram and Kamavaram were the names of the cloth or clothing produced thereat. In the Palnad area of Guntur district, people of middle and lower middle classes were engaged in spinning and weaving

1. 1969 *Ibid*.
2. 1969 *Ibid*.
3. Umakantha Pandita, (Ed.). 1955 *Palnativira Charitra*, p.17.
4. 1955 *Ibid*.
5. Sir Henry Yule,(Ed.) 1903 *The Book of Ser Marco Polo*, the Venitian, concerning the kingdoms and Marvels of the East, Vol.I, pp.360-361.
6. John Irwin, *Homage to Kalamkari*, Marg Publication, p.79.
7. Epigraphia Indica,XII,pp.183-184.
8. Appa Rao, V., 1947 *Reddy Sanchika*, p.195.

of cloth. Especially women spent their leisure hours at the spinning wheel which inspired the Telugu poet Srinatha to remark, after his first visit to Palnad, that even Rambha, if she visits Palnad, must rotate the spinning wheel. Here the implication is that most of the ladies were employed in spinning yarn and that some of them were as beautiful as the celestial nymph Rambha.

During the Kakatiya times, the kings, nobles and well-to-do sections wore attractive and elegant dresses. In private, however, the King did not look very much different from other distinguished nobles so far as the dress is concerned.

In the sculptural representation whether it be a King, a noble or a commoner, all are depicted wearing short dhotis reaching to the knees. The front pleats of the dhoti were taken to the back from below and tucked in tightly. A long band of cloth was also tied round the waist with a looped knot over the navel and one of its ends was left loose, dangling between the thighs. This garment is generally referred to as *Ardhoruka*[1] or *Nivi*.[2] Various shapes of *ardhorukas* are referred to in the contemporary literature viz. *Nirkavi - Pinja - Dhovati*[3] (light brown coloured), *Chandanakavulu* (Sandal-wood coloured), *Karakamchu, Jodukuppasamulu*[4] etc. A cloth tied round the waist and tucked back from underneath is known as Koupinamu. Above *Koupina* a fine white transparent cloth was tied.

The upper garment consisted of a long cloth. In the literature it is mentioned as *Duppati* or *Kavipachchadamulu*, Kavi Duppatalu, *Velipattu - Pachchadamulu* etc.

The literature is conspicuously silent on the stitched garments of the males. But it is evident from the sculptural representations that the males sometimes used long loose tunics. In a panel from Warangal fort two devotees are shown putting on long loose tunics covering the body upto knees, closed at front. The Goddess Durga flanked by devotees is carved on a wall at Panugal temple. These devotees are shown wearing long loose tunics, open or closed at the front. One tunic has a border with linear patterns. Another panel at Nidikonda, carved on a *Ranga Mantappa* ceiling, depicts a group of male dancers and female instrumentalists. The dancers are shown with long loose tunics with sleeves (Fig.8d).

Turban :- (Head-dress of males). Turban or *Makuta* was the commonly used head-dress of man. If there was any distinction between the makuta of a noble or a common man, it was only in the material. Kings must have used crowns or (Makutas) made of gold, studded with precious

1. Sarma, H.D.,& Sardesai, (Ed.). 1931 *Amarakosa*, p.158.
2. Macdonell & Keith, 1958 *Op.cit.*, p.457
3. Prabhakara Sastry, V., (Ed.) 1960 *Kridabhiramam*, p.14.
4. Narayan Rao, Ch., (Ed.) 1974 *Sri Panditaradhyacharitra*, p.228.

stones and pearls. The crowns carved over the heads of Gods and Goddesses in the sculptures give us an idea of those put on by the kings, particularly, during ceremonial occasions. The *Jangamas* or Saivite devotes were wearing specific types of head-dresses known as *Makutas* or crowns. This practice was in accordance with the Saivite tradition. Some of the names of the *Makutas*[1] worn by *Jangamas* are *Kambala Mukuta* (turban made of coarse woolen cloth), *Nandi Makuta* (probably like the hump of a bull), *Pulitolu Makuta* (turban of tiger's skin), *Kanchu Makuta* (of bronze), *Rudraksha Mukuta* (turban decorated with *Rudrakshas* or simply a rosary of *Rudrakshas* worn around the head), *Ragi Makuta* (of copper), *Navaratna Makuta* (turban studded with nine kinds of precious gems, signifying nine planets). Besides, the Saivite pilgrims were also wearing *Tapparas*[2] or turbans of which three types were mentioned i.e. *Soga, Boda* and *Koppu*; *Soga* probably long, *Boda* rounded and *Koppu* conical. The sculptures provide an array of turbans that were in vogue. A Viragal inside the Warangal fort is shown wearing a tiered turban having a loop and tassel-like ends lifted up (Fig.9a).

Another panel of a Saivite devotee depicts a beautiful turban with several knots in tiers and having ends with tassels (Fig.9b). We find many sculptural depictions of this type in the Warangal fort. A hero stone now exhibited in the State Museum, Hyderabad, brought from Nalgonda district depicts a beautiful tiered turban with a knob at the top, crowned by bun and flanked by tassels (Fig.9c).

Another hero stone from the same Museum depicts a rounded turban with a knot and bun at the back and the tassels in an upright position (Fig.9d).

Another hero stone shows a similar tiered turban with a top knot flanked by triangular flaps (Fig.10i).

One more hero stone also from the above Musem has a two tiered turban topped by a rounded knob and flanked by flaps on either side (Fig.10j).

Another good example of a highly decorated turban is found in another hero stone. The turban is made into a loop towards left and decorated with three bands of beads above the forehead and at the loop joint (Fig.10k).

There are several representations of *Koppu* and *Boda* type of turbans. The representation of a flat type of turban is found on a ceiling sculpture at Nagulapadu temple (Fig.10a). It may be the figure of a noble man wearing a beard and proceeding to attend the marriage of Lord Siva with Parvati.

---

1. 1974 Ibid
2. 1974 Ibid

There are three representations of *Boda* type of turbans at Nagulapadu. The first one (Fig.10b) has a rounded cap decorated with a fillet and middle rossette. The second one also a rounded type but is decorated with two jewels on either side (Fig.10e). The third type is a rounded turban like a cap, covering the ears and reaching to the shoulders (Fig.10f).

There are two good examples of *Koppu* type, both found at Panugal. The first type found over the head of a dwarf and he is having a two tiered turban topped by a small knob and decorated with a band of jewels above the forehead.

The other turban also found over a dwarf has a rounded band with a conical knob above. The band is decorated with rosettes (Fig.10d).

At the top portion of the Hanumakonda inscription in the temple of Rudreswara a standing devotee carved in front of a *Linga* covers his head with a folded long shawl. But for the *Koupina,* he is nude and dressed like a common shepherd. He is shown with a beard (Fig.10g).

One sculpture of a devotee inside Warangal fort depicts him as covering his head with a long shawl (Fig.10h).

Dress of Women :- Sari or *'Chira'*[1] in Telugu is the common dress of women from ancient times. The only difference noticed is in the mode or method of wearing. The mention of *Chira* is found in Telugu *Mahabharata, Bhagavata,* Srinatha's *Kasikhanda, Basavapurana* etc.[2] Sometimes the long cloth used as a turban is also known as *Chira* (Sari). On the door-jambs at Palampet, the lady of the donor-couple is shown wearing a sari down to here knees (Fig.11a). One end of the Sari is wound round the waist and the other end was folded to dangle down and tucked- up behind. The same mode of dressing is also seen at Padmakshi temple, at Hanumakonda by the lady in a donor-couple panel.

Another panel of Dharmapuri depicts a group of ladies playing *Kolatam* on a *mantapa* pillar. The ladies also wear saris, which are trucked-up behind. An example of a well-to-do lady wearing a sari stitched with small pearls is found on a bracket figure at Palampet temple (Fig.11b). Sometimes saris were seen with border (Fig.11d).

The saris worn by ladies in the Nagulapad temple are slightly below the knees but beautifully decorated with horizontal beaded designs (Fig.11e & f) squares having circles in the middle (Fig.11g), or vertical strokes with flowers. These saris appear like *Kalamkari* prints. The saris found at Nagulapadu contain series of swans, *Hamsakambulu,* stars *Nakshtrakambulu* or elephants, *Gajavalulu.* This is a fine example to show as to how the literature suplements the art and vice versa.

1. Ramayya Panthulu, J., 1970 *Sri Suryarayandhra Nighantuvu,* Vol.3 p.170.
2. 1970 *Ibid.*

In addition to the saris the women also wore bodice or jackets which is mentioned as *Rayika*[1] or *Kuppasamu.*[2] It was tightly stitched around the body and the neck.

Kridabhiramam mentions a tailor making fun while measuring the breast line of a young lady with his palm length.[3] Women from well-to-do families were putting on silk bodices decorated with gold flowers.[4] The jackets were usually made of cotton cloth, silk[5] or *makmal.*[6]

Ladies with veils : It is interesting to notice that there are some representations of women wearing veils over their heads. In Warangal fort the ladies are shown covering their body from head to foot with veils but only showing their faces (Fig.11i & j). This reminds us of *Abhisarika* or the lady going in search of her lover in darkness. The plastic evidence is corroborated by contemporary literary works. *Kridabhiramam* mentions a lady covered with a veil but still the movements of the pearled ear rings and the flashes of her heavy bosom are perceptible.[7] The ladies who proceed on pilgrimage to Srisailam used to put on veils in the company of several pilgrims passing through the forest.[8]

Some *Alasakanyas* from Palampet, Ghanpur and Pangal are shown wearing thin muslin cloth as veils. Sometimes musicians and dancers are also seen with veils. On a pillar of the Rangamantapa at Pillalamarri, in the Nameswara temple a female dancer, now badly damaged by vandals, has a veil of beautiful geometric patterns and fringed with tassels.

Dress of tribal ladies ; Interestingly the Kakatiya sculptors selected some tribal girls for portrayal on the temple walls. The plausible reason would be that most of the temples were situated in the vicinity of forests inhabited by tribals like the Chenchus. The *Stalapuranas* of some important temples like Srisailam, Kalahasti, Ahobilam are interlinked with tribal episodes. The tribals were regularly making pilgrimage to these temples along with those from the civilized areas.

In *Simhasana Dvatrimsika*[9] it is said that the Chenchu ladies wore rosaries of *Kuruvinda* (*Terminalia catappa*) seeds, wild flowers in their locks, dried leaves of *Palasa* (Butea frondosa) as undergarments.

For gaining merit, some Chenchus used to supply food stuffs, water, clothes, lamps, blankets, camphor, querns for making sandal paste,

1. Ramaswamy Sastry,V.,(Ed.) 1960 *Sri Ranganadha Ramayanam*, p.65.
2. Ramaswamy Sastry,V.,(Ed.) 1960 *Op.cit.*,p.235.
3. Prabhakara Sastry,V.,(Ed.) 1960 *Op.cit.*,p.33.
4. Ramaswamy Sastry,V.,(Ed.) 1960 *Op.cit.*,p.65.
5. Umakantha Pandita, 1969 *Op.cit.*, p.72.
6. 1969 *Ibid*, p.17.
7. Prabhakara Sastry,V.,(Ed.) 1960 *Op.cit.*, p.29.
8. Narayan Rao, Ch.,(Ed.) 1974 *Op.cit.*, p.231.
9. Koravi Goparalu, *Simhasana Dwatrimsika*, 1960 Vol.II p.94

sacred ash, beads, *rudrakshas* and crystals to those who visit the Srisailam temple.[1]

The above discussion will show that the tribals were intimately connected with the worship in the temple. On a pillar base at Bejjanki temple are depicted tribal women wearing shorts of dried leaves fastened to a double stranded girdle (Fig.11c).

Foot-wear: The study of foot-wear is as fascinating as the study of any facet of the material culture. Foot-wear which is necessary for the protection of the feet for both men and women, had its antiquity from the age of *Satapatha Brahmana* and the *Puranas*. Upanah[2] is a word constantly used for sandal or shoe from the later *Samhta* times onwards. According to *Satapatha Brahmana* boar-skin appears to be the chief material used for making shoes.[3] In *Kaushitaki Brahmana, dandopana* was used as a combination of *danda* and *upanah* (staff and sandals).[4] This evidence is corrorated by literary and sculptural depictions of the Kakatiya period. *Panditaradhya Charitra* gives information about Pavalu[5] (sandals) which were sometimes artistically decorated with tassels etc. The other varieties are *Pasidigodugula pavalu* (probaly decorated with gold brocade over the straps), *Lohapu pavulu* (Iron sandals), *Dantapu pavalu* (Ivory sandals), *Ragi pavalu* (copper sandals) etc. The fashion of wearing sandals which made creaking sounds were also in vogue.[6] Chappals giving creaking sound put on by a Brahmin of *Karanam* sect is mentioned in *Kridabhiramam*.[7]

The *Manini* bracket figure at the temple of Palampet wears high-heeled sandals, probably made of wood. Considering the strap like garment worn by her made of coarse fibre, projected against the background of a forest scene picturised over the frame, it may be presumed that she was a tribal beauty.

In the temple of Bejjanki, there are several representations of high-heeled sandals worn by female musicians and dancers. In a panel of dancers, both the women are shown wearing high-heeled sandals (Fig.11h). In another panel, a *Manini* in the company of a musician, is shown wearing only a single sandal on her left leg while the right one must have slipped off as she was startled and concerned more about protecting her modesty as she was about to be stripped off by a monkey shown at her back. This is yet another dramatic repesentation of the struggle of a *Manini* picturised by Kakatiya sculptors.

1. Palkurki Somanatha, *Basava Puranam* Ed Subramanyam, G.V. 1969, p.237.
2. Macdonell & Keith, 1958 *Op.cit.*, p.97.
3. 1958 *Ibid,*
4. 1958 *Ibid.*
5. Ramaswamy Sastry,V.,(Ed.) 1960 *Op.cit.*, p.228
6. Koravi Goparaju, 1960 *Op.cit.*, Part- II, p.84.
7. Prabhakara Sastry, V.,(Ed.). 1960 *Op.cit.*, p.53.

CHAPTER-VIII

JEWELLERY AND ORNAMENTS

Ornament is called *Abharana* in Sanskrit, the literal meaning is *Ä bha*[1] being light, a flash or beautiful appearance. In the Vedas we find mention of various ornaments like *Karna sobhana,*[2] *Kumba*[3] (Ear ornament), *urira,*[4] (also head ornament) *Khādi*[5] (anklet), and *nishka.*[6] *Khadi, Kadi or Kadiya* or a ringed object is still known as such and is used as an anklet. *Nishka* is also a common term which either denoted a gold coin or a necklace made of coins. In the *Aitereya Brahmana* we find the epithet *Nishkakantha*[7] and in the Rigveda there is mention of *Nishka griva*[8] both mean a person who wears a gold ornament around his or her neck.

The making of neckleces and other ornaments of gold or silver, sometimes studded with gems must have served three purposes, firstly they were used to embellish the human body and secondly, to keep the valuables like the currency and gold secure by bunching them together and carrying them along the person for safeguranding them from theft. Thirdly, they also served religious, mystical or curative purposes. Throughout the human civilization we find the practice or adorning the body and beautiying the surroundings. Ornamentaion was intended to make the physiognomy attractive to the opposite sex. All human beings are not born attractive and charming. Even physical features and colour of the body varies from person to person. Ornamentation served to cover up the deficiency of charm.

Before the advent of currency the riches of man were measured in terms of cattle,[9] the *'godhana*. Then the cattle wealth was exchanged for mobile currency like cowries, then for metallic coins. A handful of cowries were exchangad for a coin, *Pana,*[10] a term derived from Pani or hand. A gold coin was known as *Nishka or Suvarna,* because it was made of gold

1. Sir Monier Monier Williams 1979 *(Reprint) Sanskrit- English Dictionary,* p.145
2. Macdonell & Keith 1958 *Vedic Index of Names and Subjects,* Vol.I, p.140
3. *Ibid.,* p.163
4. *Ibid.,* p.164
5. *Ibid.,* p.216
6. *Ibid.,* p.454-455
7. *Ibid.,* p.454
8. *Ibid.*
9. Das, A.C., 1925 *Rigvedic Culture,* p.139
10. Chakraborty, S.K., 1973 *A Study of Ancient Indian Numismatics,* p.103

wich has an attractive or unfading colour. Gold or silver or any other kind of money, also food grains were treated by the Indians as sacred and auspicious. Making ornaments from gold and wearing them constantly was also intended to keep them safe. The houses of commoners were not strong enough to protect the valuables. There was no strong State protection; villages and cities were to be protected by the people themselves.

Important commercial villages and towns were fortified with walls around. Even during 17th - 18th centuries small fortresses know as *gadis* are commonly found in Telangana. There was also no banking system comparable to the modern practice of depositing valuables in a bank locker. Making of amulets, talisman or yantras to invoke a particular deity or to cure a particular disease was a common practice. Many times the family deities like the Goddess Lakshmi, Narayana, Parvati, *Nagas*, the Planets Sun, Moon, the mythical animals like the *makara* various mystical and geometric designs are found on the ornaments. It is believed that a particular kind of gem represents a particular planet. The belief in astrology appears to be as ancient as the Vedas. In fact *Jyotisha* is considered as one of the Vedangas. In a gold necklace found at Kotilingala datable to the Mauryan period the beads are shaped like the Sun disc, *Nandipada*, tortoise, frog etc. The tortoise is symbolic of the planet Saturn and the frog represents Jupiter or Brihaspati

Precious stones like amethyst, carnelian, jasper, bloodstone, lapis lazuli, agate (banded or plain) and quartz crystal were commonly used for making beads, pendants, ear spools etc. Some varieties of red stones like the carnelian, garnet (deep red) and ruby represent the planet Sun. The white pearl was used for the deficiency caused by the planet Moon. Coral cures the deficiencies of Mars or *Kuja*. The blue stones, *Indranila* or saphire, cure the Saturnine maladies. The amethyst which is the commonest precious stone found through out India is believed to bestow spiritual power.

The story of Indian jewellery and ornaments can be traced back to the Harappan period. The people of the Indus civilization used to adorn themselves with traditional jewellery and ornaments made of gold, silver, copper, bronze, shell and semi-precious stones. The notable types of jewellery and ornaments used during the period mainly consisted of ear rings, finger rings, pendants, bangles, wristlets, cones, bracelets, armlets, hair pins, fillets and beads of semi-precious stones.

As in other parts of India, several ornaments have been noticed from the neolithic-chalcolithic times in the Andhra region. The excavations at Budigapalli in Karimnagar district and Chagatur in Mahboobnagar district yielded evidence of shell objects etc.[1] In the the late Neolithic phase at

1. Krishna Sastry,V.V., 1983 *Proto and Early Historical Cultures of Andhra Pradesh*, p.103

Polakonda, a copper spiralled ring was found. It must have been used as a finger ornament. The sites like Palavoy, Bastipadu and Velpumadugu yielded beads of steatite, agate, carnelian and chert.[1]

There was also a variety of beads from other sites . They included beads of amethyst, carnelian, agate, chalcedony, coral, shell, glass and paste. Gold objects though rare in other sites, yet were found at Tekkalakota in the from of a pendant or ear-ornament with coils in the centre and dumb-bells at both the ends.[2]

Personal ornaments become more frequent during the Megalithic period. Beads, bangles, rings, ear ornaments and diadems of various metals are some of the ornaments of the period. The beads were made of different materials viz., terracotta, semi- precious stones like carnelian, jasper, agate, quartz crystal and materials like shell, horn, ivory, gold, silver, copper etc., and rarely glass or paste.[3]

In the early historical period, we have a variety of ornaments worn from head to foot. The main source of the study of ornaments of this period are the excavated material and ornaments represented in the sculptures and terracotta.

Coming to the Kakatiya period from 10th century A.D. to 14th cent. A.D., we find a variety of ornaments worn by females and males from head to foot. The main source for the study of the ornaments are the sculptural representations, literature and epigraphy.

Contemporary records contain references to various kinds of ornaments worn on the head : *Sekhara*,[4] *Cheruchukka*,[5] *Sasi*,[6] *Ravi - Bimbam*,[7] *Bangaru Puvulu*[8] (Flowers in strings, made of gold), *Mutyala - Jalli*,[9] *Lalaatika*,[10] *Pacchadapuganda*,[11] *Jada-Kucchulu*,[12] *Kuppela - Mutuyala - Kucchulu*,[13]

1. Sarma, I.K., 1967 "Painted Pottery from Pusalapadu, A.P. and further excavations at Cuddapah and Kurnool districts", *IndicaIV*, Part I.
2. Krishna Sastry,V.V., 1983 *Op.cit.*, p.45
3. 1983 *Ibid.*, p.99
4. Koravi Goparaju, 1960 *Simhasara Dvatrimsika*, Part-I, p.130
5. Narayana Rao, Ch.,(Ed.) 1974 *Sri Panditaradhya Charitra*, and also Umakantha Pandita's *Palnativira Charitra*, p.72
6. Koravi Goparaju 1960 *Op.cit.*, p.130
7. 1960 *Ibid.*
8. Umakantha Pandita,(Ed.) 1955 *Palnativira Charitra*, p.72
9. 1955 *Ibid.*
10. Koravi Goparaju, 1960 *Simhasana Dvatrimsika*, p.130 Part-I.
11. 1960 *Ibid.*
12. Umakantha Pandita,(Ed.) 1969 *Op.cit.*, p.72
13. 1955 *Ibid.*

Bhramarakam,[1] *Koppu-billa*[2] etc. The ornament *Sekharam* is also known as *Sigadanda* or *Koppu-billa.* It is a circular ornament worn by women in their braided hair (Koppu). *Cheruchukka* or *Papiti-bottu* (in Telugu) was a gold ornament studded with precious stones and worn in the centre of the forehead at the parting of the hair. The *Sasi* and *Ravi bimbas* were gold ornaments studded with precious or semi-precious stones resembling the crescent Moon and the Sun respectively and were worn by women on either side of the back of the head. The ornament *Mutyala-Jalli* was a hair-net woven of pearls. *Lalatika* was a forehead ornament of gold set with precious stones. *Kuppela-mutyala Kucchulu* were tassels of pearls with golden knobs worn above the ears on the head on either side. *Bhramaraka* must have been named after the shape of ornament worn by women on their plaited tresses.

The sculptural art of the Kakatiyas represents most of the varieties cited above as culled out form the contemporary literature. A bracket figure of a lady drummer in the Palampet temple is shown with a *Cheruchukka* or forehead ornament which looks like a miner's search-light, in the middle of the forehead. A big gem is probably studded in the centre of the ornament. Similarly there is another bracket figure of a lady wearing a strap like garment as a prominent *Cheruchukka* over her forehead. The disc-shaped ornament must have been studded with precious stones. *Cheruchukka* is also known as a *Cheru-bottu,* which was worn at the beginning of the parting of the hair. It is connected to a string of pearls, which is taken to the back of the head along the parting. The parting is known as *Simanta.*

Mutyala - Jalli : We come across another head ornament known as *Mutyala Jalli,* usually worn by the ladies of royalty and nobles and of the harems of the Kakatiya society. It is seen in may sculptural representations of the period. Jalli, literally means a tassel or a string of pearls attached to the disc of the hair-parting and taken to both sides of the hair upto the ear-ornaments. Many a time the ornament is shown as made of pearls.

The ladies depicted on either side of the doorway of the temple at Ghanpur are adorned with Jallies worn along the edge of the hair line over the forehead. A beautiful *Madanika* figure from Ghanpur now exhibited in the premises of State Department of Archaelology is shown having a chain like Jalli and attached to the heavy discular ear-ornament with a gold link. The ornament was probably composed of big-pearls threaded with a gold string (Fig.12b).

---

1. Koravi Goparaju 1960 *Simhasana Dwatrimsika,* Part-I, p.139
2. Prabhakara Sastry, V.,(Ed.) 1960 *Kridabhiramam,* p.22

Ravi and Sasi : The ornaments worn on either side of the parting of the hair over the forehead is known as *Ravi* and *Sasi*. The Sun and Moon are symbolic of permanancy. Here the required aspect is *soubhagya* or married life. The representation of *Ravi* and *Sasi* ornaments may be seen in a bas relief of *Salabhanjika* on the southern wall of Pachchala Someswara temple at Panugal. *Chandrika* is the other name of the Sasi (Fig.12c).

Lalata - patta : It appears that a string of pearls over the forehead was also worn by the males along the periphery of the hair without a break at the parting. This ornament was probably composed of one or two pearls or *Rudraksha* type beads. A donor-couple carved on a door-jamb at Palampet which in all probability be the representation of Recherla Rudra, the commander-in-chief under Kakatiya Ganapatideva is portrayed with rich ornamentation. The commander is shown in a standing posture and wearing a string of pearls over his forehead. Another panel from the same temple found on the pillar of *Ranga mantapa* depicts three male dancers wearing forehead ornaments in the shape of straps or *Lalata pattas* (Fig.12d).

Koppu - Billa or Chudamani : *Koppu Billa* is an ornament worn by women at the back of the head. *Koppu* in Telugu is a bun of hair and billa is a disc. A solar eclipse falling on Sunday and a lunar eclipse falling on Monday are also known as *Koppu-Billas*.

Ear Ornaments : The antiquity of the ear ornament may be traced back to very ancient times. They were made of materials like clay, semi-precious stones like quartz crystal or of metals like gold, copper or lead. It is believed till recently that it is auspicious to have long ear-lobes, reaching down to the shoulders. This tradition must have come into vogue from Buddhist times. Almost all the images of Lord Buddha have ear lobes touching the shoulders, but without ear ornaments.

The *kundalas* were given special treatment while depicting the Gods and the Goddesses. The image of Siva or his other emanations are usually depicted with two different types of *kundalas* in his two ears. There are either the *Makara and Chakra* or *Makara and Sarpa kundalas*. This is in accordance with the conceptual prescription that the form of Siva is a combination of Siva and Sakti, the *Arthanarisvara*. The *Sarpakundala* is symbolic of Siva and the *chakra* of Sakti. In case of Vishnu, there is no dissimilarity, he wears only one type in both ears - *Makara*, a mythical aquatic animal which is reminiscent of the origin of the God *Narayana*.

The practice of wearing heavy *kundalas*, sometimes half the size of the face, continued during the Kakatiya period. It is unlikely that large-sized ornaments are made of soild gold or other metals as they would cut open the ear lobes. They were probably hollow inside and covered with thin foil of gold.

They were known under different names as referred to in the contemporary records, such as *Tatankas*[1] ,*Kundalas*[2], *Ontlu,*[3] *Punju Kammalu,*[4] *Baviralu,*[5] *Kuntelu*[6] or *Kuntena kucchulu,*[7] *Choukatlu,*[8] *Pogulu,*[9] *Duddu Kammalu,*[10] *Mutyala kammalu*[11] etc.

Choukatlu : It may be the other name of *Mutyala Kammalu*, composed of four pearls. *'Baviralu* and *Kuntelu'* are large gold rings and appear to be twin ornaments worn together. *'Kuntena Kucchulu'* are rings with tassels of gold or silver, cotton, silk thread or of pearls. Some ear-ornaments like *Kammalu* were worn by both men and women but *kundalas* were exclusively worn by men.

Gopinath Rao mentions five principal kinds of ear ornaments such as *Patra, Nakra, Sankhapatra, Ratna* and *Sarpakundalas.*[12] Those ornaments made of thin sheet of gold in the shape of a leaf are called *patras;* when a conch shell is cut crosswise, a spiral ring is produced and this is known as *Sankha patra;* a jewelled circular ear ring is known as *Ratna kundala.* Finally, those made in the form of mythical *makara* (crocodile) or *nakra* or those in the form of cobra are the *Makara Kundalas* and *Sarpa Kundalas* respectively.

All these varieties are noticed in the sculptural representations.

Patra kundalas : The depiction of *Patra kundalas* or the leaf shaped ornaments are extremely rare in the sculptures. However, reference to *Tatankas* in the literature are common, A *tatanka* was probably made of *Tadi* leaves (Palm Leaves). Sometimes they were also made of ivory and the lady who wore them is considered to be a *Suvasini* or a women with a living husband.[13] In the *Kridabhiramam* the author refers to the ladies of *Medarawada* (a suburb of basket makers) who wore *'Dhavala Tala Palasa Tatankamulu'*[14] which means *Tatankas* made of palm leaves. At another place, the author addresses the lady from Karnataka as Karnata *Tatankini*. Ivory ornaments

1. Prabhakara Sastry,V.,(Ed.) 1960 *Kridabhiramam*, p.22
2. 1960 *Ibid.*, p.28
3. Umakantha Pandita, (Ed.) 1955 *Op.cit.*, p.72
4. Ibid. p.72
5. Umakantha Pandita,(Ed.) *Op.cit.*, p.72
6. 1955 *Ibid.*
7. 1955 *Ibid.*
8. Ramaswamy Sastry,V., (Ed.) *Ranganatha Ramayanam*, p.69
9. Umakantha Pandita, (Ed.) 1969 *Op.cit.*, p.72
10. Prabhakara Sastry,V.,(Ed.) 1960 *Op.cit.*, p.32
11. 1960 *Ibid.*, p.29
12. Gopinatha Rao,T.A., 1968 *Elements of Hindu Iconography*, Vol.I, Part-I, p.24
13. Subbayya Sastry, K., 1979 *Sri Suryarayandhra Nighantuvu*, Vol.III, p.671
14. Prabhakara Sastry,V.,(Ed.) 1960 *Op.cit.*, p.22

were probably the exclusive privilege of the wealthy. *Sankha patras* or those made of conch were worn by the common folk. The ornaments like *Ratna-Tatankas, Ratna- Maukti, Hemayukta-Taatankas, Mutyala kammas, Vajrala kammas* (diamond studded) as found in the literature denote the ornaments set with precious stones.

Nakra or Makara Kundalas : These are found from a very early period. At Nagarjunakonda, beautiful *Makara Kundalas* of gold have been found which are made of thin gold wire with twisted terminals for threading and minutely decorated with filigree work[1] Similar gold *Makara Kundalas* were found at Mortha Village near Narsapur with a signet ring inscribed in *Brahmi* as "Dharma Vriddhi".[2] *Makara kundalas* are also found in the terracotta and stucco figures.[3]

Kakatiya sculptures are replete with representation of *Makara Kundalas*. The idol of Chennakesava from Visnur exhibited in the State Department of Archaeology is shown wearing elegant *Makara Kundalas* with pearl tassels.

Similarly the Vishnu sculpture from Katakshapur and the Narsimha idol from Hanumakunda are shown wearing *Makara* ornaments. The male in the donor-couple on the palampet door-jamb is also shown with *Makara Kundalas*. It may be presumed that the *Makara* type was an exclusive male ornament.

Sarpa Kundalas : According to *Saiva Agamas* the celestial serpant *Vasuki* should serve as the *Sarpa Kundala* of Siva, *Takshaka* as the waist band and *Pushkara* as the *Hara*.[4] According to *Kalingapattuapparani'*, a contemporary work of Kulottunga Chola, prescribes that the serpent *Vasuki* was used as the rope around the *Meru* mountain for churning the milky ocean and the other serpent *Adisesha* which supports the entire universe on its hood, coils round the feet of the *Devi* as anklet.[5] Sarpa kundalas were also worn by *Kapalikas* and other Saivite devotees.

It is possible that the practice of wearing such ornaments is as old as the Chalcolithic times. In the excavations at Chinnamarur a coiled bracelet of thick copper wire was encountered, the ends of which are shaped as bells.[6] It might be possible that the bell ends were replaced by serpant-hood shapes during the later period. From the site excavated at Polakonda, coiled

---

1. Krishna Murthy, K., 1977 *Nagarjunakonda - A Cultural Study*, p.67
2. Krishna Sastry,V.V., 1985 Personal Communication about the Treasure Trove from Narsapur now kept in the State Museum, Hyderabad.
3. Krishna Murthy, K., 1977 *Op.cit.*, p.67
4. Gopinatha Rao,T.A., 1971 *Elements of Hindu Iconography*, Vol.II, Part-II (Reprint), p.340
5. Nagaswamy, R., 1982 *Tantric Cult of South India*, p.27
6. Chinnamarur- A chalcolithic site. Annual report of the Dept of Archaeology and Museums. 1980.

copper ear rings were found. The practice is seen continued during tje, Megalithic period. In one of the burials at Kadambapur, gold plated spiral ear ornaments are recorded.[1] In the Buddhist sculptures of Amaravati, Mathura and Singholi, the ladies are shown with massive spiral anklets.[2]

In the *Gajasura samhara murthi* panel at Palampet Siva is shown wearing *Sarpa Kundalas* in both the ears (Fig. 12f). The intention of the artist was to accentuate warring Siva as a total male. At Nidikonda, Siva as *Dakshina murthy* is seated in *Padmasana* and wears dissimilar *kundalas,* the right one being *Sarpa* and the left one a *Ratnakundala*. Among the three female figures on the door- jambs of Ghanpur temple, a *nagini* has two *Sarpakundalas* in both the ears, while she holds two serpants aloft in her hands. One more *sarpa* is wound round her knee.

Though Gopinath Rao mentioned only five main varieties of *kundalas,* it may be necessary to record one more type, namely *Chakra Kundala* which has had a long antiquity. The *Sankha patra* type mentioned by Gopinath Rao belongs to the annular or the ring type. The so-called annular beads recorded in the Megalithic context at Brahamgiri, Maski, Kesarapalli and Nagarjunakonda[3] must have been used as ear ornaments as a big hole in the middle would not make it conducive to be threaded as a bead. In fact even from the early historical sites quite a large number of annular rings made of ivory, conch, lead, copper and iron have been recorded.[4] The discular types are generally made of terracotta, quartz crystal, glass etc. However, the discular types of the early historical times look like pullyes with a groove over the rim.[5] In the Buddhist and the later sculptures these are represented as worn by both men and women.[6]

Among the ringed ones, mention may be made of the crescent shaped ornament described as *mrishta kundalas (Mattha kundalas),* by Sivarama Murthy.[7] The cresecentic ear rings have also had a large distribution in India. It is possible that these were known as *Mrishta kundalas* or the *mattha kundalas* in Pali literature, in view of the fact that they were made of *mrittika* or clay. *Matti* or *Mattha* in Pali had become *Matti* in Telugu, which means clay. These crescentic ornaments are also known as *Chandrakarnikas*. These types of ornaments are extremely rare in the Kakatiya sculpture. However, crescent shaped nose rings are still in vogue in the Karimnagar and other

1. 1974-76 State Administrative Report, Department of Archaeology & Museums, A.P.,Hyderabad.
2. Sivarama Murthy, C., 1942 *Amaravathi Sculptures in Madras Museum* p.109›
3. Krishna Sastry,V.V., 1983 *Op.cit.,* p.99
4. 1983 *Ibid.,* Pl.86
5. 1983 *Ibid.,* Pl.86
6. Krishna Murthy, K., 1977 *Op.cit.,* p.64
7. Kivaram Murthy, C., 1942 *Op.cit.,* p.109

regions. Along with the crescentic ear rings a good number of annular rings of ivory or conch are found in the excavations.

The second type i.e., disc type is largely represented in the sculptures through the ages.

Ring Type : Mention may be made of the ear ornament worn by the lady in the sculpture of the donor-couple at Palampet. It is like a broad ring with a central hole. The ladies on the pillar panels holding lotus buds have rings with central holes. In the same temple the tribal ladies are shown wearing rings.

Disc Type : These are found in large numbers in the early historical times. Of these there are two categories; one is pulley shaped with a groove in the middle of the ring, and the other has a serrated edge. The pully shaped ornaments made of terracotta, crystal or glass have a wider distribution from the Mauryan times. It appears that the ornament is known as *Dhenri* in Bengal.[1] Krishna Murthy records that the disc-shaped ornament in the Attic and the Etruscan cultures are more elaborate than the Indian examples.[2] Disc-shaped ear ornaments are seen in the sculptures at Bharhut, Amaravati and in the early paintings at Ajanta.[3]

A beautiful *Madanika* figure is carved on a bracket in the eastern portico of the Palampet temple in a standing posture with legs crossed. She is bedecked with a crown, *Tatankas, haras* etc. The *Tatankas* are large-sized and made of metal. The ornaments are very simple and devoid of any design (fig.12g). Another figure of a voluptuous huntress from the same temple is adorned with *Tatankas, Haras, Keyuras, Manjiras* etc. The ear ornament is in the shape of a disc, bearing lotus-shaped decoration; in it's centre a big gem must have been in-laid. This ear ornament can be identified as the *Kanaka-Kamalas* (fig. 12h),[4] as mentioned by Kalidasa or the circular ear rings with full blown lotus pattern. These are often ruby-set to give the appearance of a lotus, sparkle like pomegranate seeds and are the *Ratnakundalas* of the *Silpa* texts.

An exquisite *Madanika* figure from Ghanpur, now installed in the State Department of Archaeology, Hyderabad, is bedecked with a disc-type ornament which contains a central jewelled flower in the shape of marigold (Fig. 12n).

Another type of disc inlaid with gem in the centre (or pulley type) may be seen worn by a *chauri* bearer on one of the door-jambs of the Thousand Pillared Temple at Warangal. Similarly a figure of *Madanika (Manini)*

---

1. Krishna Murthy, K., 1977 *Op.cit.*, p.64
2. Higgins, R.A., 1961 *Greek and Roman Jewellery (6th Edition), pp.99,125,137-139, Pl.13e and 13f*
3. Krishna Murthy, K., 1977 *Op.cit.*, p.64
4. Sivaram Murthy, C., 1942 *Op.cit.*, p.109

at Palampet has large-sized *Kundalas* with gems studded in the inner tier. We come across a double disc ornament as on the figure of Annapurna in the State Museum, Hyderabad. The lower disc appears to have been set with pearls and decorated with radiating spokes from the central hub. These may possibly indicate the Sun and the full Moon (Fig. 12j).

A treasure-trove recently deposited at the State Museum from Narsipur (Warangal district) makes an interesting study. The hoard consists of two ear rings of gold,each made in two parts. The upper part is triangular and the lower part is discular. In the middle of the disc is the figure of the Goddess Lakshmi. As the treasure-trove is found in the levels ascribable to the Kakatiya period, this ornament may give us an insight into the fabric of the real ornaments (Plate-21).

Nose Ornament: Nose ornament is conspicuously absent in the Kakatiya sculptures right from the early period. However, we find innumerable references in the mediaeval literature like, *Palnativira Charitra, Panditaradhya charitra, Vidhinatakam* and *Ranganatha Ramayana* etc. Some of the varieties mentioned are *Mutyala mungara*[1] (Pearl ring), *Patikapu mukkera*[2] or *spatika* (quartz), *Addapu- mukkera*[3] (transverse stud) and *Mukkunattu* (nose stud).[4] In the *Vidhinatakam* and *Chatuvulu* supposed to have been composed by Srinatha, a poet laureate in the court of the Reddis of *Kondavidu*, we find an amazing variety of nose ornaments, such as *Nattu, Mukku mungara, Kempula mungara* (set with rubies), *Harumunji-mutyala mungara* (ornament studded with pearls imported from Ormuz, a Persian sea port, *Pacchala mungara* (emeralds) *Ravvala mungara* (diamond studded) etc.[5] Evidently all these nose rings might have been made of gold and inlaid with pearls and precious stones.

We find no mention of nose ornaments in the entire Vedic litertature or in the early Indian art. It is argued that nose ornaments became familiar in India from about 1000 A.D. mainly as a result of Muslim contact.[6] However, some writers tried to disprove the earlier opinion stating that the use of nose ring may be traced to 1st and 2nd centuries A.D.[7] In Soundarya Lahari, Tripura sundari Manasa Puja and Lalita Sahasranamam, the nose ring of the Goddess is eulogised in glowing terms.[8]

1. Umakantha Pandita,(Ed.) 1955 *Op.cit.*, p.72
2. Ramaswamy Sastry, V., (Ed.) 1960 *Op.cit.*, p.69
3. Sarma, M.S., 1948 *The History of the Reddy Kingdom*, p.299
4. Prabhakara Sastry,V., (Ed.) 1960 *Op.cit.*, p.48 and *Ranganatha Ramayanam* Ed by Ramaswamy Sastry, V., (Ed.) p.72
5. Singaracharya,B.V., (Ed.) 1972 *Srinathuni Chatuvulu*, p.78,81,82,85 and 89.
6. Altekar, A.S., 1959 The position of Women in Hindu Civilization, pp.301-302
7. Krishna Murthy, K., 1978 "Is not nose ornament ancient?", *Telugu Vaani*, Vol.III, No.10, pp.60-62
8. 1978 *Ibid*.

In the light of the above discussion, it may be presumed that the nose ring is as Indian as any other object but not represented in the plastic art, due to the fear that the delicate features of the nose will get damaged while chiselling or modelling.

In the Narsipur hoard now under the safe custody of State Department of Archaelogy and Museums, Hyderabad, is found a nose ring of gold from which a coral is suspended (Fig. 12k). The other objects of the treasure trove consisted of two perforated gold coins of Raya Gajakesari, gold rings etc.

Neck Ornament : Of all the ornaments, necklaces are the most commonly worn ornaments by both men and women during the medieval ages. Necklaces of any kind either of gold, copper, silver, pearl, coral, even cowries, beads of precious and semi- precious stones or seeds of lotus, *Kuruvinda* (doricus biflorous) etc, were worn tightly around the neck, while some reached down to the chest or even navel region. An amazing variety of neck ornaments have been recorded in the contemporary literature. Some of them are *Trisaras*[1] (three seried) *Mutya-Ratnala-Peru*[2] (necklace studded with pearls and rubies), *Pataka*[3] (Pendants), *Bannasaralu,*[4] *hara* studded with *precious stones or sometimes made of black beads), Mutyalya Patteda*[5] (strap-like ornament of pearls), *Ratnaharamulu,*[6] *Navaratnamala*[7] (studded with nine kinds of precious stones), Muktaphala-valulu[8] (series of necklaces),*Taraharas*[9] (large-sized genuine pearl necklaces), *Kanthe* (torque), *Graivekamu*[10] (necklets) etc. Most of these *haras* are made of gold with precious or semi-precious stones, sometimes with a single bar of gold, with or without designs. All thse varieties are worn by royalty,nobles and the wealthy sections of the society. The ornaments such as *Pusala-perlu* (garland of lotus seeds), *Guriza perlu* or kurivinda or doricus bilflorus,[11] etc, as mentioned in the litreature cited were used by the poor people. In the light of the above discussion, the *hara, sara, peru, danda,* or *mala* or *golusu* indicate long necklaces. A *hara*

1. 1958 *Bhimeswara Puranam by Srinatha,* Part-I, Verse 105
2. *Palnativira Charitra,* Ed Umakantha Pandita, 1955 p.72
3. 1955 *Ibid.*
4. Ramaswamy Sastry, V., (Ed.) 1960 Op.cit., p.65 and also *Palnativira charitra Ed by Umakantha Pandita,* p.72
5. Sarma, M.S., 1948 *Op.cit.,*p.299, *Ranganatha Ramayanam* Ed by Ramaswamy Sastry, V., p.65 and also *Palnativira Charitra* Ed by Umakantha Pandita, p.72.
6. Koravi Goparaju, 1960 *Op.cit.*, p.130
7. 1960 *Ibid.*
8. 1960 *Ibid.*
9. Ramaswamy Sastry,V., (Ed.) 1960 Op.cit., p.65 and also *Palnativira Charitra* Ed by Umakantha Pandita, pp.17, 49.
10. 1960 *Ibid.*
11. Narayana Rao, Ch., (Ed.) 1974 Op.cit., p 229 and p.235

composed of a single string of pearls or gold is known as *Ekavali,*[1] when it is composed of three strings, it is *Trisara*[2] and if it is of five strings it is known as *Bannisara.* The *pataka* may literally mean a pendant set with several varieties of precious stones. It is likely that it denoted a necklace with pendant during the later medieval period.

Pearl necklaces: A figure of *dalamalika* (alasakanya), holding a creeper with her right hand and left hand in akimbo, on the southern wall of the Pacchala Somesvara temple at Pangual is shown wearing an *Ekavali* which forms a loop below her breasts. She also wears another single stringed pearl necklace with one bigger pearl in the centre. This may be the *Sirshaka,* as mentioned by Kautilya (Fig.12.l).

The idol of Annapurna from Kasipet, now exhibited in the State Museum, Hydeabad is shown wearing a long *hara* of pearls with five pendants (Fig.13c). This may be the *Pancha Phalaka* type. Each *phalaka* is studded with nine gems, one central big gem is surrounded by eight. The same figure wears a beautiful *Ekavali* of pearls with a big *Phalaka* below the breast This is also studded with nine gems as described above (Fig.12m).

A figure of *Madanika* from Ghanpur, now exhibited in the premises of State Archaeology Department is richly adorned with different types of ornaments such as a *Graiveyaka* (strap type ornament close to the neck), *Patteda,* probably decorated with figure work and a *trisara* passing over the breast down to the navel and having a middle pendant (Plate-22). The multiple pearl stringed long *haras* on the lady bracket figures at Palalmpet have three or more pearl strings, provided with three joints on each side. The joints are in the shape of a lotus (Fig.13a & b). We find a best example of *Pataka* on the torso of Siva in Warangal fort sculptures (Fig.12.0).

Strings of Beads: The wide practice of wearing beads is testified to in the literature as well as in the sculptural art. *Panditaradhya charitra* simply mentions the existence of various kinds of beads. The other references like *gavvadandalu, Tammipusalu* (lotus beads), *Kuruvinda* beads have already been mentioned. Unfortunately it is dificult to identify the material of the beads in the plastic art. In the Palampet temple the musicians and the dancers found on the pillars of the *Sabha mantapa* are shown adorned with *Pattedas* (straps) attached with rectangular beads,possibly of seeds or glass.

Torque or Kanthi : In the literature and in the sculptural art several specimens of torque are encountered. The *Kanthi* has a great antiquity. In *Gathasapthasati,*[3] a work attributed to the Satavahana period refers to *Kanthi.*

The best example of Kakatiya *Kanthi* may be found in the figure of Annapurna. This is a simple ring-like object with a central knob or jewel.

1. Shyama Sastry, R., (Ed.) 1915 *Arthasastra,* p.86
2. 1915 *Ibid.*
3. Ramachandra, T., 1978 *Gathasaptasathilo Telugu Padalu,* p.34

Usually a clasp is provided at the back of the neck. Similar ornaments are also found on the female figures in Bejjanki temple. Kanthis are made of solid or hollow gold.

The hoard from Narsipur contained an interesting type of necklace of eleven gold beads and one pipal leaf-shaped pendant. Each bead is in the shape of a *Nagabandha* shown in dotted line and toped by a bull with a transverse hole for threading. There is also a vertical dotted line bisecting the *Nagabandha* symbol. The pendant in the shape of pipal leaf has a loop in the place of a stalk (Plate-23).

Keyuras : The ornaments worn on the upper arm is known as *Angada, Keyura* in Sanskrit or *Danda kadiya*[1] in Telugu. *Keyura* is known from the times of *Mahabharatha*.

The reliefs depict both males and females with the armlets mainly of two varieties, namely (i) a simple entwining or spiralled ring; (II) the one decorated with a beaded pattern, sometimes having a flower or a jewelled disc in the centre.

The tubular ring which is hollow inside is probably the most com mon variety, as is evident from its frequent depiction in the reliefs. The huntresses with leafy under-garments in Bejjanki temple are shown wearing spiralled armlets (Fig.14a).

A *chauri* bearer on the door-jamb in the Hanumakonda temple wears two armlets. The upper one is known as *Vanki* in Telugu consisting of a triangular bend upwards (Fig.14) The lower armlet is a jewelled strap; Inspite of its occurrence on the both male and female figures, it appears that it is more a male ornament. On the Hero Stones now exhibited in the State Museum, Hyderabad, the ornament is not found on the females whereas it is always there on the male figures.

A lady bracket figure from Ghanpur temple, exhibited in the State Department of Archaeology has armlets with a beaded pattern and semi-circular jewelled disc attached at the top facing the viewer (Fig.14d).

Of all the armlets depicted, those found on the figure of Annapuuna from Kasipet are extremely beautiful. Each consists of three rows of beads with a central nine-jewelled plaque . At the top is one more plaque in the form of a rising sun with radiating lines (Fig 14c).

Armlets of beads : The other variety of armlet is usually made of beads or *Rudrakshas*. Very often the *Rudraksha* armlets are found on Saivite mendicants, devotees, temple musicians, donors etc. A figure of a Saivite mendicant found on the pillar of the *Sabha mantapa* of Hanumakonda temple is shown wearing armlets of beads, probably *Rudrakshas*. A devotee ringing a bronze gong in a squating posture found in the Hanumakonda temple

1. Umakantha Pandita, (Ed.) 1955 *Op.cit.*, p.17 and p.72

and a male figure in the panel of the donor- couple in the Palampet temple are shown with the same type of ornaments.

Bracelets : This is the commonest ornament worn by males and females during the Kakatiya period. The simple type is a tubular ring which may either be solid or hollow. These are generaly known as *Kankanas*. These were made of different materials depending on the economic status of the people wearing them.

In the literature we find copious references to *Kadiyas*[1] *Chekatlu*[2] (Hand ornaments), *Murugulu*[3] etc. While kings, nobles and people of higher strata wore bracelets made of gold, studded with diamonds, emeralds, sapphires etc. the poorer section of the society went for bracelets made of silver, copper, shell or glass of various hues. In *Palnativira Charitra*, we find mention of *Danda Kadiyas*, *Neelalagajulu* (blue glass), *Chamala Kadiyas*[4] etc. At another place thre is a mention of *Gurjari Kadiyas* (probably imported from Gurjarat) and *"Moravanka Kadiyas"* (gingling curved bracelets).

In the sculptures, there are five principal types of bracelets i.e., (1) spiral or ring type (2) thick bracelets decorated with jewels, (3) beaded type, (4) gauntlet or tapering cylinder and (5) a chain type. The first three varieties are found commonly and need no explanation. Examples of the last two types i.e., chain type and gauntlet type are dealt here. The figure of Rati in the Palampet temple holding a sugar cane has the chain type of bracelets on her forearms (Fig.14e & f). The figure of Annapurna from Kasipet wears a gauntlet type of bracelet. The gauntlet is made of three or four plates and jointed together with clasps (F9g14g). Several gauntlets of silver of the post-Kakatiyan period are found in the State Department of Archaeology and Museums, Hyderabad.

Finger Rings : Finger Ring is known as *Ungaramu*,[5] *Mudrika*[6] (Signet ring) and *Anguliyaka*[7] (Finger ring). They are made of gold, silver, copper, conch, ivory etc. and studded with precious or semi-precious stones. We find the representation of finger rings in the sculpture. However, it is not possible to identify the design and pattern of the rings.

In the *Manini* and other types of *Alasakanya* figures in the Palampet temple, the maidens are shown wearing rings on all the figures including the thumbs. There are also coiled rings on the fingers of bracket figures (Fig.14h).

---

1. Umakantha Pandita, (Ed.) 1955 op. cit p.17 and p.72.
2. Ramaswamy Sastri,V.,(Ed.) 1960 *Op.cit.*, p.65
3. Koravi Goparaju, 1960 *Op.cit.*, p.130
4. Umakantha Pandita, (Ed.) 1955 *Op.cit.*, p.17 and p.72
5. Koravi Goparaju, 1960 *Op.cit.*, p.130
6. Srinatha, 1958 *Bhimeswara Puranam* Vol.I, verse 117
7. Koravi Goparaju, 1960 *Op.cit.*, p.129

Chest Band : This is associated mostly with the divine and royal figures. In the sculptural art three varieties of chest bands are noticed. One is a strap-like ornament decorated with tassels and jewelled cusps. The best example for this is found on a torso of a royal or divine figure with broken head, hands and legs found lying in the Warangal fort. The figure of Vishnu has strap-like chest band with beaded edgings.

On the figure of *Virabhadra* recovered inside the Warangal fort, the chest band is curved upward in a triangle (Fig.14i) In the wall figure of Lakshami Narayana in the Pacchala Someswara temple at Panugal, one figure has a chest band of several strands and the other figure has a pearl-studded one (Fig. 14j). Interestingly the figures of Lakshmi in both the panels do not have *Kucha bandhas*.

Mekhala : *Mekhala* is a girdle or belt worn by men and women. Formerly the girdle was worn by the upper caste people only. According to *Grihya Sutras* a *mekhala* worn by a Brahmin should be made of *Munja* grass. A *Kshatriya* should wear a *Murva* and *Sana* or hemp by a *Vaisya*[1] Mounji bandha is one of the sixteen sacraments or *samskaras* for a Hindu . As such, the origin of this particular ornament is more ceremonial and functional than decorative; functional in the sense that it is useful for wearing a Kaupina which protects the genitals.[2] In Telugu literature, we find several terms such as Nadikattu (middle band), *Molanūlu* (waist- thread), *Katisutra*, *Vaddānamu* etc.[3]

The *mekhala* (girdle) is profusely represented in the Kakatiya sculptures. The *Katisūtra* or the thread over the loins is generally depicted over the *mekhalās* on both the male and female figures. The *mekhalas* sometimes consist of three bands of pearls knitted to a strap or sometimes two bands, each having several strands of pearls. This is probably a *'rasana'* or *rasanakalpa*, as mentioned in *Raghuvamsa*[4] and *Mrichakatika*.[5] The *Katisutra* or chord found over the *rasana* is the *hemasutra* or the gold cord. Sivarama murthy opines that *rasana* is so named from the chain type with numerous links composed in it.[6]

One of the bracket figures in the Palampet temples (upraised hands mutiliated) has a broad waist-band with three *valayas*, each composed of several strands of beads, each having a central gem or a rosette. Similarly,

1. Macdonell & Keith 1958 *Vedic Index of Names and Subjects*, Vol.II, p.177
2. 1958 *Ibid.*
3. 1958 *Bhimeswara Puranam by* Srinatha, Vol.I, Verse 117; *Ranganatha Ramayanam*, Ed. Ramaswamy Sastry, V., p.65.
4. Sivarama Murthy, C., 1942 *Op.cit.*, p.113
5. 1942 *Ibid.*
6. 1942 *Ibid.*

the *nartaki* bracket figure from Ghanpur is depicted with a similar *mekhala*. The lower band with a series of festoons is suspended over the thighs.

An excellent specimen of *mekhala* is found over the torso of a male (or female) recovered from the Warangal fort. A curvilinear *katisutra* is found over the *mekhala*. The *mekhala* is a three banded one, the top band is embossed with floral designs, the middle one is a woven thread of filgree work; the lowest band is decorated with jewels in the shape of diamonds. The clasp in the middle is shaped like a lionine *kirtimukha* clutching a bead patterned ring in its mouth. Festoons of beads attached to the lowest band are suspended over the thighs down to the torso (Fig. 14n and plate 24).

The lady *chauri* bearer on the door-jamb of the Panugal temple has a single band of a broad girdle knitted with a series of beaded rings. Three circular gems carrying pearl festoons are fastened to the gridle. A broad *katisutra* pointed in the middle is found over the *mekhala* (Fig. 14 k).

A three banded *mekhala* each having a series of beaded string with a nine gem studded plaque in the centre having suspended tassels and festoons, is found on the figures of Channakesava from Katakshapur. (Fig. 14m).[1]

Here it may be noted that most of the divine figures are shown with three bands of girdles. This is reminiscent of the description of the Goddess in the *Lalitasahasranama*[2] as having three folds below her stomach formed due to the heavy weight of her bosom. These three *valayas* encircling the nine *avaranas* form the essential features of *Sri chakra* which may represent the three worlds.

Anklets : The anklets formed an important feature of ornamentation, the antiquity of which may be traced from very early times. The term *'Khadi'*[3] found in Rigveda denotes an anklet or an armlet. In the *Sutras 'Manjira'*[4] probably meant a cow or a river. *Manjira* also means a post around which strings of the churning stick passes. Sivarama Murthy states that the *Manjira* anklet is so called since it resembles the coiled strings on the churning stick, entwining the legs above the ankle and *nupura* is the one which produces the sweet sound.[5] In the Buddhist sculptures we find heavy spiralled anklets. In the contemporary Telugu literature various names such as *Andiya or Ande, Kadiya, Manjira, Hamsaka, Panjevu,*[6] are found.

1. This sculpture is now in the state Museum, Hyderabad, Andhra Pradesh.
2. Ramamurthy Sastry,Ed. 1964 *Lalita Sahasranama Stotramu*, Verse 15, p.61, 89 and 90.
3. Macdonell & Keith 1958 *Op.cit.*, p.216.
4. Sir Monier Monier- Williams 1979 *Op.cit.*, p.774
5. Sivarama Murthy, C., 1942 *Op.cit.*, p.114
6. Umakantha Pandita, (Ed.) 1955 Op.cit., p.17 and p.72 and also in *Kridabhiramam* Ed. by Prabhakara Sastry, V., p.70

The *khadi* or *kadiyams* are those worn above the anklets, and *andiyas* or *hamsakas* are worn over the feet. There are two main varieties of *khadiyas;* one is a tiered ring with beaded fillet as found on the *nartaki* bracket figure at Palampet (Fig. 15b). The second type consists of a ring with beaded design having suspended festoons (Fig. 15a & c).

The male dancers, on one of the pillars of the Palampet temple, wear the usual type of rattles in four rows. Below the rattle band are heavy anklets with a beaded pattern (Fig. 15d).

The *Manjira* or the feet ornament was also worn by male warriors as found in a triangular panel found inside the Warangal fort (Figs. 15 f, g & h). However, there are numerous references to a special ornament known as *Gandapendera* worn by men of great literary excellence. However, in *Palnativira Charita,* Nalagama Raja - the cheif of Macherla, is said to have adorned himself with *Gandapendera* on his legs.

Toe Rings : Toe Rings or *Padamudrikas*[1] are exclusively worn by married women in the Hindu society. These are otherwise known as *mattiyalu, pillendlu*[2] (a ring worn on the fourth toe of the ladies) *Vira maddiya*[3] or *Vira mudrika* is one worn to the first toe of the feet. The lady figures on the pillars at Bejjanki temple are shown wearing toe rings on first and second toes. Another representation of the toe-rings are found on the toes of Annapurna, exhibited in the State Museum, Hyderabad. (Fig. 15i).

1. Koravi Goparaju 1960 *Op.cit.,* Part-I, p.130
2. Narayana Rao, Ch., (Ed.) 1974 *Op.cit.,* p.235
3. Subbayya Sastry, K., 1979 *Op.cit.,* p.317.

CHAPTER-IX

COIFFURE

From ancient times Indians have bestowed extreme care on the beautification of their hair. Even during Vedic times a variety of hair styles were in vogue. They are the *opasa,*[1] *kaparda,*[2] *kumba,*[3] *kurira,*[4] *dakshinata-kapardhi, pulasti,*[5] *sikhanda,*[6] *sikha,*[7] *simanta*[8] etc. *Opasa* probably means plaited hair, especially of women. *Prithustuka* may mean broad braids and *visitastuka,* loosened braids. It (Kaparda) may also mean wearing the hair in plaits. The term *jata* was exclusively used for Siva as *Kapardhi,* wearing braided hair. If braids are on the right side, it is known as *Dakshina Kaparda. Kumba* might have been derived from a pot or *kumbha.* Originally it may also have meant a horn, as such the hair made into a bun like a pot or a horn known as *kumba. Kurira* might be an ornament worn on the hair or a mode of hair dressing. *Pulasti* denotes wearing the hair plain or combed as opposed to *Kapardin.*

Sikhanda denotes a tuft or lock as referred in the later *Samhitas* and *Brahmanas. Sikha* or *Siga* is a knot of hair, worn on the top of the head. Wearing a top-knot was a sign of mourning in the case of men and women alike. *Simanta* denotes the parting of hair. According to *Katyayana Grihya Sutra,*[9] the hair and beard excluding *sikha* should be removed to perform a sacrifice. The *Grihya sutras* prescribe different rules for arranging the hair of a child. In Boudhayana Grihya Sutras,[10] the boy may keep one, three or five *sikhas* according to the custom of the family. In the *Natya sastra* of Bharata,[11] the hair styles of the women are described according to the

---

1. Macdonell & Keith, 1958 *Vedic Index of Names and Subjects,* Vol.I, pp.124-25.
2. Ibid, p.135.
3. *Ibid,* p.163.
4. *Ibid,* p.164.
5. *Ibid,* Vol.II, p.8.
6. Ibid, Vol.II, p.377.
7. *Ibid,* Vol.II, p.378.
8. *Ibid,* Vol.II,p.451.
9. *Ibid,* Vol.II, p.378.
10. *Ibid,* Vol.I, p.135.
11. Ghosh, M.M., 1950 *Natya Sastra,* p.420.

regions from which he hailed. The women from Malwa wore curly hair, from Gauda had a top knot or plaited hair, from Abhira the women had two plaits which were sometimes wound around the head. The women of South India wore their hair in the shape of a water vessel (*Kumbha*), held together by an ornament. The *Vishnudharmottara Purana* describes different modes of hair dressing, namely *Kuntala, Dakshinavarta* (plaited hair towards right), *Taranga* (wavy), *Simha Kesara* (mane-like hair falling on the neck), *Vardhala* (inter-twisted), *Jata* (Chignon).[1]

We find plentiful references to hair dressing in the medieval Telugu literature, such as *Koppu*[2] (pot like), *Jada*[3] (plaited hair), *Jadimudi*[4] (plaited hair made into a bun), *Jaru Koppu*[5] (bun having flowing hair below). *'Palnativira Charitra'*[6] mentions that Manchala wore pearl tassels at the end of her plaited hair. In the *Virata Parva* of *Andhra Mahabharata* Sairandri (Draupadi) introduces herself to Sudheshna as an efficient hair dresser, who could do varieties of hair dresses and prepare various kinds of garlands[7]

Male Hair Styles:

The study of hair dresses of the Kakatiya period may be categorised into two sections - male and female hair styles. Both the males and females were having long hair. The common people such as warriors, musicians etc. are shown donning a bun at the back. In the Rudresvara temple at Palampet, the warriors in a war scene have done their hair into a bun. *Sikha* or *Siga* is a knot of hair worn on the top of the head. A panel representing an ascetic with *Sikha* type hair dress is found at Tripurantakam temple. The knot is simple and arranged in tiers. This type of hair-do is repeatedly found in the temple sculptures of Warangal fort (Fig. 16n).

Loose hair fallen on the shoulders :- In a ceiling panel at Nidikonda a Saivite devotee is shown with loosened hair, which is allowed to fall on the shoulders (Fig. 16. m).

Another mode of hair dressing is to have long hair with ringlets dangling on the nape and shoulders. The *adhistana* friezes at Palampet temple representing the soldiers have this type of hair-do. The coiffure is shown secured by a forehead band. (Fig. 16. o & p).

Kaparda or matted locks tied into a knot on the top of the head. Lord Siva is also known as *Kapardi* as he is said to be donning a *Kaparda*

---

1. Krishna Murthy,K., 1982 *Hair styles in Ancient Indian Art*, p.15.
2. *Srinathuni chatuvulu*, p.78. Singaracharya,B.V., (Ed.) 1972
3. *Ibid*, p.79
4. *Ibid*, p.79.
5. *Ibid*, p.78.
6. *Ibid*, p.79.
7. *Andhra Mahabharatam*, Ramanujayya,B.V.,(Ed) 1939

or the dishevelled matted locks. A *chaturmukha* linga in the courtyard of Somesvara temple inside Warangal fort is represented with four faces of Lord Siva (Isana, Vama Deva, Aghora and Tatpurusha). All the four heads are having matted locks. Another representation of Kaparda is found on the head of a Saivite mendicant, carved on the wall sculpture at Palampet Temple.

The mane-like coiffure may be identified as the *simha- kesara.*[1] On a door-jamb at Pachhala Somesvara temple at Panugal a beautiful *madanika* is accompanied by a male dwarf. The dwarf is shown with coiffure mentioned above. The hair is falling on the shoulders like a lion's mane.

Clean Shaven head :- In the reliefs we find ascetics, and wrestlers with clean shaven heads. On a wall sculpture in the Palampet temple, the wrestlers are shown with clean shaven heads, which appears to be a requisite for the wrestlers so that the opponent does not catch hold of the hair.

A top knot in a conical shape :- On a wall sculpture at Pachhala Somesvara temple a dwarf is shown wearing a conical shaped top knot on the head. Another panel from the same temple represents a dwarf with a loose knot with coil at one end resting on the shoulders. Wearing a knot seems to be very popular among the commoners of the Kakatiya period.

Beards :- In several reliefs the Saivite devotees are shown with beards. However, beards were not favoured by common men. On a ceiling panel in the Palampet temple the devotees are shown with long grown beards. We have many sculptural representation of this feature.

Female Hair Styles :-

Decoration of hair forms the most important aspect of the ladies dress. The Hanumakonda *Niroshtya Kavya* epigraph[2] mentions that the hair of the peasant women in the act of being dressed gave the appearance of the spread-out plumes of the peacock. Kalidasa refers to this style as *barha-bhara-kesa.*[3] Not only the literature and epigraphs,but the sculptural representations as well bear ample testimony to the great care bestowed on dressing and arranging the hair in different patterns.The sculptures give us a fair idea of the various hair styles of the women. A panel representing a beautiful *Madanika* carved on a ceiling at Palampet temple is shown wearing a knot. She has combed her hair back and tied with a band round the head.(Fig.16.a)

---

1. Sivaramamurthy,C., 1955 "Sanskrit Literature and Art, Mirrors of Indian Culture", *M.A.S.I.*, 73, p.65.
2. Epigraphia Indica,XXXVI,p.216.
3. Agrawala, V.S., 1949 "Art Evidence in Kalidasa", *JUPHS*, Vol.XXII, p.89.

Another figure of Madanika, exhibited in the State Archaeology Department, Hyderabad, is adorned with a beautiful knot. She has combed her hair back and secured it into an oval shaped bun.(Fig.16.b).

A figure of a lady attendant carved on a door-jamb in the temple at Hanumakonda has combed her hair back and secured it into a knot. The knot is arranged in tiers, which are closely interspersed with pearls and strings of gold. It may be identified as a *Dhammila*[1] type of hair style (Fig. 16. d, Pl. 25).

Another panel depicts a lady in the porch of the temple Pacchala Somesvara, in which she is shown wearing a beautiful halo-like roll, with parting in the center. The hair is secured into a big roll and decorated with a band of flowers or *Pushpapatta* (Fig. 17c, Pl. 26).

Another Panel representing a lady *chamaragrahi* found in a niche in the temple of Pacchala Somesvara is shown wearing fan- like crescentic roll. The tiers seem to be interspersed with flowers or jewels (Fig. 17. b, Pl. 27).

Side knot:---On a pillar in the Bejjanki temple, two dancers are shown wearing side end knots behind the right ears,. They combed their hair to one side and secured it into a bun (Fig 6.c). Conical side knot is still in vogue in north coastal Andhra Desa.[2]

Another type of hair style seems to be worn by a lady in the Warangal fort sculpture. She has combed her hair back and tied it into a big side-bun. This type of hair style is known as *Jarumudi* in Telugu, which seems to be very common.

Varieties of loose knots:---A Madanika carved on a bracket in the Palampet temple is wearing an elegant loose knot on the nape. She has combed her hair back and secured it into a bun (Fig, 16. e)

Another panel depicts a lady with a loose knot in the Warangal fort sculptures. She has combed her hair back and twisted it into a big loop and the remaining hair gracefully flows over the shoulders (Fig, 16. F, Pl, 29). This style may be identified as *Kesapusa*[3] or a noose

A huntress depicted in the wall sculpture at Palampet is shown wearing a simple knot. She has combed her hair back and secured it into a knot like a whorl (Fig. 16. g).

A dancer who is tying her rattles around the flexed left leg is shown with her hair beautifully combed and made into a left side-bun. In the same

1. Sivaramamurthy,C., 1942 Amaravari Sculptures in Madras Museum.P. 107.
2. Even today this type of knots are worn by the Agency women at Araku valley in Visakhapatham district, Andhra Pradesh.
3. Sivaramamurthy, C., 1942 op. cit., P. 106.

panel the male drummer playing *mridanga* with both hands has a right side-bun.

On a wall sculpture in the Pacchala Somesvara temple at Panugal a lady is shown wearing a double bun. She has combed her hair back and arranged in two tiers (Fig. 16. h.)

Anoher type of hair style is represented in the temple at Palampet. A lady is depicted on a door-jamb with a double knot. She has parted her hair in the center, combed her hair back and secured it into a double bun. (Fig. 16.1).

A panel in a wall sculpture in the temple of Pacchala Somesvara at Panugal. depicts a scene--- in which a lady engaged in dressing. She has made her hair into a long plait the ends of which are held in her hands while a lady attendant shows a mirror lifted up to the level of her face (Fig. 16. j. P1.28).

In a *Ramayana* panel, *'Tara Vilapam'*, at Nidikonda, Tara the consort of Vali has her long hair loosened down to her hips without plaiting, This type is rare in the sculpture, but shown only to indicate mourning. Sometimes Saivite, mendicants are also shown with long loosened hair or *Ekaveni*[1] (Fig. 16.k).

Karanda type:- Karanda type of hair style appears to be rare during the Kakatiya period. Karanda means a wicker basket of flowers in the shape of a honey comb or cone with receding tiers. A closer example of this type seems to be worn by a female devotee in the Warangal fort sculputures. She has combed her hair upwards and secured it into a ball-shaped knot. The knot seems to be decorated with a rosary of *Rudrakshas* (Fig. 17. a).

Another representation of Karanda hair style is found on a pillar in the Thousand Pillared hall in Hanumakonda. Here a panel depicts a king offering obeisance to a sage. The figure with a parrot-head and human body may represent Suka Maharshi. The king is represented with a *Karanda* type of hair style with his hair combed and secured into a top bun.

On a wall of the temple of Pacchala Somesvara, a *Madanika* is represented with coiled hair made into a side-bun. Some ringlets dangle on the forehead. We find this type repeatedly in the sculptural art of the period. In the Palampet temple most of the *Alasaknyas* on the brackets are shown wearing loose knots, arranged in coils, either to the left or the right of the head.

Curled hair:- The curly hair style occurs frequently in the reliefs. The best example is that of a *nagini* or a lady with the serpent who is represented with curled hair, having small ringlets near the forehead. We have further

1. 1942 Ibid.

evidences for curled hair. Many of the figures are shown depicted with *bramarakas*[1] or small ringlets dangling on the forehead.

The discussion in the preceding pages gives an idea of the great care bestwed on dressing and arrranging of the hair. Long hair being a pre-requisite for elaborate hair dressing by both men and women, people of all walks of life wore long hair which also required extreme care for preservation and promote its growth. It was also the practice to apply scented oils made form *champak* and other fragrant flowers. *Kridabhiramam*[2] describes a lady of the *Karanam* caste selling oil scented with *champak* flowers in the streets of Warangal. The hawking voice of the lady, it is stated, was as mellifluous as the song of a cuckoo. The different knots of hair seem to have been decorated with wreaths of flowers known as *Pushpapatta* or strings of flowers, *Patrapatta* (strings of leaves) or by various gold or silver ornaments studded with precious gems and pearls. However, people of lower strata have perforce opted for flowers and leaves.[3]

1. 1942 *Ibid.*,and Gatha Sapta Sati, p.111.
2. *Kridabhiramam,* (Ed.) Prabhakara Sastry, V., 1960 p.32
3. *Palnati Veeracharitra* Ed. Umakantha Panditha 1955. p.72

CHAPTER-X

GAMES AND AMUSEMENTS

Contemporary literature and sculpture provide us lot of information about the games and amusements that were in vogue in the Kakatiya society.

Following are some of the games mentioned by Palkurki Somanatha in *Panditaradhya Charitra,*[1] *Ragunju Pogunjulata, Gudigudi Gunjambulata, Appalavindulata, Chappatlu, Sarigunjulata, Serabontalata, Chitlapotlata, Gorantalata, Dagudumutalata* etc. But for a few of the above games, most of them are extinct in the present day society.

Palnati Viracharitra[2] mentions *Gummadikayalata* (Pumpkin play), *Cherukula Pandemulu* (Sugar cane contests), *Pokalata* (Betal nut play), *Mutyamula Bantulata* (Pearl balls game), ferocious animal fights, *Rukalakuppalata* (Play with piles of coins) etc.

The game of tops was probably a favourite of the boys. In *Palnati Viracharitra* Balachandra expresses his wish to play tops. His mother Aitamma sent for the goldsmith and ordered to prepare tops of gold, studded with precious stones and the strings made of gold and silver. She also explains as to how the game should be played. She stated that royal streets, main roads and habitational places are not fit for the game. Outskirts of a village or town are the most suitable places for the game of tops.[3]

The most popular game was dicing or gambling. In the ancient period it was known as *Akshadyuta* as the dice were marked with circles and dots in the shape of an eye-ball. We have many references throwing light on this game. This game was described in *Panditaradhya Charitra*[4], as Pachikalu. The chess board is referred to as *Phalaka*. The terms mentioned are *Daya* (one), *Duga* (two), *Ittigi* (three), Chowkamu (four) etc. *Gachchakayalu* (Molucca beans or fever nut), balls, birds, caged falcons, parrots formed the pawns.[5]

In *Simhasana Dvatrimsika,*[6] one gambler boasts that in the game of dice (chess?) he may lose the elephants, horses, ministers, charriots to his

---

1. *Sri Panditaradhyacharitra*, NarayanaRao, Ch., (Ed.) 1974 p.106.
2. *Palnativiracharitra, Umakantha Panditha, (Ed.) 1955 pp.37-38.*
3. Umakantha Panditha (Ed.). 1955 *Ibid*, pp.41-44.
4. Narayana Rao, Ch. (Ed.) 1974 *Op.cit.*, p.86.
5. Umakantha Panditha, (Ed.). 1955 *Op.cit., p.45.*
6. *Simhasana Dvatrimsika* Koravi Goparaju, Reprint 1960 Vol II P.85

opponent but ultimately he would check the king with a mere Bantu (Pawn). The above work discourages gambling by stating that people who are addicts lose their wealth, morals, truthfulness and good name, and the author gives examples of the legendary figures like Nala and Dharmaraja who lost everything in gambling.[1]

This was the most trecherous of the ancient games. Generally gambling dens were attached to the houses of prostitutes. Lovers of this sport used to stake whatever they possessed and finally they were made paupers due to cheating by the prostitutes.[2]

Next we come across the game of dolls particularly indulged in by the girls. The dolls were usually made of ivory, wood, glass or clay. They used to build toy houses and celebrate marriages of dolls.[3]

Another interesting pastime referred to is swimming. Nannechoda[4] refers to this in his work *Kumara Sambhava,* wherein he refers to the swimmers who gained proficiency in the display of back-stroke while they were swimming. Another variety of water game was mentioned, particularly indulged in by women. They used to throw water on each other with syringes known as *Karayantras* or *Jalayantras* filled with scented water.[5]

It was also indulged in by the royalty, especially during the summer season. It is elaborately described in the work *Vikramakadeva Charitra*[6]. The king Vikramaditya VI, spent his time with his women in bathing chambers (dhāragriha) constructed with crystal floors and arrangments made for water springs emitted through the interstices to cool down their bodies from the scorching heat. Swimming was also enjoyed by them.

Kanduka-Krida or the game of ball seems to have been a very popular sport of the period under review. The work *Kridabhiramam*[7] makes mention of this game as played at dusk by girls. Jingling sounds of bangles, bracelets and anklets was produced while playing this game. The balls were made of pearls[8] and flowers.[9] One of the *madanikas* at Palampet is represented as doing *Kandukabhinaya* (Dance gesture), Her right hand is raised above her head and holds a *Kanduka,* perhaps made of flowers.

1. *Simhasana Dvatrimsika,* Koravi Goparaju, 1960 *Vol.II, p.85.*
2. *Kridabhiramam,* Prabhakara Sasdtry.V,. (Ed.). 1960 pp.30-31, and also Koravi Goparaju, 1960, *Simhasana Dvatrimsika,* Vol. II, p.85.
3. *Kumara Sambhavam* by Nannechoda, Ramaswamy Sastry,V., (Ed.). 1961 Ver.69.
4. 1961 *Ibid,* Ver.84,p.259.
5. 1961 *Ibid,* Ver.50,p.253.
6. *Vikramankadeva Charitram* by Bilhana, Buhler, G., 1897 Ver.15-19.
7. Prabhakara Sastry, V., (Ed.). *Op.cit.,* p.84.
8. Upakantha Panditha (Ed.) 1955 *Op.cit.,* p.38.
9. *J.O.I.,* Vol.XXIII,No.3,p.220.

In an inscription of Nayanapalli in Guntur district Ganapatideva is praised as *Prithvisvara- Sirah - Kanduka - Kridavinoda*, enjoying the game with the decapitated head of Prithvisvara.[1]

Next we come across some of the pastimes of our period. Mention may be made of *Meshayuddha* (Ram-fight), perhaps liked by one and all of the society during the Kakatiya period. In *Kridabhiramam* the same is witnessed by Tittibha Setti and his friend, while wandering in the city of Warangal.[2] In *Manasollasa* the chapter entitled Mesha Vinoda opens with the discription of different varieties of rams. The ram with the head turned aside and with black head is suitable for the fight. They are to be looked after very carefully, nourished with good food and have to be kept in a dark place. Wine should be given to them for making them excited. To make the fight fierce, birch-bark was thrown on their faces. When once it loses the game it becomes impossible to make it fight again. The fight generally takes place for some wager. The flag of vicotory was snatched away by the successful party and the money put as a wager on the competition was also taken away by the successful party.[3]

The fight between two rams is picturesquely described in *Kridabhiramam*. Before taking to the play ground, the two animals were washed and adorned with jingling bells. They silently follwed their masters to the ground where the competition was to be held. During the fight, each fierce encounter raised dust over the ground. Even with bleeding noses they hit each other with great force but never ran away from the ground. After a tough fight, the two finally would collapse.[4] Another favourite pastime was *Tamrachuda Vinoda* (Cock-fight). Chalukya Somesvara, the author of *Manasollasa* describes different kinds of cocks as also some special characteristics of the cocks meant for fighting. The selected one should be nursed by experts with excellent food and water and trained. Mud mixed with salt was appiled to the comb, then a notice of challenge inviting for competition was stuck to a post or a banner held high.

The ground should be cleared and besmeared with cowdung. Small squares were drawn with *Rangoli*. A preceptor chanted *mantras* to propitiate deities. After invocation, the competitors released their cocks. The author prescribes the months from *Kartika* to *Phalguna* as proper time for the fight. After the game was concluded, celebrations were held. The people like *Vadakas, Nartakas* and other experts in the art of cock-fight were honoured. The party winning the fight should be ready to snatch away the flag of the other who lost the game.[5] Another method of fighting may be gleaned

1. *S.I.I.*, Vol.X, p.376.
2. Prabhakara Sastry,V., (Ed.) 1960 *Op.cit,pp.63-64.*
3. *Manasollasa*, Shrigondekar, G.K., (Ed.) 1939 Vol.2, p.294.
4. Prabhakara Sastry, V., (Ed.) 1960 *Op.cit.,pp.63-64.*
5. Ibid, p.237

through *Kridabhiramam*[1]. Specially trained cocks belonging to the "coconut and crane" racial affinities were brought to the ground. The cocks lift their heads, fluttered their wings and cackled loudly. Then they hit each other fiercely with their beaks, even when blood was oozing out from their bodies. They try for a chance to attack and wound the opponent with a sharp knife tied to the back of the leg. Even when stomach, legs are torn by the kinfe they never leave the ground. They fought like the mythical personalities *Vāli-Sugriva, Vinda-Anuvinda* and *Murari-Chānu,* who fought on single leg. Finally, greatly exhausted they fell down loosing their consciousness to the ground.

On one occasion the pastime *Tamrachuda Yuddha* (cock-fight) took a serious turn and led to the great historic battle of Palnadu between Nalagama Raja and Brahamanayudu.

There is representation of the cock-fight incised over a medallion on the wall, said to have been built by the Hindus in the Raichur fort. On the same slab there is a Kannada inscription dated to the reign of Rani Rudramadevi. The panel shows two cocks engaged in fighting with a man standing behind, probably encouraging and instigating the birds.[2]

Even in our present society the villagers enjoy the amusement of cock-fights occasionally on the festival days like *Makara Sankranti,* the day on which the Sun enters the sign of Capricorn.

The other pastimes are fights of he-buffaloes, tigers, elephants ets.[3]

Apart from the above mentioned sports Chalukya Somesvara describes *Lavaka - Vinoda* (Quails fight), *Paravata Vinoda* (pigeons fight), *Sarameyavinoda* (Dogs fight), *Syena - vinoda* (hawk-fight), *Gaja-vyaghra-vinoda* (Elephant-tiger fight), *turaga-vyaghra vinoda* (Horse-tiger fight), *matsya-vinoda* (fishing) etc.[4]

Mrugaya-vinoda or hunting was perhaps a very popular amusement enjoyed by the royalty. Numerous methods of hunting are mentioned in the ancient texts. A contemporary work *'Simhasana Dvatrimsika'* makes mention of three varieties of hunting, viz., *dīpampu-veta, dāmena-veta* and *tera-veta.*[5]

Depampu-veta, probably derived from *Deepa-mriga* or a deer; in this type of hunting a decoying deer was probably used to serve as a bait. According to *Manasollasa* the deer were so trained that at the slightest sign from the master, they came back to him with wild deer without themselves falling a prey to the temptations of food or opposite sex. The king was accompanied to the forest by trained deer and a few hunters.

---

1. Prabhakara Sastry V.1960 *op.cit,* pp.75-76.
2. 1929-30 *Hyd.Arch.Ann.Rep.,p.20.*
3. Lakshmiranjanam,K., (Ed.). 1960 *Sri Siddesvara Charitra,* p.153.
4. Shrigondekar,G.K., (Ed.) 1939 *Op.cit.,* vol.II,pp.244-264.
5. Koravi Goparaju, 1960 Op.cit., p.36-37.

The other method *dāmena-veta* was a method of hunting with restraint. The hunter chased the deer in such a way that the deer may not get water or grass throughout the day. They became exhausted and unable to run away even when the hunter was sighted. Gradually the hunter came nearer and nearer. Thus struck with hunger and thirst, the deer surrendered to the hunter and was easily captured.

Hunting with nets was known as *tera-veta*. Nets were placed on a soft patch of grassy land with the corners tied to nails. After thus spreading the net at a place, the hunter followed the deer after setting a trained dog lose on the herd. While running through the net the herd was closed in and easily caught.[1]

Vikaramaditya VI used to enjoy hunting expeditions accompanied by his wife and other ladies of his harem near a tank in the forest during the cold season. This type of hunting is named as *Paniyaja*. Big pits were excavated near water places in which people hid themsselves from the beasts. The participants were dressed fully in green. The beaters then spread the grass before the trained deer, in order to tempt the wild ones with food or opposite sex. While coming near the tank or while eating grass the game was killed with an arrow. Immediately the place was cleared by beaters, without leaving stains of blood for the next hunt.[2]

Contemporary works spoke of other hunting expeditions near water sheds or a tank in the forest, where deer, falcons, cranes, pigeons and other water birds were killed. Fishing of different varieties, viz., *Korraminu, Vaaluga, Bedasasambu, Velimetta, Godise, Royya, Kuntumukku* etc.,[3] is also described.

Wrestling was another chosen amusement during the Kakatiya period. According to *Palnativira Charitra* wrestlers also accompanied a war processsion.[4] The chronicle *Pratapa Charitra* records that competitions were held in the court of Prataparudradeva daily, as an evening pastime.[5] *Ranganatha Ramayana* describes an interesting fight wherein two wrestlers come to the arena like lions coming out of cages. They try for an opportunity to catch hold of each others' thighs, beat each other on belly, forehead, head and chest. Sometimes one wrestler caught the other in the clutch of the thighs to incapacitate him. They rolled together on the ground. Sometimes they tore their backs with nails, beat each other on their back, nose, arms, head etc. Finally they would be badly injured in the fight and blood ozed out of their head, nose, mouth and other parts of the bodies and both of them collapsed to the ground.[6]

1. Koravi Goparaju,1960 *op.cit p.244.*
2. Shrigondekar, G.K., (Ed.). 1939 *Op.cit.*, vol.II,pp.264-304.
3. Koravi Goparaju, 1960 *Op.cit.*, Vol.I, pp.44-5.
4. Umakantha Panditha, (Ed.). 1955 *Op.cit.*, p.5.
5. Lakshmiranjanam, K., (Ed.). 1969 *Ekamranatha's Pratapacharitra*, p.20.
6. Ramaswamy Sastry,V., (Ed.). 1960 *Sri Ranganatha Ramayana*, pp.295-6.

In the *Virata Parva* of *Andhra Mahabharata* composed by Tikkana, there is a reference to the *mallayuddha vinoda* between Bhima and Jangama. The author narrates the rules according to which wrestling was fought. Special types of lower garments known as *Challadams* and *Kasikoka* were worn by the wrestlers.

The game started in a courtyard with friendly hand-shakes by the opponents. They would then perform some feats and somersaults. They rolled in a circle while slowly loosening their hands, and tried for an opportunity to catch hold of each other. They held each other tightly and beat terribly. Finally Bhima sat on the supine body of Jangama who fell down totally exhausted. The king Virata decalared Bhima victorious.[1]

Not only in literature but also in sculptures we have vivid representations of wrestling bouts. In the Ramappa temple at Palampet a wrestling match is depicted on one of the exterior panels of the *mukhamandapa* towards the left of the southern porch. The panel consists of four different scenes of the fight. From left to right the first one depicts a man shown in a half kneeled posture holding the right leg of his opponent with his left hand and squeezing his head with his right hand while the second man held the head of the first with both hands.

In the second panel one wrestler lifts up the opponent by holding his lower legs tightly. The third panel shows one wrestler standing on flexed left leg and the right one bent upwards and encircling the left leg of the opponent. The opponent is shown holding the head of the first and twisting. In the fourth one the body of the lower man is shown wriggling in a tight leg clasp of the one on the higher level (Pl.30).

Another bas-relief also from Ramappa temple contains another powerful representation of *mallayuddha* on the back wall to the west. In this scene one wrestler is shown squatting on the ground with his right leg flexed and bent backward while the left leg clasps the upper man who is wriggling the head of the former with his left hand and dangerously bending the right hand backwards. The body of the lower wrestler is already tightly entwined by the legs of the upper one. There is a standing figure problably a referee by the side of the wrestlers with his right hand lifted to announce victory or cautioning the fighters to stop. (Fig.31).

Manasollasa cites three kinds of wrestlers. The best one is called *Jyeshthika*, the second best is *Antarjyeshthika* and the third is known as *Govāla*. One should be below thirty two years of age to enter the race. The work prescribes the following exercises for the wrestlers. In order to gain stamina and confidence, one should practise weight lifting, walk a *kros* (two miles) a day vigorously and practise swimming. He should also practise '*Sthambha-Srama*' or exercise of pounding the pillar. Early in the morning a

1. Ramanujayyaa, B.,(Ed.) 1939 *Sri Andhra Mahabharatam*, p.145.

wrestler should practise four chief movements (or Sthānakas), under the supervision of his teacher. They are movement to front, back, right and left. Wrestling matches were arranged by the kings in arenas or open air theatres.[1]

Like *Mallayuddha* another amusement was *Ankayuddha* or duel fighting, much favoured during the period of the Kakatiyas. The players were known as *Ankakāras*. They were maintained by the kings or feudal chiefs and also by the temple authorities.

Manasollasa defines *Ankakāra* as a person who duels with another carrying the same weapon. According to the text there are altogether eight kinds of *Ankās*. In *Ranganatha Ramayana*[2] there is reference to duel fight or *Dvanda - Yuddha*. The author describes a fight between *Angada* and *Narāntaka*. They fought by means of arms. They would beat each other on the crucial parts of the body such as head, chest, stomach, thighs and even blood flowed in streams from their bodies. Finally *Narānataka* was killed by *Angada*.[3]

Snake charming was a common man's amusement. Details of this kind are found in *'Kribadhiramam'*[4]. The snake charmer plays Nagasoram' (Nagasvaram) or the blower, squats in the middle of the street; While displaying different types of snakes which also included a cobra, he played Various ragas like *'Naga Sindhu, Prabheda, Nanavarata, Gandharva, Laharika* and *Sankarabharana*.[5] ragas on the *nagasora* instrument

Another pastime was *Gangireddulata*,[6] in which a bullock is bedecked with colourful clothes and jingling bells fastened to the legs and to the collar round the neck. Then they would induce the bull to do feats and whirl round. Even now such bullocks are taken round the streets on the festival occasions.

Magic and jugglery were also popular. *Simhāsana Dvātrimsikaavi*[7] refers to magic many a time as *Indrajāla* and *Mahendrajāla* and included the same in the sixty-four fine arts.

Some amusements were used to be shown on the day of *Sivarātri* at Srisailam, such as playing on stilts and on ropes, shadow plays showing selected scenes from the *Rāmayana* and *Mahabhārata*. This is also known as show of leather puppets or *tolubommalāta*. *Prachanna Veshamulu* is another sport in which one or a pair of men go round each day in the make-up of

1. Shrigondekar, G.K., (Ed.). 1939 *Op.cit.*, Vol.Ii, p.229.
2. Gona Buddha Bhupathi, *Ranganatha Ramayanam* Ed P. Laxmi Kantham 1989 p.368
3. Ramaswamy Sastry, V., (Ed.). 1960 *Op.cit.*, pp.368-69.
4. Prabhakara Sastry V Ed 1960 op.cit pp61-62
5. Prabhakara Sastry, V., (Ed.). 1960 *Op.cit.*, pp.41-43.
6. Umakantha Panditha, 1955 *Op.cit.*, p.20.
7. Koravi Goparaju, *Simhasana Dvatrimsika*. Reprint 1960 Vol II p.112

different roles and imitate different stock characters in life with short dialogues.[1]

Different types of circus feats were performed by *Mailārabhatas* with religious fervour and fanatism at the temple of Mailāra Deva in Ainole. The author of *Kridadhiramama* very graphically describes these terrible feats. Some devotees would hop in the space, some would jump from a considerable height into a pit fixed with sharp spikes, some would swing in the space with iron hooks driven into the skin of their backs and some would lit camphor in their palms of both hands and offer *harati* to the deity. While men perform such terrible feats, the women show the *Gondali* type of dance and *Murdhābhinaya* (a form of dance with various gestures of head). Some ladies would do other feats like hopping back into a water tank and pick up a nose-ring kept therein. The other female feat was to thread black glass beads or (*Nallapusalu*) with their tongues.[2]

1. Narayana Rao, Ch., (Ed.) 1974 *Op.cit.*, p.256.
2. Prabhakar Sastry, V., (Ed.). 1960 *Op.cit.*, pp.47-48.

CHAPTER XI

CONVEYANCES

The progress of mankind through the ages was made possible by his gradual control over nature. When man attained the stage of food production from the life of savagery, he started domesticating animals such as cattle, sheep, goat, horse, elephant, etc., for producing food and for consumption of animal flesh. Whe he produced food in excess he felt the need for transporting the food from the place of production to his homestead or to the place of disposal or market. This need compelled him to invent conveyances. The early modes of conveyance were of course, carrying on heads, using the beasts of burden and then using the wheeled carts drawn by oxen. Several terracotta figurines of bullock carts have been found in Harappan sites and continue to occur even in the Satavahana sites. The cart was used not only to transport his produce to the market or to his home but also to carry him and his family over long distances. A miniature cart with a female figure dated to 3rd millennium B.C. from Mohenjodaro reveals that oxen were a means of trasportation in the proto-historic period when people practised storage economy.

The same method of trasportation by bullock carts continued in the Kakatiya society. A few representations depicting the cart are found in the sculptures at Nagulapadu and other places. A bullock cart with a rider seated over the yoke is found on a panel carved on the architrave in the main temple of Nagulapadu. The cart was probably drawn by buffaloes(Fig.18.b).

An interesting representation is found by the side of an inscription on the Raichur fort-wall in which several pairs of buffaloes are shown dragging a huge stone slab from the quarry to the place of construction. Here the conveyance is shown with two pairs of wheels, drawn by several pairs of buffaloes. The riders are shown whippping or driving the animals. At the back end of the huge stone block is shown a wooden roller or lever held by several men, intended to push the conveyance forward. The artistic treatment in the delineation of the strenuous march of the animals is beautifully achieved by depicting some animals lolling out tongues out of their mouths. Some with bent waists and others with curled tails lifted up indicate that the animals were put to great strain. A pair of buffaloes were yoked to the cart and the rest of the pairs were linked by means of a chain.

The driver is shown seated on the top of the block, holding the reins in one hand and a whip in the other (Fig.29).

Inside the Raichur fort, there is a long Kannada inscription[1] on a gigantic stone slab which records the conquest of Raichur and the erection of the fort by Raja Vithala under instructions from Rani Rudrama of Warangal. This is dated 1216 Saka era corresponding to 1294 A.D.[2] There is ample evidence in the contemporary literature and lithic records that carts were used extensively in the Kakatiya society. *Palnativira charitra* refers to roofed carts many a time. The marching army of Brahma Nayudu included huge carts provided with tented roofs to carry attendants along with boxes, taped cots, wooden seats, spittoons, decorated boxes to keep umbrellas, Kashmirian musk, sandal wood, camphor, caged birds like parrots etc. The same work informs that the army of Malidevaraja reached Karyampudi on tented carts carrying various kinds of necessities.[3]

The Tripurantakam inscription[4] of Kakatiya Ganapatideva records the remission of taxes (Sunka) on 300 *'Perika'* oxen in the town of Tripurantakam now in Prakasam district. These oxen belonging to the temple were probably utilised as draught animals. Owners of the oxen were known as *'perikavaru'* and the oxen as *perika yeddulu* (yeddulu means oxen). Various kinds of articles carried in gunny bags, large or small, were known as *'perikalu'*.[5] Though Thurston[6] opined that *perikas* formed a separate caste they are in fact only a sub-division of the balijas, whose main occupation was to carry salt.[7]

The records also bear testimony to the prevailing custom that some people lived by trasportation business alone to earn their livelihood by hiring out their oxen to the traders or to general market-yard and they were subject to the tax levied by the Government.[8]

Horse :- The horse is an important animal among beasts of burden from the ancient times. The agility and swift movement of the horse fascinated man to domesticate it and utilise it for multifarious purposes. The horse has a high antiquity in India. It is referred to many times in Rigveda.[9] The Vedic people considered it as a sacred animal and used it for scrificial rites.

---

1. 1929-30 Annual Report of Archaeology Department, p.20.
2. 1929-30 *Ibid.*
3. Umakanta Pandita, 1955 *Palnativiracharitra*, pp.3-4.
4. 1929-30 *Ibid.*
5. *S.I.I.*, Vol.X, p.304.
6. Thurston, E., 1909 *Castes and Tribes of Southern India*, Vol.VI, p.184.
7. 1909 *Ibid.*
8. S.I.I., Vol.X, p.304.
9. Subba Rao, M., 1974 *Rigveda Aryulu*, pp.134-135.

According to the *Brahmanas*[1] the Horse Sacrifice or the *Asvamedha* was performed by kings with the intention of proclaiming sovereignity over other kings. The possession of horses in the battle fields greatly strengthened the army and it formed one of the four-fold divisions of the army (*Chaturanga bala*).

Even to day in many parts of South India people offer votive figurines of horses to the village Gods and Goddesses in fulfilment of vows. They believe that the Goddesses or Gods would bestow robust health on the sick and that he would become as strong and active as a horse.[2] In Tamilnadu some terracotta figurines of horses are modelled to a height of ten feet.[3]

The depiction of horses in various postures is a common theme in the Kakatiya temple sculptures. The sculptures represent the horse as being used for riding and drawing chariots. Horse-riding appears to be a favourite pastime in the Kakatiya period. Mention may be made of the representation of *Asvasthara* over a loose sculptured slab at Warangal fort displaying a procession of horse riders. The horses are shown with rich trappings, the saddle is trellised and bordered with small jingling bells. The saddle was probably made of leather. The bridle consists of a thin strap into which is attached a forehead piece, a check piece and a nose band. The reins appear to have been knotted on to the bit. The use of bridle provides excellent control over the horse. Apart from the saddle and bridle, the horse was further embellished with a breast band. Small jingling bells are attached to the saddle, breast band and side band near the front line of the saddle. Decoration with floral designs with hanging tassels are seen in the side and breast bands.

In the temple of Surabhandesvara at Kondaparti, there is a ceiling panel showing a horse with a rider flanked by ladies in *anjali* pose. Below the horse are shown warriors holding shields and swords. The horse rider may probably represent *Chaunda Senapati* - one of the Commanders-in-chief of the King Ganapatideva. In this scene the horse is shown bedecked with saddle, back band with tassels, and ornamental strap around the neck, and blinkers or *akshimala*. It is probably made of leather to cover the eyes of the horse against insects and mosquitoes. The horse bit is attached to the reins held in the left hand of the rider. He is also shown using the stirrups, probably made of thick cloth of leather hung by means of a twisted rope (Fig.18.a), Pl. 12.

---

1. Macdonell & Keith, 1958 *Vedic Index of Names & Subjects*, Vol.II, p.14.
2. Personal communication from Krishna Sastry, V.V., Several terracotta figurines of horse have been collected from the temple of a village Goddess at Kotilingala in Karimnagar district. Similarly some terracotta figurines were collected from Joramma Temple near Laxettipet, Adilabad district.
3. Stephen P. Huyler, 1985 *Village India*, pp.104-105.

Another relief from Warangal fort clearly shows the stirrup consisting of triple ropes. The torso of the rider and the head of the horse are badly mutilated. The straps of the stirrup are shown attached to the saddle.(fig.18.c).

The antiquity of stirrup in India goes back to very ancient times. Many western scholars believed that the stirrup was an invention of the Chinese or of Central Asian origin possibly associated with the Sakas or the Romans.[1] But the recent excavations of protohistoric burials in South India unearthed horse stirrups at a number of places. By this it is evident that stirrup was widely used in South India several centuries before the Christ.[2]

Apart from the sculptural representations, contemporary literature and epigraphs of the period also throw much light on the use of horse. In *Palnati Viracharitra*[3] we find that Kakatiya Rudradeva despatched a contingent of army consisting of one thousand horses and infantry to King Nalagama in his war against Mallideva. In *Sivayogasaramu* it is said that Induluri Annayya, a son-in-law of Rudramadevi invaded Kalingadesa with a large army consisting of one lakh twenty thousand horsemen.[4] The work *Pratapa charitra* records that the army of the King Prataparudradeva consisted of one lakh horses.[5] According to Amir Khusrau, Prataparudradeva had a strong army consisting of 100 elephants, 9,00,000 archers and 20,000 horses.[6] Amir Khusrau gives a graphic account of horses. "The horses seemed to leap in the field of vision out of the realm of imagination. The marine horses could swim through the sea as if it was a cup of water. Their eyes were like crows, with black linings, as they looked at *Shabdiz* with contempt. There were dark horses with white faces, like the moon rising up in the horizon of the night; white horses with black hoofs, like an eclipse overshadowing the Sun, horses with black patches which reminded one of the clouds scattered by the winds, and bay horses with red marks like the air full of roses. Their essence was from the wind, and rain could do them no harm; their bodies were of fire and you could not make their effigies out of wax. They wore shoes of iron and could nevertheless, dance in the air. The limbs were like reeds, and they could not, therefore, be drowned in water. Their breasts were wide like the foreheads of the munificent, while their ear-holes were small like the eyes of the stingy. Like true mystics, they could step on air and walk over the surface of water. Barley was permitted to them, but not whips".[7]

---

1. Dhavalikar, M.K., 1973 *Ajanta - A Cultural Study*, p.124.
2. Krishna Sastry, V.V., 1982 *Sunday Chronicle* (October 31st, 1982), Magzine Section,p.1.
3. Umakanta Pandita, (Ed.) 1955 *Op.cit.*, p.34.
4. Rama Rao, M., (Ed) 1939 *Kakatiya Sanchika*, pp.10- 20.
5. Ekamranatha, 1960 *Pratapa Charitra*, p.16.
6. Amir Khusrau, *Ashiqua*, p.69.
7. Amir Khusrau, *Khazainul-Futuh*, *J.I.H.*, Vol.IX, p.63.

In the above lines we can easily see through the unbounded poetic imagination of eqestrian science (*Asvavidya* or *Asva sastra*). In Nakula's *Asvasastra,* it is stated that horses of the best kind possessed of the following traits; white spots all over the body, over hoofs, face, a well built body and a graceful gait, horses with a red or dark colour of the body should have white ears, hoofs, face and legs. White spots in the shape of a lotus petal or a pitcher, plough, flag, goad (*Ankusa*), conch shell, umbrella, *swastika* etc., indicate wealth and victory to the owner of the horse. A mark of the full moon, crescent, the sun or stars, is considered very auspicious.[1]

Before the introduction of the gun powder into India the cavalry force had a predominant place in the army. Some of the lithic records describe the cavalry of the Kakatiyas in eloquent terms.

The Hanumakonda inscription, dated 1162 A.D., records that the world was reduced to dust by the hoofs of the excellent and high horses of Rudradeva.[2] The same record mentions "the horse troops of Rudradeva do not jump over the sky out of consideration for the sky being the place of Vishnu, and do not rest their feet on this earth out of consideration that the earth being a cow, they are all victorious, filling all the quarters with their prancing on the battle field, frightening enemies, making them run and killing them every day.[3]

Another copper plate of Queen Rudramadevi eulogises the cavalry of Viriyala Sura as assaulting the Space enclosed by the quarters, become submerged in the clouds of dust which was thrown up from the earth by the trampling with chisel-like edges of hooves of multitudes of (his) horses[4]

The study of the equestrian movements is important to the horsemen. Victory depends on the movements or paces taken by the horse. It is known from the records that the horses of Rudradeva had very charming bodies and neighings, and very fast with bodies endowed with firmness, long living and versed in the five kinds of paces.[5] The five paces are known as *Panchadharas* or the five movements in which the cavalry of Rudradeva was trained. According to Kautilya[6] the movements are (i) the circular movement (*Valgana), (ii)* slow movement with the head and ears kept erect (Nichairgata), (iii) jumping (langhana), (iv) gallop (dhorana), and (v) response to signals (Naroshtra).

In the work Nakula's Asvasastra[7] the five dharas or gaits are as follows:-i) *Vikrama* - ordinary gait, ii) *Pulaka* (?), iii) *Purnakanthi*-moving with

1. Nakula's *Asvasastra* (Unpublished manuscript, Tanjore), p.50.
2. *H.A.S.*, No.13, p.12.
3. *H.A.S.*, No.13, p.14.
4. *H.A.S.*, No.6, p.8, (Katagiri plates).
5. *H.A.S.*, No.13, p.14.
6. Shyama Sastry, R., (Ed.). 1915 *Arthasastra,* p.148.
7. Nakula's *Asvasastra,* (unpublished) Manuscript, Tanfora p.51

the face upright, iv) Tvarita - moving fast of its own accord, v) *Niralamba* - moving after being beaten. The inscriptions record that there were special officers appointed by the state viz., *Turaga- sadhanika*[1] , *Asvasahini*[2] etc. The terms *Turaga- Sadhanika, Asvasahini* etc., denote the employees whose duty was to train and maintain the horses.

From sculptural representation it is diffecult to say anything precisely regarding the breed of the horses. Marco Polo writes "........there is no possibility of breeding horses in this country......For even when a great blood mare here has been covered by a great blood horse, the produce is nothing but wretched wry-legged weed, not fit to ride. ....A great part of wealth of the country was wasted in purchasing horses. .... this king wants to buy more than 2000 horses every year. The reason why they want so many horses every year is that by the end of the year there shall not hundred of them remaining, for they all die off. And this arises from mis-management."[3] Further he states: "the reason why a good number of horses from foreign countries were imported into India was that most of them died in less than a year on acount of the people who do not know in the least how to treat a horse." In the medieval ages most of the horses were imported from the countries like Bahlika, Kambhoja, Persia, Arabia etc.[4]

Elephants :- In ancient India elephant was one of the symbols of sovereignity. Therefore, it was the most favoured beast of the king. Elephants played an important role and a position of paramountcy during the period of our study. Many sculptural representations of the horses are found in Kakatiya temple sculptures. They were richly ornamented with exquisite designs and elaborate trappings. (Fig.18.e).

There is a beautiful relief of an elephant at the entrance to the Thousand pillared temple at Hanumakonda. The neck, the forehead and the trunk of the elephant is richly ornamented. A pallet is hung by pendants or jingling bells around the neck. There is a similar ornament on the forehead. The belly is surrounded by plain trappings studded with octagonal iron pieces. Two more chains are found on either side with huge hanging bells probably made of bronze.

Very often we find *adhisthana* mouldings decorated with elephants in procesion or war posture etc, as found at Ramappa, Kusumanchi and Warangal fort the *Gajastara* motif at Warangal consists of elephants mounted by the mahouts and at the back a warrior is in a chasing position. The howdha on the elephant, like that of a saddle of the horse, consisted of a thick padding covered with a piece of embriodered cloth secured by girth.

---

1. *S.I.I.*, Vol.X. No.465.
2. *Ibid*
3. Henry Yule, Col., 1875 *The book of Ser Marcopolo, The Venitian*, Book-III, p.378.
4. Krishna Murthy, K., 1977 *Op.cit.*, p.214.

Bells were suspended from the saddle. Some panels contain a *Chhatra,* posssibly for protection from sun and air. Besides the sculptural representations the contemporary literature and epigraphs give description of the elephants.

Amir Khusrau in his usual poetic strain describes Indian elephantry thus, "They were like hills, so high that vermilion on their foreheads gave a red lining to the clouds, they are like clouds so much above the ground that water took a long time to trickle from their backs. The Creator of Ether had hidden 'fire' in them just as lightening is hidden in the clouds".[1]

Elephants are referred to in the inscriptions as *'Saila Sringapruthu-tunga-Maatanga', 'Sailendrayita Kunjaram'* etc.[2] An inscription at Yenamadala dated 1249-50 A.D.. records that Mahadeva fell asleep in a great battle on the two temples of a female elephant and awoke to find himself reclining on the bossom of a celestial nymph.[3] The same tradition is preserved in the *Pratapacharitram* which describes him as a doughty warrior who invaded the Sevuna kingdom and perished in an attack on Devagiri, the Sevuna capital, while fighting seated on the back of an elephant.[4] Another inscription records that Tailapadeva, the Crest-Jewel of the Chalukyas, was skilful in riding elephants.[5] A well known commander-in-chief of the Kakatiyas, Jayapa was a distinguished soldier and appears to have been specially skilled in training the war elephants and overseeing their employment on the field of battle. He bore the title *Gajasahini.*[6] The other title *Gandhahasti Gajasahini*[7] found in another inscription also denotes the careful training given by these employees who were specially employed by the Government to train and maintain the elephantry.[8]

The work *Palnativira Charitra* gives a beautiful description of a caparisoned elephant before taking it to war. The forehead of the elephant was painted with *Panchavarna* (five colours). The upper part of the head (*kumbhasthala*) was adorned with a *Patta* bedecked with pearls. The trunk and the fore-feet were festooned with golden chains. A multi- coloured velvet cushion was placed on its back and a blanket under belly. The word *chowdolu,* was explained as a howdha by the commentator of this work. Erected on the elephants' back it resembles a miniature house from which the soldiers discharged the arrows. Its top was surmounted by golden *kalasas.*

1. *J.I.H.,* Vol.IX, pp.74,78,79 and also *Khazainul-Futuh* by Amir Khusrau, p.75.
2. *Epigraphia Indica,* Vol.III, p.101.
3. *H.A.S.,* No.13, pp.16, 123, 175.
4. Ekamranatha, 1960 *Op.cit.,* p.139.
5. *S.I.I.,* No.X, p.409.
6. H.A.S.,No.19, pp.18-20.
7. *Ibid,*
8. *Ibid.*

Bells were were hung down from the elephant's body by means of short silken threads, suspended from the howdah. Sharpened knives were fastened to the tusks with which they could do great harm.[1] The work mentions the use of golden (metallic) ladder (*puttadi nichchena*)[2] to reach the back of an elephant which was arranged by the servants.

Camels :- Camels were also used as beasts of burden. Unfortunately none of the panels represent the figure of a camel in Kakatiya temple art. But the contemporary literature mentions the use of camel as a beast of burden to transport the packed loads and tents to the war.[3] It can be concluded that the use of the camel as a means of transportation is not in common vogue, but only used in the times of war to transport essential goods, war drums etc.

Palanquin:*(Sibika)* :- Palanquin was mostly used by nobles and opulent classes of the society. Usually it was carried by four men who were known as Boyilu[4] . Contemporary literature gives numerous references to the palanquins of our period.

Unfortunately none of the Kakatiya temple sculptures depict the palanquin. But in the later periods particularly Vjayanagara, we can find a variety of palanquins with exquisite designs and decorations as well as in the sculptured reliefs and paintings.[5]

According to *Sri Sddhesvara Charitra,* [6] a medieval work, learned Brahmanas like Sakavelli Mallikarjuna Bhatta used to come to the court of King Prataparudra in palanquins, The court jesters like Lokesu Bachayya who were forty in number, about 500 *Kshatriya* warriors like Sankara Raju and Kedara Raju, about 200 dancing women who were like angels in beauty headed by Sirigiri Mallu, Kaleswarapu Ganga etc., used to arrive at the court of King Prataparudra in palanquins decorated with diamonds. Tikkana Somayaji,[7] the great Telugu poet of *Andhra Mahabharata,* arrived in a palanquin to the court of Kakatiya Ganapatideva. *Basava Puranam*[8] narrates a dispute of *boyilu or palanquin bearers. The* palanquins used by rich people were profusely decorated with jewels.

The Karimanagar inscription records that Rudradeva made Gangadhara a Minister of State and presented a palanquin, white parasol, jewels and clothes to him.

---

1. Umakanta Pandita, (Ed.). 1955 *Palnati Viracharitra,* p.30.
2. 1969 *Ibid,* pp.29,43.
3. 1969 *Ibid,* p.30.
4. Subrahmanya Sharma, G.V., (Ed.) 1969 *Basava Puranam,* P.235
5. Saletore, R.N., 1982 *Art of Vijayanagara,* (See Pl.5.) *Sri Siddhesvara Charitra,* p.17
6. *Sri Siddhesvara Charitra,* p.17
7. *Ibid*
8. Subrahmanyam Sharma, G.V.,(Ed.) 1969 *Basava Puranam,* p.235

Chariots :- Ratha in the Rigveda[1] and later *Samhitas*[2] denotes a chariot. It became quite common during the time of *Mahabharata* in which we find a detailed description. The *Arthasastra*[3] deals with different varieties of chariots and their measurements.

Ratha[4] denotes a chariot or car and may literally means a vehicle or carriage. In *Rigveda*[5] sometimes it was used as wagon or cart. The artisan who built the chariots are known as *Rathakaras*.[6] In course of time it appears they have formed into a separate sub-caste. *Atharva veda*[7] mentions about the *Rathajnana*, the knowledge or science of making *rathas*. It also includes the knowledge of driving the chariot in times of war. It appears that a special type of wood (*Rathadaru*) was used for building *Rathas* as stated in Panini.[8] In the *Mahabharata* the army was divided into *srenis* according to the chariots.[9] The heroes who were adepts in the science of chariot were awarded titles as *Ardha ratha, Samaratha, Maharatha, Atiratha*, etc.[10] When Karna was categorised as *Ardharatha* by Bhishma, he felt deeply hurt and left the scene abruptly. In order to safeguard the *Ratha* and *Rathikas* some warriors known as *chakrarakshakas*[11] (literally wheelguards who were Maharathikas themselves) were appointed. Sri Krishna and Salya are said to be *Mahasarathis*. In *Mahabharata*[12] *Yudhamanyu Uttamoju* and *Kiritee* were appointed as *chakrarakshakas*. Both of them were *Maharathis*. Over the canopies of some famous warriors special flags were hoisted. Even the horses had special colours. Their bows, conches had different names. The heroes used to perform *Viravrata*[13] (a religious function) before proceeding to the war. The great hero of *Mahabharata*, Bhishma had a flag with the figure of a palm leaf over the ratha and canopied by white umbrella. The great teacher of military science, *Acharya* Drona used to have a flag bearing an altar. His horses were red. Duryodhana had a serpent on his flag.

The chariot was also a favourite vehicle of the medieval kings and formed as one of the four wings of the army. In *Virata parva*, Tikkana

1. Macdonell and Keith, 1958 *Vedic Index Vol.II, pp. 201, 203 and 488..*
2. 1958 *Ibid*, Vol.I, pp.96, 104, 246 and 401 and also Vol.II, pp.203, 204, 220 and 265.
3. Kautilya, Asthasastra, Syama Sastry, R., (Ed.) 1915 *Op.cit.*, p.175.
4. Sir Monier Monier Williams, 1979 *Sanskrit- English Dictionary*, p.865.
5. Macdonell & Keith, 1958 *Op.cit.*, Vol.II, pp.201-203.
6. 1958 *Ibid*. p. 203
7. Sir Monier Monier Williams, 1979 *Op.cit.*, p.865.
8. 1979 *Ibid*.
9. Lakshmirajanam,K.,(Ed.) 1970 *Andhra Mahabharatam*, p.13.
10. 1970 *Ibid*.
11. 1970 *Ibid*.
12. *Ibid*.
13. *Ibid*.

Somayaji[1] mentions the chariot as having profuse ornamentation. *Kridabhiramam*[2] describes that the *Rajavidhi* (main throughfare) was busy in the daytime with the movements of chariots, horses, carts and elephants. The distinction between the *Ratha* and *Sakata* (cart) is not much except that the nave or hole in the wheel of the chariot was greater than in that of the *Sakata*. (Macdonell & Keith, 1958 *Op.cit.*, p.203).

The chariots were familiar to the Kakatiya sculptors as it was used extensively as stately vehicles, war chariots, festival chariots etc. A panel depicts war chariots on the ceiling of the *Navaranga mantapa* in the Siva temple at Nagulapadu. The frieze consists of four chariots being drawn by horses. Each chariot has two pairs of wheels. The wheel consists of a rim (*pavi*), a felly (*pradhi*) (consisting the *nami*) spokes (*ara*) and the nave (*nabhi*). The wheel is fitted to the end of the axil. The nave must have been made of wood. The spokes are conspicuously absent. The rims must have been made of iron. The body frame is of open type and the horizontal shaft is very thick with a platform on which the warriors were to stand or sit. The arrangement of the platform may provide a clear vision to aim the arrow (Fig.18.d and Pl.32). This type of war chariot has a basket type body-frame, and four wheels with simple design without spokes. The railings are conspicuously absent. Similar type of chariot is carved on the ceiling of Navarangamantapa at Palampet temple (Fig.18.f, Pl.33).

A panel depicts the procession of the chariots carved on a loose slab, lying in the Raichur fort with a Kannada inscription belonging to the Kakatiya period. The freize throws light on the festival chariots of our period (Fig.20).

The panel shows six chariots drawn by humped bulls with decorative collars round their necks. The body frame of railing which is placed on the axil is designed with four petalled flowers and placed on solid wheels with an umbrella-like canopy to provide cover to the rider of the chariot. All the six chariots are ornamented with flags and banners of different designs and symbols of royal insignia of the kings. It is observed that the rider of the first chariot is wearing a heavy turban. The rider in the second chariot is shown wearing head- rest resembling a modern felt-hat. The third is the repetition of the first one. The fourth chariot has two riders, one driving and the other in a standing posture. The fifth one is much worn off and hence difficult to identify. The rider of the last chariot is putting on head-dress in the fashion of a night-cap.[3]

Some of the epigraphical records mention the use of the chariot in war time. The Boothpur inscription[4] records that Malyala Gunda destroyed

1. Lakshmiranjanam, K., 1970 *Op.cit.*, p.29.
2. Prabhakara Sastry, V., (Ed.)1960 *Kribabhiramam*, P.36.
3. 1926-27 Annual Report of the A.P. State Archaeology Department, p.8.
4. *H.A.S.*, No.13, p.145, verse 15.

the phalanx of the chariots and the elephants of the enemies. Another epigraphical work, *Niroshtya-Kavya*[1], which is incised over a hill near Hanumakonda, states that "the heavy chariot covered with numerous blue cloths and resounding with small bells resemble the clouds pierced by lightnings and accompanied by thunder".

It was generally believed that the chariots disappeared from about 7th century A.D. from the Indian army.[2] It can now be concluded on the basis of the artistic representations and epigraphical records that the chariots continued to be in vogue even during the Kakatiya period.

Water Transport :

The antiquiuity of sea-borne trade may be traced to the Harappan civilization as attested to by the commercial relation between Meluhha, the Indus city and West Asia (Dilmun) during the third and second millennia B.C.[3] In South India we have ample numismatic evidence for a brisk maritime trade. Some of the Satavahana coins particularly of the time of Yajnasri Satakarni[4] dated to 2nd century A.D. depict a "ship with two masts." Large number of Roman coins found in South India is enough proof of commercial contacts between Rome and India.

The Kalingas[5] were famous navigators who established commercial contacts with many foreign countries. The Chinese used to mention any navigator from the east coast of India as 'kling', a word taken to mean Kalinga. *The Periplus of the Erythrean Sea* is the first record of an organised trade with the East by the Western world. It was a guide book for foreign traders. Ptolemy[6] recorded that Mousopalle (Motupalli ?) was a metropolis of inland pirates. It is highly probable that Motupalli in Prakasam district or some extinct town in the vicinity had a port through which a major part of the trade of the 'Maisolia' region passed through in the early Christain era.

A large proportion of internal trade and commerce used to be carried through the rivers because of lack of proper roads. Even the few existiing roads passed through thick jungles thronged by wild animals and highway robbers. Moreover, road journey was costly and cumbersome. The goods had to be transported by carts drawn by oxen or buffalo. Horses were very few and practically monopolised by the kings to be used in times of war.

---

1. Epigraphia Indica, XXXVI,p.217.
2. Dikshitar, V.R.R., 1948 *War in Ancient India,* p.165.
3. Elizabeth, C.L., 1979 Sumar, Coastal Arabia and the Indus Valley, Journal of Economic and Social History of Orient, Vol.II,pp.121-135, Leiden.
4. Sarma, I.K., 1980 *Coinage of the Satavahana Empire,* p.32
5. Sarma, M.S., *Andhra Vignana Saraswamu,* Part-III, p.525.
6. Majumdar, S.S., 1927 *Macrindle's Ancient India by Ptolemy,* p.180.

Even the horses imported from Persia and Sind were not properly looked after because of lack of knowledge. Many became useless within a period of one or two years.

Elephants were used for movement of the cargo but it was very slow. The speedier, cheaper and safer journey was through the rivers and oceans. India, with a net work of perennial. navigable rivers, was at an advantage regarding water transport and the lessons of navigation were learnt at home.

According to Pliny[1] , the voyage to Ceylon in the former days was made by vessels constructed by papyrus and rigged with ropes after the mannner of the vessels on the Nile. The ships were built with prows at each end to obviate the necessity of their turning about in channels of extreme narrowness. The tonnage of these vessels was 3000 amphorae (Greek or Roman two handled vase). The Indian rivers were crossed by small boats made of wattle and covered with animal skin to make them water tight. These are known as *puttis*. Even horses could be transported through these *puttis* during times of war. Small boats made of planks and the joints sewn with ropes of coir were used for carrying cargo along the sea-coast. John of Mantecorvino[2] was not much impressed with Indian boats. In his words "Their ships in these parts are mighty frail and uncouth, with no iron in them and no caulking. They are sewn like clothes with twine..... every year therefore there is mending of these ..... And they have a frail and flimsy rudder like the top of a table ..... in the middle of the stern; .... they have but one sail and one mast and the sails are either of matting or of some miserable cloth. The ropes are of husk".

According to *'Periplus'*,[3] bigger vessels were known as *Sangara*, made of single logs bound together, but those which made the voyage to *Chrys* and to the Ganges were called *Colandia* which were very large. The third variety were boats or smaller ships coasting along the shore.

The vessels[4] of the Persian gulf were known as *Jase* (*Jahaz*). These were fastened only with stitching of twine, and iron was not at all used (Friar Odoric 1321-22 A.D.).

The Chinese vessels[5] that travelled to India were of three categories; the biggest called *Junk* (*Jong*), the middle sized *Zao* and the third *Kakam*. The greater ships had from three to twelve sails, made of strips of bamboo woven like mats. Each had a crew of 1000 men, viz. 600 sailors and 400 soldiers. Each ship had four decks and numerous private and public cabins for the merchant passengers with closets and all sorts of conveniences. The

---

1. Nilakanta Sastry, 1939 *Foreign Notices of South India*, P.49.
2. 1939 *Ibid*, p.190.
3. Schoff, W.H., 1974 *The Periplus of the Erythrean Sea*, p.46.
4. 1947 *Ibid*.
5. Nilakanta Sastry, 1939 *Op.cit.*, p.242.

oars or sweeps used on these great junks were more like masts rather than oars, each was pulled by 10 to 30 men (Ibin Battuta- 1325-1354 A.D.).

The reasons for the use of coir rope as binding material instead of iron nails, and the method of making the rope is recorded by Ibin Battuta[1] in these lines. "The natives (of Maldive Islands) macerate the rind (of coconut) in pits dug on the sea-shore and then beat it with mallets; then the women spin, they make thread from it for sewing together the planks of ship. It is with such cords that the ships of India, China and Yemen are sewn, for the Indian ocean is full of rocks and if a vessel joined with iron nails strikes against rocks it would fall to pieces, whereas, if it is sewn with cords it gains a certain elasticity and does not break. After the boards were joined together and tied fast with coir rope the seams were smeared with a native resin so that the water cannot leak through". The resin was ambergris, a wax like grey or black substance found floating in the tropical seas and present in the intestines of sperm whales.

The South Indian ships[2] were very big with a crew of 200 to 300 men. Each vessel carried 6000 bags of pepper. Two or three smaller boats accompanied the ship and ten smaller boats were hung to the ship for provision at the time of voyage. There were 60 rooms in the ship and the interior was divided into 13 water-tight compartments so that the ship would not sink even if a compartment was damaged. Nicolo De Conti[3] noted that each South Indian merchant had a fleet of 40 ships, each costing 15000 gold coins.

In making sea voyages the Indian mariners were guided by constellations such as the greater bear and the little bear (Ursa Major and Ursa Minor) during night voyages. The Ursa major was known as the *Sapta Rishi Mandala* (the Rishis are *Marichi, Athri, Angirasa, Pulasthya, Pulaha, Kratu* and *Vasista*). Two of the stars in the constellation were known as pointers, towards the pole star (Polaris). Ursa minor is the constellation including the North pole and the Polaris situated at the top of the tail of the bear.[4]

Pliny[5] remarks that "in making sea voyages the Taprobane mariners make no observation of the star and indeed the greater bear is not visible to them, but they take birds out to sea with them which they let loose from time to time and follow the direction of their flight as they make for land".[6]

1. 1939 *Ibid*, p.285
2. Marco Polo, Cited by Komaravali Subba Rao in *Avachi Tippaya Setti, Reddy Sanchika* 1947, p.191.
3. Nicclo decconti, Cited by Komaravalli Subba Rao, Ibid.
4. *Reddy Sanchika*, p.191.
5. Sastry, N., 1939 *Op.cit.*, p.49.
6. Radhakumud Mookerji, 1912 *A History of Indian Shipping and Maritime Activety from the Earliest Times.* Longmans, Green and Co., London, p.73.

In Dighanikaya (a Buddhist text) there were clear references to ocean navigation in India of the early historical times and the evidence of the use of birds by mariners for discovering the proximity of land. It is likely that the ancient Indians with a profound knowledge of Astronomy and Astrology could identify the directions by observation of stars. It may not be true that they were solely guided by the birds. Marco Polo[1] observes "in this country (Malabar) you see more of the north star, for it shows two cubits above the water."[2]

Fahien[3] informs us "there is no knowing east or west (during voyage), only by observing the sun, the moon and stars was it possible to go forward. If it was dark and raining the ship went as she was carried by the wind without any definite course. In the darkness of the night, only the great waves were to be seen, breaking on one another and emitting a brightness like that of fire, with huge turtles and other monsters of the deep. The merchants were full of terror, not knowing where they were going. The sea was deep and bottomless and there was no place where they could anchor and stop. But, when the sky became clear they could tell east and west again and went forward in the right direction. If she (ship) had come on any hidden rock there could have been no way of escape".

The Indian mariners[4] did not go on voyages all through the year but chose certain periods for sailing in the different directions. From the beginning of the April to the end of October the winds were westerly, so that no one can sail towards the west and again they sail easterly from the month of October. From the middle of May till the end of October the wind blows so hard that ships which by that time have not reached the port whither they are bound, run a desparate risk and if they escape it is a great luck:.

Indian sailors must have known and used the monsoons or periodic winds from a very early period. These were of two types, the South-West monsoon winds, blowing from the latter part of April to the middle of October and the North-East from about the middle of October to April. The season of South-West monsoon in India and neighbouring countries is the period of heavy rain-fall. The sailors select the season for voyages when the wind is favourable, if otherwise they keep along the shores.

The other important problem for the sailors was the menace of pirates who were well organised from very early times. Ptolemy[5] mentions Mousopalle as the metropolis of the pirates. The pirates used to take with them their wives and children and stay over the sea for the whole summer.

---

1. Yule, Henry, Col., 1875 *Op.cit.*, p.378.
2. 1875 *Ibid*.
3. Sastry, N., 1939 *Op.cit.*, p.76.
4. 1939 Ibid, p.190.
5. Majumdar,S.S., (Ed.) 1927 *Op.cit.*, p.180.

Fleets of 20 to 30 of their vessels joined together, and then they formed a sea cordon, i.e., they move off till there was an interval of 5 to 6 miles between ship and ship, so that they cover about 100 miles of sea and no merchant can escape them. When a vessel was sighted a signal was given to other ships by fire or smoke and then the rest of ships come closer and seize the merchants and plunder them. The merchants were well aware of this piracy and they went on sea well armed.

In the Charter of Security[1] issued by the Kakatiya Emperor Ganapatideva, it was recorded that the kings formerly ruling Motupalli used to take away by force the whole cargo of the maritime traders whose ships were thrown to the shores by cyclonic storms. Marco Polo[2] also mentions this obnoxious custom that if a ship be driven by stress of weather to some other port than to which it was bound, it was sure to be plundered. If a ship touched the port to which it was bound originally they receive it with all honour and give it due protection.

But for the epigraphic and literary sources, none of the panels of this period depict a ship or a boat. However, we find an interesting scene depicted on the mantapa of the Devi shrine at Srisailam, which can be dated to the post-Kakatiya period in which a long flotilla type of boats with eight men holding the rowing pads. On either end of the boats are seen two men in a standing posture supervising the rowing operations. They are shown carrying long swords over their shoulders.

1. Epigraphia Indica, vol.XII,pp.196- 97.
2. Henry Yule, 1875 *Op.cit., p.378*

CHAPTER-XII

WEAPONRY

We have ample literary evidences which give a fair idea of the arms and weaponry in ancient times. The early literature such as the Vedas, the Puranas, *the Ramayana, Mahabharata* and some of the Buddhist *Jatakas, Arthasastra* of Kautilya contain exhaustive treatment of the subject. Ancient writers have classified arms and weapons under various heads.

According to Arthasastra,[1] the superintendent of Armoury will be made responsible for employing experienced workmen of tried ability to manufacture weapons, wheels, mail armour and other instruments used in the battles. It is prescribed that the weapons shall be kept in suitable places. They should be frequently dusted and transferred from one place to the other and also be exposed to the sun. Transfering of weapons from place to place was probably recommended so that they are not detected easily by the enemy at times of war.

Kautilya gives a list of several kinds of immovable and movable weapons. The immovable machines or the *Sthira yantras,* are *Sarvotabhadra, Jamadagnya, Bahumukha, Visvasaghati, Sanghati, Yanaka, Parjanyaka, Ardha Bahu, Urdhva Bahu etc. The moveable weaponry were the Panchalika, Devadanda, Sukarika, Musala, Hastivaraka, Talavrinta, Mudgara, Gada, Spriktala, Kuddala, Asphatima, Audhaghatima, Sataghni, Trisula* and *Chakra.* He also mentions some weapons with sharp edges like plough shares. They are the *Sakti, Prasa, Kunta, Hataka, Bhindiwala, Sula, Tomara, Varahakarna, Kanaya, Karpana, Trasika* etc.

Bows are made of four kinds of materials namely palmyra, bamboo, daru, wooden bone or horn. These are respectively known as *Karmuka, Kodanda, Druna* and *Dhanus.* Bow strings are made of *Murva* (Sansviera Roxburghiana), *Arka* (Catotropis crigantea), *Sana* (Hemp), *Gavedhu* (Coix Barbata), *Venu* (Bamboo bark) and *Sanyu* (Sinew), *Venu, Sara, Salaka, Dandasana* and *Naracha* are different kinds of arrows.

The edges of arrows might be made of iron, bone or wood as to cut,rend or pierce.

The *Mahabharata*[2] speaks of a fourfold classification of weapons. They are *Mukta, Amukta, Muktamukta* and *Yantramukta*. Mukta in Sanskrit means liberate, or deliver and *Muktaka* is a missile which is to be delivered or

---

1. Shyama Sastry, R.,(Ed.). 1915 *Arthasastra,* p.123.
2. Lakshmiranjanam, K., 1970 *Andhra Mahabharatam,* p.11 and also *War in Ancient India* by Dikshitar, V.R.R., p.93.

thrown or cast against an enemy. It also means to set forth, emit or discharge. As such, these weapons are divided according to their movability. The *Mukta* weapons are probably the missiles, lances or arrow heads or any other weapons which can be discharged against the enemy whereas the swords, the battle axes come under the category of *Amukta*. The weapons that were delivered by means of a machine are known as *Yantramukta*. Some artisans had specialised in making arrows and bows. The iron smiths made arrow heads. The bows are made by the carpenter. In *Aitareya Brahmana*,[1] we find a detailed description as to how the gods manufactured the bow. In *Mahabharata* it is said that Arjuna's bow popularly known as *Gandiva* was made of bamboo. The bowman used to wear a leather cover on his left hand to hold a bow and draw back the arrow in right hand along with the string. The leather cover for the left palm is intended for protection against abrasion due to the speedy delivery of the arrow. It is said in *Adiparva* of Mahabharata that the bow strings are made of barks of trees, guts or sinews and jute fibre. During the couse of the battle, breaking of bows and cutting of the strings are often mentioned. When once a bow is broken, there was arrangement to substitute it at once with another bow.

In the literature and the inscriptions, contemporary to the Kakatiya period, a large number of weapons are recorded viz., *Ankusa*[2] (Goad-like weapon), *Asi* (sword), *Bhindiwala* (a rod with heavy top), *Bhusundi*[3] (Octagon-headed club having broad knots, body and good handle). Its two principal movements were jerking and whirling, (it is also known as *Musundi*).[4] The other weapons are *Gada*[5] (a long heavy rod or mace), *Chakra*[6] (a disc sometimes shown with serrated edge in the late sculptures), *Khadga*[7] (sword), *Karavala*[8] (a particular type of sword, which could be wielded in whatever way one wanted), *Kanaya*[9] (a metallic rod both ends of which are triangular), *Ksurika*[10] (a short sword or razor-like weapon), *Khetaka*[11] (shield), *Krakacha*[12] (a saw-like weapon), *Kuthara*[13] (a kind of axe), *Mudgara*[14] (a hammer

1. *Aitareya Brahmana*, VII. p.19.
2. Ramaswamy Sastry, V., 1960 *Sri Ranganatha Ramayanam*, p.422.
3. Kumaraswamy, K., (Ed.) 1954 *Prataparudriyam*, Part-II,P.139.
4. 1954 *Ibid*
5. Ramaswamy Sastry, V., (Ed.). 1960 *Op.cit.*, p.422.
6. 1960 *Ibid.*
7. Umakanta Pandita, 1955 *Palnati Viracharitra*, p.28-29.
8. 1955 *Ibid*
9. Ramaswamy Sastry, V., (Ed.) 1961 *Bhaskara Ramayanam*, p.161.
10. 1961 *Ibid.*
11. Ramaswamy Sastry,V., (Ed.). 1960 *Kumara Sambhavam by Nannechoda*, p.314.
12. Ramaswamy Sastry,v.,(Ed.), 1961 *Op.cit.*, pp.165-166.
13. Umakanta Pandita, 1955 *Op.cit.*, pp.28- 29.
14. 1955 *Ibid.*

or mallet-like weapon), (pointed rod or club or a long staff often made of Khadira), *Yashti*[1] (pointed rod made of *khadira*, (mimosa catechu), *Naracha*[2] (a kind of arrow made of iron), *Parigha*[3] (a battering ram or an iron bar or beam used for locking or shutting a gate, an iron club), *Parasu*[4] (a scymitar or a hatchet, a battle axe *Pattisa*[5] (same as *Parasu* but shaped like a trident at both ends), *Parasvadha*[6] (battle-exe, hatchet etc., it is wielded as a weapon chiefly by the nobility), *Phalaka‹* (a shield), *Prasu*[7] (a weapon 24" long with two handles), *Trisula* (a trident), *Tomara*[8] (a rod with an arrow like edge or a lance, javelin probably of a shorter kind),*Sakti*[9] (a metallic weapon four hands long and like the leaf of Karavira (Mimasa catecha) and provided with handle like a cow's nipple or lance, spear, pike, dart or sometimes used as a flag staff), *Sula* (a pointed rod without any fixed length) etc.

Bows: There are numerous sculptural representations of bows of the period. They may be mainly classified into two categories (1) A bow with a single curve and (2) a composite bow.

A bow with a single curve:- A bow made from a single piece of wood is called a 'simple bow'[10] or a bow with a single curve.

This is the common type of bow which was used by ordinary people like hunters, huntresses, tribal people and also by soldiers in the army.

On the door-jamb of the temple at Jakaram, a hunter is shown holding a simple bow in the left hand and an arrow in the right hand. The bow has a curved stave with pointed ends in which the chord is fastened. The fatigued lady is leaning against a wall with her left leg raised up, from which a thorn is being removed by an attendant (Pl.36). On a pillar in the temple at Bejjanki, similar bows are held by two tribal girls wearing garments of leaves. The girl on the right side holds the bow in her left hand and arrow in her right. Her crossed left leg is being relieved of a thorn by a squatting attendant (Plate 37).

On one of the pillars of the *Mandapa* at Dharmapuri, a battle scene is represented wherein the foot soldiers are represented carrying bows with single curves. The staves were decorated with linear patterns. In another representation over a pillar of the *Navaranga mantapa* at Palampet, a warrior

1. Ramaswamy Sastry, V., (Ed.), 1960 Op.cit., p.29.
2. H.A.S.,No.19, p.47.
3. Ramaswamy Sastry,V., (Ed.). 1960 *Op.cit.*, p.422.
4. 1960 *Ibid.*
5. Kumaraswami, K., (Ed.) 1954 *Op.cit.*, p.139.
6. Ramaswamy Sastry, V., (Ed.). 1961 *Op.cit.*, p.29
7. Kumaraswami, K., 1954 *Op.cit.*, p.139.
8. 1954 *Ibid.*
9. Ramaswamy Sastry, V., (Ed.). 1960 *Op.cit.*, p.422.
10. Pant, G.N., 1978 *Indian Arms and Armour*, vol.I, p.117.

is shown discharging the arrow with his right hand and the bow is held in his left hand. The stave is simple and the upper end is decorated like the tail of a fish. The soldier is flanked by ladies on either side (Fig.21c).

2. Composite or jointed bow:- The bow made of wood, horn and sinew was called a 'composite bow'.[1] A good number of representations of the composite bow are found. This kind of bow appears to have been used by the royalty, charioteers, royal hunters, huntresses etc. The battle scenes represented in the ceilings of the *Navaranga mantapas* of the temples at Palampet and Nagulapadu depict the composite bows held by charioteers. The staves are made of multiple joints possibly welded with cylindrical metallic pieces. The metallic cylinders are mainly intended as a safeguard against the bow breaking in the middle while in use. It also provides a good grip to the archer (Fig.21f).

A battle scene from *Ramayana* depicted on a pillar, probably brought from the delapidated Mahamandapa of the Ghanpur temple now exhibited in the State Museum, Hyderabad, A.P., shows Rama and Lakshmana holding composite bows in their left hands. The staves are shown jointed together by a central piece. The stave is beautifully decorated with floral designs.

The carved frieze found towards the eastern porch of the *mahamantapa* contains a figure of a huntress with her right leg slightly bent and the left crossing the right. She holds a composite bow in her left hand and an arrow in the right. An attendant on her right is removing a thorn from her left foot. There is another attendant on her right holding a fan-like object probably to relieve her fatigue. The lady is shown in a frame of creepers and flowers and leaves probably to indicate forest scene. The miniaturised figures of attendants, the profuse ornamentation on her body are indications of her royalty. This proves that royal ladies also participated in hunting.

The stave of the bow is made of two curved pieces jointed to a central piece. At the upper tip of the stave a piece of cloth is tied which looks like a banner. The string of the bow is seen clearly fastened tightly to the ends of the staves (Fig.21d).

A bracket figure by the side of the eastern portico of the same temple represents a charming lady, profusely ornamented with *chakrakundalas, haras* etc. She holds a composite bow in her left hand and an arrow in her right. An attendant is shown removing a thorn from her left foot. The creepers and the ornamentation over the fauna behind the lady is indicative of a jungle scene. The attendant is also seen holding a multiple jointed bow in her right hand (Fig.21e).

Somesvara prescribes in his *Manasollasa* that the bow must have the quality of *'Uthchalana'*[2] or moving up or bounding up. It may have three,

1. 1978 *Ibid*, p.118.
2. Shrigondekar, G.K., (Ed.) 1939 *Manasollasa*, Vol.II, p.8.

five, seven or nine joints. The terminals of the bow should be finely decorated so that it is a pleasure to hold. He suggested that the beautiful bow made of bamboo be coated with red-lead or vermilion or shellac and mounted with senew strings. It may be decorated with golden tassels and various jewels.[1]

Arrows: Arrows are represented many a time in the panels along with bows. They can be classified into two types, one of which consisting of a long slender shaft and a pointed head as found in the huntress scene depicted near the porch at Palampet. The other type has an elongated triangular head in the shape of a spear (Fig.21j).

In *Ranganatha Ramayana* while describing the duel between Rama and Ravana, the poet mentions several heads of arrows like the '*Silimukha*' (tipped one), *Sardulamukha* (Tiger shaped), *Ushtramukha* (camel shaped), *Sūkaramukha* (boar faced), *Uragamukha* (serpent shaped), *Karivairimukha* (lion head), *Danti*' (tooth or elephant tusk shaped), '*Gridhramukha*' (eagle-faced), *Agnimukha* (emanating fire), '*Ulkamukha*' (meteor), *Vidyunmukha* lighnting like, *Grahamukha* (planet shaped), *Mihiramukha* (Mihira is water or water emanating), *Dahanamukha* (burning head), '*Chandramukha*' (crescentic) etc.[2]

The art of archery was frequently referred to in the inscriptions and in the Muslim chronicles. An inscription at Hanumakonda thousand pillared temple records that Rudradeva shattered Dommaraja more than once by hundreds of his arrows.[3] Another epigraph describes that "unfailing shower of arrows of Namadeva fell over them (enemies) even before they could think of running away."[4] Nanaya of the Bhoga family reputed to have the expertise of breaking into fragments any stationary or mobile target of any size with his shower of arrows.[5]

A quiver is generally referred to as *tuna* or *tunira* in the ancient texts. A few representations of quivers occur in the Kakatiya temple carvings. They are all indentical in shape with tapering sides. On the ceiling of *Rangamantapa* at Nagulapadu and Palampet are shown quivers as mentioned above.

The quiver was generally fastened at the back by means of leather or such other straps. Sometimes two quivers are also shown slung over the shoulders.

A pillar sculpture of the Kakatiya period, now exhibited in the State Museum, Hyderabad, shows a representation of a battle scene from *Ramayana*. The warriors, as also Rama and Lakshmana, are seen carrying two quivers

1. 1939 *Ibid*.
2. Ramaswamy Sastry, V., (Ed.) 1960 *Sri Ranganatha Ramayanam*, p.427.
3. *H.A.S.*, No.13, p.17.
4. Ibid, p.120.
5. *H.A.S.*,No.9, p.21.

over their shoulders on either side. Probably they might have been made of wood or leather.

Swords: The sword appears to have come into vogue comparatively later than the bow. But next to bow, the sword is the most important weapon of warfare.

The terms *Asi, Khadga, Karavala* and *Kshurika* indicate short swords with a broad razor-like blade. Along with the celestial emblems like the Sun, Moon and the religious emblems like *nandi,* sword is also found as a symbol of royalty on the seals of Garavapadu and Khandavalli copper plate sets of Kakatiyan times. Here, a sword is depicted upright before a *Nandi.* There are other epigraphs like the Vardhamanapuram inscription of Malyala Gunda, Thousand Pillared Temple Inscription of Rudradeva, Pusuluru epigraph of Cheraku Bollaya Reddi, where the Sun, Moon and the sword are represented. The blade of the sword is plain, sometimes with a curved end and upright.

Apart from literary and epigraphical evidences, we have varieties of swords represented in the sculptures.

The swords of the period may be divided into five categories viz., long swords, short swords,curved swords, extraordinary swords and lastly daggers.

Long swords:- Generally long sword with a straight and pointed blade, appears like a modern *Kirich.* The blade has a parallel groove and is double edged. The handle is sometimes provided with a round pommel and a quillon.

On the door-jamb at Palampet temple a donor-couple is depicted, which may possibly be the representation of Recherla Rudra and his consort, who was a general under Kakatiya Ganapatideva. He is shown standing with a long sword in his right hand and embracing his consort with his left hand. The sword besides having protective quillon has a mid-rib all through (Fig.22 and Plate34).

Another scene depicts a battle scene on the ceiling of the *Rangamantapa* of the same temple in which a warrior is shown fighting with a long sword held in his right hand and thrusting it into the body of the enemy (Fig.22d).

The panel at Nagulapadu on the ceiling of the *mandapa* contains a row of warriors, carrying swords and shields in their hands. The swords are medium sized and have double edged broad blades and the handle contains a round pommel, plain grip and collar guard.(Pl. 35)

The same type of sword carried by a lady is depicted on a slab at Ghanpur temple. The sculpture is now disfigured.

Short swords (*Ksurika*):- This type of sword was commonly used by the army. It is also found in the hands of the devotees. In general the swords have small pointed and double-edged blades. The hilts have cylindrical pommels, plain grip and collar guard. These swords are used particularly for thrusting, piercing and cutting purposes (Fig.22.o,p & q).

From the ruins of the Warangal fort a number of panels representing small swords carried either by warriors or Gods and Goddesses are noticed. On the capital of a *mandapa* pillar, a lady mounted on a lion is shown carrying a short sword and a shield.

An architrave of a ruined temple at Warangal depicts two warriors with short swords in their hands (Figs.22k & 1). In some temple sculptures of Palampet and in the hero stones of the Kakatiya period exhibited in the State Museum of Andhra Pradesh small swords are found in the hands of the warriors. The Khandavalli copper plate contains a seal with a short sword having a pointed end.

Curved swords :- The warriors of our period also used various types of curved swords. Some swords have a forward bend, some have two or three bends in the shape of sickles while some resemble a serpent (Figs.22c,f & i).

On the ceiling of the *mandapa* at Palampet a battle scene is represented in which the warriors are shown fighting with different types of curved swords.

On another frieze on the *Gajasthara* moulding of the *adhisthana*, a scene depicts a warrior fighting with elephants with a curved sword in his right hand and convex shield in his left. The sword has a forward bend found on an architrave of Surabhandesvara temple at Kondaparti, which depicts a warrior carrying a serpent (wavy) shaped sword.

Extraordinary shaped swords with a spear :- In the temple of Heroes at Karempudi (Guntur district) there are some iron swords, which according to the local tradition belong to Brahma Nayudu and Balachandra, who were the heroes of Palnad battle fought in the year 1182 A.D.

These are some of the most extraordinary types of swords with multiple prongs, tridents, swords with broad cutting blades, curved knives, straight sided daggers with mid-ribs etc. The tridents with multiple prongs are shaped like human faces probably to represent Agni or Rudra with emanating tongues of flame. Bells are suspended at the lower ends.

Daggers (*Asi-Putrika*) :- A good number of representations of daggers occur in the stone sculptures. In the State Museum of Hyderabad, there is a large collection of hero stones, which are dated to 12th-13th centuries. The heroes are shown carrying the daggers over their waist-belts. In general the daggers have thick blades, tapering to a point with prominent ribs. The hilt has a knobbed, flattened pommel and a quillon. Sometimes the dagger is seen in a sheath. The sheath is decorated with linear patterns and attached to a piece of leather strap.

According to Somesvara[1], the length of the dagger is to be measured by *Angusthaparvas*. (Finger-breadths). Further on, he describes certain strategic positions for fighting with the dagger. He says the best dagger to be used by the king should be four *Vitastis*[2] in length.

Spears and Javelins: Of the numerous representations of spears, it is difficult to identify exactly the examples of particular types of spears and javelins. The frequent occurrence of the spears indicates the use of the weapon in the warfare.

The spear has a high antiquity in South India as spear heads of iron have been found at Hallur[3] etc., dating back to 1st millennium B.C. if not more. The common term for the spear in the epic and post-epic literature is *Sakti*.

In *Mahabharata* it is described as a terrible weapon made of iron, sometimes adorned with gold and beryl and sometimes with bells.[4] The *tomara* was sometimes identified as a javelin. According to *Nitiprakasika*, *tomara* is a weapon with a wooden body and a metal head.[5]

On the ceiling of the *navaranga mantapa* at Palampet temple, a battle scene is represented in which some of the warriors are shown carrying the spears across their bodies, held in both hands (Fig.23a). Sometimes it would be carried by Gods and Goddesses also as an attribute.

In general, the spears had long shafts and pointed heads. The head of the spear consists of a pointed blade with a sharp edge. On the blade the presence of a mid-rib is to be seen clearly. The head is fixed to the shaft in a socket and the socket covers the tang of the shaft. The shaft is decorated with linear patterns.

Lance (*Sakti*) :- The lance is prescribed to be of six cubits length and provided with an iron body and should have six facets.[6]

There are a few excellent specimens of lances, carved in the temple sculptures, generally wielded by cavalrymen.

On some of the loose sculptures from Warangal fort cavalrymen are depicted as carrying lances. On one of the stone sculptures a hero is shown weilding a lance. Generally the lances have long shafts, provided with iron-heads or a blade consisting of six facets.

---

1. Shrigondekar, G.K., (Ed.). 1939 *Op.cit.*, Vol.II, p.26.
2. Length measured between fully stretched tip of the thumb to the tip of small finger
3. Nagaraja Rao, M.S., 1971 *Proto Historic Cultures of the Tungabhadra Valley*, p.1.
4. Ramaswamy Sastry, V., (Ed.). 1960 *Op.cit.*, pp. 33-49.
5. Chakravarti, P.C., Ed. 1972 *Op.cit.*, p.166
6. 1972 *Ibid*.

Battle axe :- A hatchet with a round cutting edge is the battle- axe which is generally referred to as *Parasu*. It was the chief weapon of Parasurama. Several representations of battle- axes are found in the plastic art of our period. In the Hindu mythology Lord Ganesa is always associated with the battle-axe (Fig.23e).

The battle-axe was provided with wooden handle having a knobbed top and a crescentic blade hafted to it by introducing the butt end of the axe into a cleft wooden handle.

Mace (Gada): Mace is one of the deadliest and commonest of ancient weapons which was used for crushing the enemy. It is also an attribute of Lord Vishnu (Fig.23f). The weapon may be small or broad, having small metal foot, shoulder and a head. Sometimes the head was inlaid with precious jewels. *'Bhusundi'* is also a type of mace which contains an octagonal head and having broad knots, body and a good handle. It was used for jerking and whirling. It was also known as *musundi*. The weapon as depicted in the Kakatiya sculptures mostly in images of Lord Vishnu has a long handle attached to a cogged spike at the end. The left hand of the God rests over the tip of the handle. In a mutilated figure of Vishnu found in the Warangal fort, the heavy mace is provided with a massive handle and the head is provided with vertical teeth. The teeth were strengthened by a middle band. The spike above the mace tapers which could also be utilised for thrusting into the body of the enemy like a dagger.

There is one more specimen of mace from Dharmapuri (Karimangar district) held by Varaha Murthy in his proper right hand. The weapon has a smaller roundish head with vertical iron straps or teeth but ending in a knob.

Chakra or Discus: It is a circular disc with a quardrangular hole in the centre. It was used variously for cutting, piercing, felling or whirling. The antiquity of the *Chakra* may be traced to the wheel of the Sun God. In the later period, it is represented as the *Dharma Chakra* of Buddha. In Hindu mythology it is also associated with Vishnu and Krishna. During the Kakatiya period the representation of *Chakra* is much stylised. In the *Samapada stanaka* murthy Vishnu from Visnur in Warangal district the God holds *Chakra* in his back left hand. The *Chakra* has a double beaded design on the periphery and a lotus design with eight petals in the centre.

Vajra: Since antiquity *Vajra* has been the favourite weapon of Indra (Fig.23g), said to have been made out of the bones of *Dadichi*. During the early period it was shaped like a circular disc. In later times it assumes the shape of a dumb bell or *damaru*. *Vajra* also has the meaning of thunder bolt. Sometimes it is represented as a double trident, two tridents in opposite directions, middle prong of the lower one is made longer to be held in the hand grip.

Weapons of Defence: Of the weapons of defence, shields have been profusely represented in the sculptures. Basing on their shapes, shields have been classified as below.

Round type :- There are a few examples of this type. On the ceiling of a *navaranga mandapa* at Nagulapadu a battle scene is depicted. The warring soldiers are shown with swords in their right hands and round shields in their left hands. Another pillar at the State Museum, Hyderabad (from Panugal) depicts a round shield (Fig.23h).

The shields have plain surfaces and possibly made of leather, and are provided with a handle at the back. Some would have pearl or beaded decorations round the periphery.

Oblong type :- Oblong shields occur very frequently, They have either a straight or cruved surface. Some are small while some are very big, in size (Fig. 23i).

On the ceiling of the *navaranga mantapa* of Palampet temple several shields of the above type have been depicted.(Pl.38)

The shields having plain surfaces are sometimes decorated with beaded patterns along the borders (Fig.23j). At the rear side of the shield a curved handle is provided sometimes with a verticle strap. Representation of this variety can be seen at Warangal, Hanumakonda, Nagulapadu, Panugal etc. The shields of this class may probably be the *'kavata'* category of the *Arthasastra*[1].

Squarish type:- This can be seen at Ramappa temple on a parapet wall of the *mantapa*. There is a squarish knob-like projection at the bottom middle of the shield, which was apparently intended to safeguard the genital area of the soldier. On the surface of the shield, linear patterns are visible. The panel at Ramappa temple represents a man, probably a devotee, shown in standing posture. He is shown carrying a sword in his right hand while the left hand rested on the top of the shield (Fig.23k).

According to Chalukya Somesvara, one hundred skins of cows, or twenty skins of horses or eight skins of oxen would be as strong as the elephant's skin when tanned by proper methods for making the shield. He cites some practices by which one can pierce through a very hard target.[2]

Body armour:- There are copious references to body armour or *kavacha* in literature, inscriptions and representations in the sculptural art. The Pillalamarri inscription[3] refers to the use of armour (*kavacha*) as one of the most important weapons of defence. It records 'when manifold and unavoidable missiles were poring in with speed from that great warrior

1. Shyama Sastry, R., (Ed.) 1915 *Op.cit.*, p.126
2. Shrigondekar, G.K., (Ed.) 1939 *Op.cit.*, Vol.-II, p.27
3. *H.A.S.* No.13. p.130

Bhimanayaka who was well known for his dexterity, the new armour covering the bodies of enemy soldiers proved utterly useless and was torn to pieces like pieces of cloth'.

In the temple of Tripurantakam there are two hero stones shown wearing helmets with armours attached to them at the back. One of them wears helmet in the shape of a head-gear from which hangs the body armour over his back (Fig.24b). At the left side top corner of the panel the hero is shown riding a horse towards Heaven after death in the battle.

In the second slab, the hero holds two daggers with mid-ribs, one in his right hand thrust into his chest which comes out of his back. The other one is simply held in his stretched left hand. The hero has a turban like helmet from which dangles the body armour pushed to his back. A semicircular plate hanging from his waist is probably intended to protect his genital part (Fig.24a).

Yantras:- In ancient times *yantras* played an important part in conducting battles. *'Arthasastra'*[1] mentions *Sthira* (fixed) and *Chara* (movable) *yantras* to be used in the battle field. In the *Puranas* we have frequent references to *sataghnis* which literally means that it could kill hundred people at a time. The *sataghnis,* it appears, were fixed on the gates of the forts, walls and fortified towns. Bhishma[2] prescribes that the gates of the fortresses should be protected by heavy *yantras*. Monier Williams states *'Sataghni'*[3] as a deadly weapon used as a missile, supposed by some, to be a sort of fire arm or rocket, but described by the commentator of the *Mahabhurata* as a stone or cylindrical piece of wood studded with iron spikes.[4] In ancient India, the art of warfare had reached a very high water mark. According to Megasthanes[5] the Andhras possessed numerous villages, thirty fortified towns and an army of one lakh infantry, two thousand cavalry and one thousand elephants. This statement has been amply corroborated by the presence of fortified Satavahana habitation sites in the districts of Kareemnagar, Warangal etc.

It appears that the fort walls were constructed with a width of more than ten feet. The Satavahana forts consisted of two fortifications, the outer one being mud wall and the inner one of stone or brick.

During the Vishnukundin period the fort wall (noticed at Keesaragutta datable to 4th century A.D.) was constructed to a thickness of ten feet.

---

1. Shyama Sastry, R., (Ed.) 1915 *Op.cit.*, p.126
2. Lakshmi Ranjanam, K., (Ed.) 1970 *Op.cit.*, p.17
3. Sir Monier Monier Williams 1979 *Op.cit.*, 1049
4. Lakshmi Ranjanam,K., (Ed.) 1970 *Op.cit.*, p.17
5. (Mc Crindle, J.W., 1877 *Ancient India as Discovered by Megasthanese and Arrian*, Calcutta, pp.137-141),

There were also water gates, so that people living inside could fetch water through these gates.

The bastions of these forts must have been strengthened by the provision of fixed *yantras* as suggested by Kautilya.[1]

Yantras appears to be an essential feature of fortification. It was meant both for offence and defence . In the *Valmiki Ramayana*,[2] there is also a mention of *yantras* used for both delivery of stones and raining arrows on the enemy. The *yantra* may be a catapult, *ballista*. In *Mahabharata*[3] it is said that the walls and gates of the city were protected by both the *yantras* and the *sataghnis*. These *yantras* and the *sataghnas* have wheels, spikes and bells. *Sringikas* were probably hollow- horns of oxen or buffaloes filled with burning oil and other ingredients which were flung at the beseigers. Throwing of burning oil on the enemies was continued even during the late medieval times. Inside the fort of Golconda of Qutab-Shahi period, there are some cells by the side of the main gate which are said to have been used for storing oil to be burnt at the time of siege.

The Kakatiyas of Warangal have built many forts and strengthened the already existing forts in their kingdom. Mention may be made of the forts on the top of Hanumakonda hill, Ramagiri, Malangur, Medak, Bhongir, Nalgonda, Polakonda, Kaulas and Warangal etc. It is said that the fort at Golconda was the work of Kakatiyas before Sultan Quli the founder of Qutb Shahi dynasty came to Golconda. The representation of Gandabherunda over the northern gateway of Golconda fort may be an additional proof.

The *Nitisara* of Prataparudradeva enjoins that strong guards should be posted at the fort gates for day and night watch.[4] The garrison of the fort be posted with heavy guards at all strategic points, such as the defiles and passes through the hills in the neighbourhood or in the fort. Efficient men must guard the audience hall. Talavaris should be moving through the roads and lanes. Talavari, in ancient times, enjoyed judicial or magisterial powers. It is possible that it was so during Kakatiya period also.

The narratives of the Muslim Chroniclers throw lucid light regarding the seize operations of the fort. The *'Tarikhi- Alai'*[5] of Amir Khusrau informs us that, after a long journey, the imperial army reached Telinga (Telangana) and occupied the hill of Hanumakonda (the earlier fort of Kakatiyas), from where all the edifices and gardens in the Warangal fort were visible. The army encamped there for a few days and completed all the necessary

1. Shyamasastry, R., (Ed.) 1915 *Op.cit.*, p.126
2. Chakravarti, P.C., 1972 *Op.cit.*, p.173
3. 1972 *Ibid.*, p.160
4. Yazdani, G., 1960 *The Early History of Deccan*, Vol.-II, p.667
5. Elliot and Dowson, 1964 *The History of India as told by its own Historians*, Vol.III,P.80

preparations to seize the Warangal fort. Then the Naib Amir ordered the "western stone balls" to be thrown at the wall from every direction to demolish it and reduce it to powder. The *manjaniqs* and *aradas* were brought into use. They erected very high embankments or storeys in the vicinity of the fort and the result was the garrison of the fort was placed in a lower elevation. One of the faces of the fort which was one hundred cubits in length was so battered down with heavy stones, that it no longer covered the Hindus and afforded them protection. The earth was battered down from the mud fort wall which filled up the ditch from the very bottom upto the middle of the wall, and the walls were pounded to dust by the stones discharged. Thus, it became an easy task for the Imperial army to capture the outer mud fort, and then they swam across the ditch to reach the inner stone fort. They made a vigrous attack on one of the stone bastions which so alarmed Rai Laddar Deo (Prataparudra Deva, the last Kakatiya Emperor) that he offered terms of capitulation.

'Barni' also gives a very vivid account regarding the seige of Warangal fort. He observes that Malik Naib Kafur ordered his soldiers to invest first, the earthen fortress. Accordingly, there was severe fighting every day between the besiegers and the besieged. The *maghribs* were played on both the sides; many were wounded. This went on for some days, till the daring and adventurous men of the army of Islam planted their scaling ladders and fixed their ropes. Then, like birds they escaladed the towers of the mud fort. which was stronger than the stone one, and by cutting down the defenders with their swords, spears and axes they made themselves the masters of the fort. After occupying the mud fort they moved towards the inner stone fort and by storming, they captured it successfully.[1]

It is very interesting to take cognisance in this connection of some of the seige engines referred to by the Muslim chroniclers.

Gargaj:- Dr. Oman says that 'it was a wooden moveable tower often used in the seige during medieval period'.[2] Men posted on its top carrying missiles, shot them down over the defenders to clear the way for an assault.[3] The tower of *gargaj* was fitted with a draw bridge which at a propitious moment, was let down on the walls of the fort and served as a path for a column of stormers. But it had many disadvantages. It was very heavy and hence cannot be moved easily. If it stuck in the debris or a ditch it became an easy target for the defenders.[4]

Sabat:- Nizamud-Din states that a *sabat* was a roofed lane, high enough to accommodate an elephant rider with a lifted lance in his hand and

1. *Ibid.*, pp.202-233
2. Gopala Reddy, Y., 1967 *The Kakatiyas and Their Age*, Ph.D., Thesis (Unpublished).
3. *Islamic Culture*, Vol.-XI, p.477
4. *Ibid.*

sufficiently wide for ten horsemen to pass abreast. It commences at a gun - point distance from the fort wall and was gradually built forward so that it ultimately touched the latter. The besiegers advanced under the cover of this passage, breached the walls of the fort and entered it.[1]

Manjaniq:- This was probably the most effective and commonly employed seige engine. It hurled with irresistible force huge pieces of rock, stones, earthen or iron balls, vessels filled of naphtha or 'Greek Fire' or casks containing foul material, scropions and poisonous reptiles, from a string attached to a huge beam worked by three different principles of torsion, counterpoise and tension.[2] The beam was held down tightly, and when it was suddenly released it cast off the missiles contained in the sling with tremendous force. There were various types of *manjaniqs* varying in their construction, size and power. The *'maghribs'* and *'aadas'* were the other types of the same machine.

Catapult:- It was a magnified cross-bow, fixed on a frame and worked by several men by means of pulleys and ropes and was used for discharging heavy bolts and long shafts at objects out of the range of ordinary arrows and javelins and with greater force.[3]

The *'Nuhsipihr'* of Amir Khusrau refers to the use of mine in connection with the seige operations that were employed by the Muslims to reduce the fort of Warangal.[4] Under this device, the besiegers removed as much earth as they could from beneath some exposed corner of fortifications, and shored up the hole with beams. The space between the beams was then filled with straw, brush wood and some combustibles, to which fire was set at required moment. When the suports were consumed, the wall crumbled downwards into the hole and a breach was provided". [5] But this device was not applicable to the forts built on hills and rocky foundations.

1. 1879 *Abul- Fazal, Akbar-Namah-II,* p.318
2. *Islamic Culture,* Vol.-XI, p.475
3. *Ibid.,* p.476
4. Elliot and Dowson, 1964 *Op.cit.,* p.559
5. *Islamic Culture,* Vol.-XI, P.477

CHAPTER-XIII

FLORA AND FAUNA

In the Kakatiyan sculptural art, the flora is less represented as compared to fauna. The most important literary evidence for flora has been found in *Panditaradhya Charitra*[1] which records various cereals, medicinal plants, flowers and trees etc. They are as follows: *Vakudu* (Solanum jaquini), *Ragi* (Eleusine Koracana), *Machipatri* (Artamesia absenthium), *Neredu* (Eugenia Janebalana), *Jammi* (Prosopis spicigera), *Kanchana* (Bauhinia acuminata), *Velaga* (Feronia elephantum), *Vavili* (Vitex trifolia), *Ummetta* (Datura metel), *Maredu* (Aegle mamelos), *Ganneru* (Nerium odorum), *Nelli* (Inoigofera tinctoria), *Sampenga* (Michelia champaca), *Mucidi* (Drospyris), *Somidi* (water creeper), *Gogu* (Cannabis sativa), *Asoka* (Saraca indica), *Pogada* (Mimus opselengi), *Malle* (Jasminum zambac), *Chamanti* (Chamomile plant), *Molla* (Jasminum pubescens), *Tummi* (Leucos linifolia), *Jilledu* (Calotropis jigantea), *Rela* (Cassia fistula), *Guruvinda* (Abrus Precatorius), *Vonna* (Acarusalamus), *Mulaka* (Solanum indicum), *Jaji* (Myristica fragrans), *Papara* (Citrulls colocynthis), *Kaluva* (Sweet smelling water lilly), *Kimsuka* (Butea frondosa), *Krovvi* (Lausonia alber), *Gummadi* (Camelira arbotia), *Kalivi* (wild fruit like jack), *Tangedu* (Cassia auriculata), *Gamte* (Clitorea lernatia), *Chengalva* (Lilly), *Regi* (ziziphus jujuba), *Mamidi* (Ficus Glomerata), *Kharjura* (Phoenix sylvostris), *Himtala* (Anona squanamosa), *Jeedi* (*Semecarpus ana cardiumem, marking nut*), *Medi* (Ficus glomerata), *Danimma* (Punica granatum), *Balusu* (Weberazetranda canthium parvilorium), *Tumiki* (Diospyros embryopteris), *Arati* (Banana or Plantain), *Gaja nimma* (Citrus limonum), *Kala juvvi* (N.Sativa), *Draksha* (Vitis vinitera or grapes), *Madi Phalam* (Citron), *Raavi* (Ficus religiosa), *Vepa (Margosa)*, *Budama* (Bryonia calloa or green fruit), *Jambeera* (Lemon), *Panasa* (Indian Jack tree), *Chandana* (Sandal or Santalum album), *Mandara* (Hibiscus rose), *Pippili* (Chisdica roxburghi), *Thadi* (Palmyra), *Madhavi* (Echites caryophyllata), *Lavanga* (caryophyllus aromatieus, clover), *Takkola* (Hibsus abelomoschus), *Ketaki* (Mogali) (Pandanus odoratissmus) etc.

---

1. Narayana Rao, Ch.,(Ed.) 1974 *Sri Panditaradhya Charitra*, pp.238-239, and also *Sri Ranganatha Ramayanam* (Ed.), by Ramaswamy Sastry, V., p.214.

The principal trees depicted on the Kakatiya temple bas reliefs are as follows:-

The Pipal tree (Ficus religiosa):- Pipal or *Asvattha* is one of the most sacred trees from the Rigvedic times as it produces fire when churned.[1] It is found more than once in the reliefs. On the ceiling of the Palampet temple is found a group of sages observing penance under an *asvattha* tree. The tree is correctly represented with its pointed single leaves. This tree grows in the sub-Himalayan forests from the Punjab eastwards to Bengal, Orissa, Central India, South India.[2]

The Banyan Tree (Ficus Bengalensis):- This is popularly known as *Nyagrodha* in ancient literature. It is repeatedly represented in the sculptural art of the Kakatiyas. In one of the panels in the Palampet temple a huntress is depicted in a standing posture. Behind her is seen a *nyagrodha* tree. In another panel on a pillar at Dharmapuri is seen a forest full of banyan trees. In India it is commonly found in sub-Himalayan forests viz., Bihar, Central India and South India.[3]

The mango tree (Mangifera indica):- On the ceiling of the temple at Nidikonda, there is the battle scene between Rama and Ravana in which a group of *Vanaras* along with Lord Hanuman are shown uprooting mango trees. The mango leaves and fruits are often depicted in the decorative panels, found at various Kakatiya temples.

The Banana (N. sapientum):- Banana is regarded as a sacred and auspicious plant offered to the Gods and Goddesses during worship from ancient times. It is very widely depicted in the anicent sculptures of India. Kakatiya sculpture is no exception to it. Almost all the temple door-jambs and sculptural panels of the Kakatiyas are decorated with this plant. Suitable examples come from the temples of Katakshapur, Palampet, Ghanpur, Ramanujapuram etc.

In the Warangal fort, the pilasters of the *toranas* are seen carved with this plant. Sometimes the plants are depicted unusually with double bunches of fruits on either side.

After the mango, this is commonest fruit found in India and is cultivated throughout the country except in the north- west.[4]

The Asoka (Saraca indica):- This tree is depicated more than once in the bas-reliefs. A panel representing Sita sitting underneath the *asoka* tree

1. Vsudeva Sastry , V., 1973 Vastuguna Prakasika (Materia Medica in Telugu).
2. Sir George Watt, 1908 The commercial Products of India, Being an abridgment Of *"The dictionary of the Economic Products of India"*, p.538.
3. 1908 *Ibid*, p.536.
4. Warmington, E.H., 1928 *The Commerce between the Roman Empire and India, p. 147.*

in the *Asoka vana* can be found on a pillar in the Nidikonda temple. Another relief representing the same theme can be seen on the ceiling of the temple at Nagulapadu. References to this tree are found in plenty in the ancient literature. It has red flowers and is used for worship.

The Palmyra tree (Borassus flabelliformis) :- It is known as *Tala* in Sanskrit and *Tadi* in Telugu. In the epic, Ramayana,[1] there is a frequent reference to *Saptatala chedhana* which means piercing seven tala trees at a time with a single arrow by Lord Rama. This, feat is repeatedly shown in the reliefs of Kakatiya sculpture.

The feat of Rama piercing seven palmyra trees is depicted on the ceiling of the Nagulapadu temple. The scene is repeated in the temple sculptures of Palampet, Ghanpur, Pillalamarri, Panugal, Bejjanki and in the sculptures of Dharmapuri temple. It is a commonly grown tree all over India. It is grown extensively in the Warangal region for extraction of toddy.

Sugar cane (Saccharum officinarum) :- It appears quite often in the sculptural representations. In the Palampet temple the Goddess *Rati* is seen carved on a wall holding a sugar cane across her body. A similar depiction is also seen in the sculptures of Panugal temple. The cultivation of sugar cane is very common all over India.

The Seetaphal (Anona souamosa):- It is a rare carving, seen only in two reliefs. A scene of forest from *Ramayana* most probably representing a theme from *Kishkindha kanda* is carved on a pillar of the Dharmapuri temple. In this scene, a few monkeys are shown plucking and eating these fruits. it grows very commonly all over India.

Cocount tree (Cocos nucifera) :- It is a tropical sea-side palm- tree with curving stem. Its representation in the sculptural art is also very scanty and is seen only once in the reliefs. In the Jakaram temple, a sculpture is carved on a door-jamb depicting a nude lady in standing posture with a serpant over her shoulders and two large cocount trees on either side. The coconut trees on the relief can be easily identified with their curved stems.

Nagajemudu (Xerophyte or cactaceae) :- It is a prickly and fleshy plant with modified stems which serve as leaves. The leaves are in turn reduced to spines. It is known as *'Nagachemudu'* (a medicinal plant used for curing asthma, carbuncles, blood motions[2] etc.). This is considered by Saivites as a sacred plant for worship.

A carving on the brackets in the Palampet temple has a representation of a huntress, elegantly standing cross legged with a male attendant removing a thron from her feet. Further, a nagachemudu plant is seen behind her.

---

1. Srinivasa Siromani, 1956 *Valmiki Ramayana, Kishkinda Kanda,* p. 44.
2. Vasudeva Sastry, V., 1973 *Op.cit.*, p.532.

The plant is shown with serpent hood-shaped leaves with wild creepers surrounding it. The entire panorama is indicative of a forest scene.

Pine apple:- One of the sculptures at Naglapadu represents a beautiful lady holding a pine apple fruit in her hands. From its spiny and rough external appearance and also the size it can be conclusively identified as the pine apple fruit. This is fairly extensively grown in South India and its habitat extends to all parts of India.

FAUNA

Birds: The birds are probably a favourite theme of the Kakatiya artists and Indian artists in general from early times. It can be observed in the plastic representation at Bharhut, Sanchi, Amaravati, Nagarjunakonda etc. Birds have been carved with great care in graceful postures. The following are illustrated:

Parrot (Psittacula karameri): The parrot occurs as a decorative motif. In almost all the temples parrot is shown with a lady (*Suka Sarika*). On a pillar in the temple at Palampet, a lady is shown holding a parrot. On one of the pillars in the Thousand Pillared *mantapa,* a lady is shown feeding a parrot.

A beautiful late Kakatiya drop pendant of stone brought from Pragatur, Srisailam area, now exhibited in the State Archaeology Department, Hyderabad, represents a lotus flower surrounded by sixteen parrots.

Peacock (Pavo cristatus): The peacocks are repeatedly depicted in the reliefs. In the Warangal fort, almost all the decorative panels and *toranas* are adorned with peacocks.

The *adhishtana* friezes at Palampet, Kusumanchi, Ghanpur, Pillalamarri etc. have similar decoration. Peacock known as *Mayura* in Sanskrit is considered to be the vehicle of *Kumara* or *Skandha,* the God of War. During the Kakatiya times the sound made by the peacock was considered to be an auspicious omen. The sighting of cock, *Bharadwaja* (skylark) bird, jackal and peacock are considered very desirable before the start of the journey.[1] This might be one of the reasons that beautifully carved peacocks are mounted on the *torana* gateways at Warangal.

The cock (Gallus domesticus):- Cock fight is a popular game of the Kakatiya period. Over the Raichur fort wall (which was constructed during the reign of Kakatiya Rudrama Devi) a medallion is carved showing the cock fight. Two cocks are shown engaged in a fight and a man instigating them.[2]

---

1. Prabhakara sastry, V., 1960 *Kridabhiraman*, p. 17.
2. 1926-27 *Ann. Rep. HYd. Arch.*, p. 17.

Hamsa or the swan (Cygnus flor):- The *Hamsa* is always associated with the Goddess Saraswati. On a triangular decorative motif in the Warangal fort, the Goddess Saraswati is seen mounted on a swan. Another panel brought form the Warangal fort and exhibited at the State Museum, Hyderabad, represents the Goddess Saraswati seated on a *Hamsa*.

In Rigveda *Hamsas*[1] are said to be capable of separating *Soma* from water and in later literature *milk*[2] from water. It is described as the vehicle of Brahma as also Saraswati, his female counterpart. They may represent the river Saraswati when depicted separately. The bird also indicates the Universal Soul or Supreme Spirit (typified by the pure white colour) identified with Narayana, Vishnu, Siva etc. It may also indicate a man of supernatural qualities born under a particular constellation; also an ambitious monarch.[3]

Animals:- Among the wild animals the following are seen in the sculptural representation.

Elephant (Elephas indicus):- The elephant appears to have been a favourite subject of the Kakatiya sculptor. This animal is represented in almost every possible posture in the reliefs. They are shown in standing, walking, running and sitting postures. Almost all the temple friezes are carved with elephants as decorative motifs.

The *adhishtana* freize at Palampet temple displays a number of elephants in the battle array. Some are shown crushing the soliders underneath their legs, while some are shown pulling down the warriors from the horsebacks. Similar freizes were found at Ghanpur, Nagalapadu, Kusumanchi and Pillalamarri temples.

Inside the Warangal fort are found many panels decorated with elephants, especially at the entrance of the temple. Two huge elephants adorned with rich ornamentation are seen installed.

The elephant is venerated as an auspicious animal from Vedic times. It is believed that the universe is supported by four elephants, known as *Bhadra, Mandra, Mrga* and *Misra*.[4] The vehicle of Indra, who is said to be the Guradian Deity of the east, is the elephant *Airavatha*.

In the Buddhist literature Lord Buddha is described as taking the shape of a white elephant when he entered the womb of his mother, *Maya*[5]. In the Buddhist sculptures the *Yakshas* who hold the the weight of the Stupa are somtimes depicted with elephantine hands, legs and ears.

1. Sir Monier Monier Williams, 1979 *Sanskrit- English Dictionary*, p. 1286.
2. 1979 *Ibid*
3. 1979 *Ibid*, p. 1295
4. 1979 *Ibid*
5. 1979 *Ibid*

In the *Puranic* literature, Ganapati or *Vinayaka* having the head of an elephant is worshipped for removing obstacles.

Elephants are the largest and strongest of all the animals in India and they occupied a prominent place in the art of warfare. From the early times, they were considered as a symbol of sovereignty. As depicted in the plastic art, the elephants were employed in various walks of life for a variety of purposes like processions in the state functions, transport, in the war etc.

Lion (Felis leoguzeratenis): The depication of lion can be seen very frequently as a decorative motif as well as royal insignia. The pillar capitals, brackets and friezes are always depicated wtih lion motifs. Inside the Warangal fort there is a pillar capital showing a warrior killing a lion. A meticulous delineation of the lion is to be seen in this panel.

The Indian lion[1] was exported to Rome possibly for wild sport.

Wild boar:-(Sus scrofa): It is depicted less frequently with only two reliefs representing it. A loose sculpture found at Kondaparti depicted Lakshmi Narasimha above which the ten incarnations of Lord Vishnu are seen carved. One of the ten incarnations namely *Varhavatara* is shown representing the boar.

Jackal: (Vulpes Vulgaris): The jackal is also represented in the reliefs. Inside the Warangal fort a relief representing the figure of the Goddess Chamundi is seen along with a jackal.

Other animals include the Indian stag, black buck, monkey and rat which occur quite frequently.

Stag: (Cervus axis):- The stag and deer are commonly seen in the sculptural representations. Many a time they are shown associated with the *yoginis* or lady devotees. In the Palampet temples, Parvati is carved on a beam of the ceiling in a meditating posture with a stag sitting by her side. Below the seated figure of Parvati one could see a boar on the right and an atelope on the left while a tortoise is seen below. A little above are seen two horses galloping on the hind legs.

Another panel on a pillar at Dharmapuri temple represents a forest scene in which could be seen stags along with other wild animals.

Monkey: The monkey was a favourite subject of the Indian artist form the anicent times. They are encountered very frequently in our period. In almost all the panels, monkeys are shown pulling down the garments of beautiful ladies.

Mouse:(Mus Musculus):(Mushika):- Mus, Mushika are the names of mouse occurring in the Rigveda[2] and the Yajurveda[3] *Samhitas*. The mouse

1. Warmington E.H 1928 op-cit,p.149
2. Macdonell & Keith, 1958 *Vedic Index of Names and Subjects*, Vol. II, p. 170
3. *Ibid*

appears very commonly in the sculptural depication as a vehicle of Ganapati, the remover of obstacles.

Demestic animals:- Among the domestic animals, horses, bulls, cows, rams, buffaloes and dogs are widely represented in the sculptural art.

Horse:(Equus Caballus):- Next to the elephants, the horses are frequently depicted in the reliefs. More often than not, the horses are depicted in battle scenes used by soliders and in certain cases they are seen in royal chariot processions.

In the Warangal fort many sculputers are carved with soldiers riding on well caparisoned horse backs.

The ceiling of the temples at Nagulapadu is carved with a scene depicting a chariot procession in the war. The chariots were drawn by the horses.

Bulls:(Bos Indicus):- Bulls were held sacred by the Hindus from the ancient times as the 'Nandi Vahana of Lord Siva'. In the Harappan culture one can find representation of bulls on the seals. The ceiling of the Palampet temple is carved with a number of bulls. They are profusely decorated with ornaments.(Plate 39).

Cow:- The cows are seen commonly in the sculptural art. A pillar in the *Ranga mantapa* of the temple at Palampet beautifully portrays Lord Krishna surrounded by herds of cows mesmerised by the music emanating from his flute.

In the temple at Ramanujapuram all the pillars of the mantapa are decorated with sculptures of cow-herds. Some of the carvings have depicted them as engaged in a fight.

Buffalo: (Bos Bubalus):- The buffaloes are represented many a time in the sculptural art of Kakatiya period.

Goddess *Mahishasura Mardhini* is always shown as the killer of the buffalo demon in the sculptures. We find these sculptures in the Warangal fort and in the wall sculptures of the Pachchala Somesvara at Panugal.

The theme *Mahishasure Mardhini* is repeatedly represented in the sculptures of Kakatiya period killing a buffalo demon.

Dog:(Canis Familiaris):- The dogs are depicated in a number of reliefs and is a common sight. It is often associated with hunters. In the Palampet temple one of the brackets is shown representing a huntress along with a dog. A similar theme is represented in the sculptures of Ghanpur, Pillalamarri, Dharmapuri and in the fort of Warangal.

Ram:(Ovis bovidae):- The ram is represented only once in the reliefs. On the ceiling of the temple at Palampet is represented *Navargrahas* along with their vehicles. Among them, Agni is shown mounted on a ram.

Reptiles:- The commonest among the reptiles are the cobras which are encountered in a number of panels. The door jambs of the Kakatiya period are always represented with a voluptuous lady holding a hooded cobra above her head. She may be identified as a Saivite yogini performing a tratric rite. The door jambs of Jakaram, Katakshapur, Palampet, Ghanpur, Ramanujapuram etc., are carved with a lady holding a cobra in her hands.

Aquatic creatures:- Among the aquatic creatures, fish, crocodiles and totoises are frequantly represented in the reliefs.

Fish and tortoises are always shown as a part of the ten incarnations of Lord Vishnu. A Chennakesava figure form Visnur exhibited in the State Department of Archaeology. Hyderabad, depicts the ten incarnations of Lord Vishnu among which the fish and the tortoise are seen very clearly. Some times the tortoise is shown associated with the river Goddesses in the reliefs.

Crocodile:(Crocodylus nilotious):- (Makaras): Crocodiles are found in the sculptural art as a decorative motif.

The gateways of the Warangal fort are adorned with arches bearing *makara toranas*. The tail of the *makara* is adorned with beautiful floral design and many *toranas* are decorated with *makaras*. Another panel depicting *makaras* on the sea water can be seen in a *Ramayana* panel on a *mantapa* pillar at Dharmapuri.

Mythical animals:- The mythical animals represented in the reliefs are limited in variety and are mainly used as decorative motifs. They include lions with human head and vultures with human body and so on. The brackets of Ghanpur temple depicts a lion with human head. In the Hindu pantheon demi-gods are represented in semi-anthropomorphic forms viz., *Garuda, Nagas, Kinnaras* etc.

The treatment of fauna in sculptures is extremely delicate. The Kakatiya sculptors have meticulously and effiiciently depicted the animal kingdom in the reliefs. The animals illustrated are well conceived and animated. The elephants in the reliefs are most successfully treated. Similar is the case with the horses. But the most spirited of all the animals shown are the monkeys.

CHAPER-XIV

RESUME

The period of the Kakatiyas who ruled Andhra Desa from Warangal may be rightly considered as the second Golden Age after the Satavahanas in this part of the country. They started their rule form 10th century A.D. which came to an end with disastrous consequences to South India in the first quarter of the 14 century A.D.

The long and peaceful yet eventful regin of the Kaktiyas saw the flowering of art, architecture, music besides the overall development in the fields of agriculture, irrigation, trade, commerce etc.

The Kakatiyas probably belonged to one of the branches of the Rashtrakuta families, known in the inscriptions as *Vrishni* or *Vishti* with the banner of Garuda. During the last quarter of the 10th century A.D, some far reaching political changes occurred in the Deccan. After the fall of the Rashtrakutas, the Chalukyas of Kalyana assumed the guradianship of Deccan resulting in the change of political subordination of Kakatiyas. They became subordinates of the Chalukyas of Kalyana till the time of Tailapa-III. The first important ruler of the Kakatiyas was Rudradeva, a great warrior and an able administrator. Rudradeva was succeeded by Mahadeva (1198-99), his younger brother. Mahadeva lost his life in the war with the Yadavas of Devagiri. His son Ganapathideva, who succeeded to the throne, was probably the greatest ruler of the dynasty. Besides his military exploits, his long reign of sixty three years saw the constructuon of great temples, tanks and forts of strategic importance. He changed his capital from the hill fort of Hanumakonda to the land fort of Warangal. Rudramamba, the daughter of Ganapathideva was the next ruler who endeared herself to the people. The last king of the line was Prataparudradeva whose millitary and architectural achievements were no less brilliant than that of his precessors. His glorious reign as well as the rule of the Kakatiyas came to a momentous end in 1323 A.D. with the invasion of Warangal by Ulugh Khan under Ghiasuddin Tughlak.

The Kakatiya temples provide a fertile field for a student of architecture, for an analytical evaluation and also to have a glimpse of the original contribution as deviated from the Chalukya styles. Though there are good number of Kakatiya temples, the sculptural representation of architectural forms are rare. A linear representation of a Kakatiya temple form on the inscribed pillar at Pusulur is of great significance. The linear sketch represents a cross-section of the temple which contains the *garbha-griha* and *mantapa*. The representations of these simple shrines are numerous. The other examples are found at Warangal fort, Panugal, Ghanpur, Dharmasagar, etc. Similarly the representations of the pillared *mantapas* are found at Hanumakonda, Ainole, Palampet and Ghanpur. The sculptural representations of the pillared hall are rare but the excavations in between the *toranas* inside the fort of Warangal unearthed some excellent examples of multistoried pillared halls in bold reliefs. The representations of the pillars are profusely noticed at different places which surpass the pilasters and pillars of both North and South India. Some of the pilasters represented in the carved panels are provided wtih the brackets which are of two types; the first represents a moulded bracket and the other contains figural representation. Beautiful representation of *vyala* brackets are represented at Palampet and Ghanpur, the inspiration for which must have been derived from the Chalukya architects.

Similarly there are profuse representations of *vimanas*-all the three types, namely the *Nagara, Bhumija* and *Dravida,* besides a composite type wherein the above three styles are harmoniously blended. An excellent representation of the composite type is found on the eastern wall of the Surya shrine in the Thousand Pillared temple at Hanumakonda. On the Pusuluru temple pillar a stepped pyramidal *vimana* is depicted. Similar representations of the *vimana* are found in the temples of Naganur, Panugal, Palampet and Ramanujapuram. Interestingly, the composite type which is a combination of Nagara and Dravida styles is found only in the sculptural representations but not in the actual specimens.

The *Kapota* or the cornice is represented on the pillars of Dharmapuri temple. In this case, the *Kapota* is shown not only projecting considerably from the pillars supporting it but is also shown in section.

The art of the Kakatiyas which is mainly represented in sculpture may be classified into various items such as (icons or *Dhruva Beras,* 2) Images within *Devakoshtas,* 3) Images in the minor shrines, 4) sculptures on walls, pillars, lintels and ceilings, 5) non-iconic human forms decorating the outer walls of temples, 6) animals and birds, 7) decorative friezes etc.

Among the main images, mention may be made of the various incarnations of Siva such as Virabhadra, Bhikshatana-murthy, Nataraja. Among the forms of Vishnu, Chennakesava was the most favoured incarnation during the Kakatiya times. The images of Annapurna are exquisitely carved among those of the mother Goddesses.

The *madanikas* or the bracket figures, found on the outer pillars of *Sabha mandapas* to support the cornices at Palampet and Ghanpur, are unique and the most remarkable examples of the Kakatiya period. These are evidently *Alasakanyas* or the "Indolent maidens".

The antiquity of narrative panels may be traced from the Buddhist period, the purpose of which was to convey the gospel of Buddha in a visual form. This created a lasting effect on the minds of common folk. The Kakatiya sculptor selected episodes from Siva's penance, *Bhagavatha* and *Ramayana* for portrayal of narrative panels. The penance of Parvati, *Andhakasura samharamurthy, Tripurantaka samharamurthy,* the *Gajasura samharamurthy, Samudra mathana* by the *Suras* and *Asuras,* felling of *Sala* or *Tala* trees by Rama and *Taravilapa* after the death of Vali in the hands of Rama, are some of the narrative panels which deserve a critical appreciation.

Fine arts such as music and dance have reached glorious heights during the period of the Kakatiya rule. Artists were patronised by gifting of houses to drummers, dancers and musicians attached to temples by feudal lords and the Kakatiya kings. Music was distinguished into two forms-*Desi* and *Marga*. The earliest reference to the *Desi* style of music is found in Nannechoda's *Kumarasambhava*. *Panditaradhyacharitra* enumerates a large number of *padas* (songs) of *Desi* style. Mention may be made of 'Tummeda padalu' which were sung while harvesting crops or transplanting the seedlings. The other popular *Padams* are the *Prabhata padam, Paravata Padam, Nivali Padam, Gobbi Padam, Vennela Padam, Sandhyavarnana Padam,* and *Gunavarnana Padam* etc.

The *Dwipada* metre in Telugu poetry was invented to propagate devotional music in *Desi* style. The *Basavapurana,* the *Panditaradhyacharitra of Palkurki Somanatha and the Ranganatha Ramayana* of Ranganatha, *Palnativiracharitra* by Srinatha were all composed in the above popular style of Dvipada metre.

The other popular folk music from was *Yakshagana* which is also a *Desi* style. *Yakashagana* is a special branch of Telugu literature sung during the moonlit nights in the presence of large crowds with accompaniments and gestures in a semi-dramatic manner.

The *Marga* form of music was the classical and more sophisticated style. Palkurki Somanatha exhaustively deals with this style in his *Panditaradhyacharitra* and *Basavapuranam*. Later, Sarangadeva contributed considerably for this style in his *Sangitaratnakara*.

The musical instruments have been classified into four categories, 1. *Tata,* 2. *Anaddha,* 3.*Sushira,* 4. *Ghana*. All the above four varieties appear to have been in vogue during the Kakatiya period as depicted in most of the Kakatiya temples. There are plenty of sculptural representations of vinas which is decidedly the most favourite musical instrument.

Nadasvara is a South Indian sister instrument of the northern *Shehnai* but much longer in size. The *ninkrina,* and *pongi* are the other accompaniments for a *nadasvara* recital. In sculptures, *nadasvara* is found at Hanumakonda and Ramappa temples. *Basuri* or the flute has a hoary antiquity. This is also found profusely represented in the sculptures. *mridanga* or the *Pakvas* is seen in the temples of Palampet, Ghanpur etc. The *sankha* and the *nagaswara* are the other wind instruments.

The mridanga the *damaru* are the *anaddha vadyas*. Among the *ghana vadyas*, there are gongs, cymbals, *Jalatarangini, Kirikitti, Hudukka, Gharghara, Jhankara* and *Ghallana*.

The Kakatiya period may be regarded as the golden age in the history of dance and drama. The contemporary writers like Palkurki Somanatha, Jayapa and Srinatha have elaborately dealt with various dance forms. Similarly we find copious references to music, dance and drama in *Basavapurana* and *Panditaradhyacharitra*. The latter refers to popular *Desi* style of dances performed on *Sivaratri* day at Srisailam. The other popular *Desi* forms are *Vedayata, Kodangiyata, Perini* etc. In *Palnativiracharitra* we find mention of some *Desi* forms of dances. A more detailed account of various dance forms is found in *Nrittaratnavali* of Jayapa who was the Commander-in chief under Kakatiya Ganapatideva. The *Desi* type of dances which were current during his times were *Gondali, Perini, Prenkhana, Rasaka, Charchari, Dandarasaka, Sivapriya, Kandukanritya, Bhandika, Ghatisasri, Charana, Bahurupa* and *Kolatta*. The exquisite sculptures in the temples at Palampet, Ghanpur, Nagulapadu, Nidikonda, Pillalamarri, Bejjanki, Dharmapuri, Kottapalli and the sculptured fragments lying in the middle of the Warangal fort contain delicately carved figures in charming and graceful dance poses which is an eloquent testimony to the dizzy heights to which the art of dance reached.

The coustumes and footwear are essential needs of people next only to food. The need of clothing was realised by the Vedic people as can be inferred from various references in the literature of the period such as *vasa, Survasa, Durvasa, Arjunavasa, Sukra-vasa* etc. Similar references are found from the *Brahmanas* and the *Puranas*. From the sculptures of Kakatiya period it may be inferred that whether he be a king or nobleman or a commoner they wore only short *Dhotis* reaching upto the knees. Similarly the contemporary literature refers to several kinds of undergarments such as *Chandana-kavulu, Karakanchu kavulu, Kuppasamulu,* and *Koupina* etc. The upper garments are known through the literature as *Duppati, Pacchada* etc. Turban was the commonly used head-dress of men. The royalty, noblemen, and commoners have been depicted as wearing truban with full display of jewellery according to the individual capacity, taste and custom. The *Jangamas* or the Saivite devotees were donning turbans of *Saris, Kambalas* (made of fur or wool), *nandi* type of turbans of tiger skins, of bronze, of *Rudrakshas*, copper and brocaded ones.

Sari was the common dress of women. Palkurki Somanatha records 57 varieties of *saris* in *Basavapurana,* which were named after the places they were woven or by the mode it was worn. For instance, *Chiri* is a simple sari whereas *Mahachiri* might be a longer one. *Ratnapattu, Sankupattu,*

Marakatapattu, Netrapattu, Velipattu might be the different kinds of silks used to make saris. *Chandratapa, Indranila, Sandhyaraga, Meghavanne,Rudrakshavanne* may indicate the colours of the Saris.

On the doorjambs of the Palampet temple, the lady in the panel of the donor couple is shown wearing a sari up to the knees and the mode of dressing might be *Kaccha.* Similar dressing is seen on a bas-relief at Padmakshi temple at Hanumakonda. Along with saris, bodice and jackets were worn by ladies. Some women put on tight jackets, whereas some wore loose jackets. Bodices were made of cotton cloth, *Makhmal* (velvet) On special occasion they wore silk.

Footwear appears to be a common feature of the people of the Kakatiya society. Serveal sculptures particularly the *Alasakanya* bracket figures at Palampet are shown with high-heeled shoes, fully decorated. *Panditaradhyacharitra* gives corroborative evidence by mentioning some sandals known as *Paavalu,* which were artistically decorated with tassels. The work also refers to footwear made of gold, iron, copper and ivory. They were also made of wood and leather.

Personal ornaments served to embellish the body and enhance the beauty and secondly to carry the valuable bunched currency (*nishka haras*) and gold on the person for fear of theft and thirdly for serving religious, mystical and curative purposes. The head ornaments were *Sekhara, Cheruchukka, Sasi* and *Ravi bimba, Mutyala jalli, Lalatika, Jada kucchulu,Bhrmaraka* etc. The ear ornaments are the *Kundalas* which were sometimes as big as half the size of the face. The contemporary literature records several types of ear ornaments like *Tatankas, Kundalas, Ontlu, Punjukammalu, Baviralu, Kuntena-kucchu, Choukatlu, Pogu, Mutyala kamma* etc. However, the five different ear ornaments mentioned in the *Silpa Sastras are Patra, Nakra, Sankhaptra, Ratna and Sarpa kundalas.*

Nose ornament is conspicuously absent in the sculptures in spite of profuse references in literature such as *Mutyala Mungara, Spatikapu Mukkera, Addapu mukkera, Mukkera nattu, Mukku mungara, Kempu mungara, Harumanji mutyala mungera* (nose ornament made of pearls imported from Ormuz) etc.

The neck ornaments were commonly donned both by men and women. Literature preserves some terms like *Trisara,Ratnala-peru, Pataka, Banna sara, Patteda, Ratnala-hara, Navaratna-mala, Kanthe, Graiveyaka* etc. The commoners used to wear strings of beads made of cowries, lotus or *kurvinda* beads or sometimes of *Rudrakshas.* The *Keyuras* or those worn on the upper arm are known as *Dandakadiyas* The bangles are referred to as *Kadiya, Chekatlu, Murugu, Gaju* etc. Similarly, there are profuse references and representations of finger rings, chest-bands, *mekhalas* or waist bands, anklets. Toe-rings are known as *Valayas, Mettes, Viramudiyam, Pillindlu* etc.

Indians have bestowed much care on beautification of hair from early times that a variety of hair styles are found in the Vedic literature such as *Opasa, Kaparda, Sikha* etc. The medieval literature is equally vociferous on the styles in which we notice the terms as *Koppu, Jada, Krovvirulu, Jidimudi, Jaru Koppu.*

Some royal harems used to enlist the services of best hair- dressers. Among the male hair styles as represented in the sculptures a simple knot at the back sems to be common. *Kaparda* which is another type of dressing was adopted by both men and women. The *jatas* or matted locks are common among the Saivite devotees. The main types of hair dresses represented in the plastic art are *Kesapasa, Dhammilla, Jatas, Sikhanda* etc. It appears that keeping of long hair required elaborate hair dressing and great care was to be bestowed to preserve and promote the growth by applying various kinds of oils. *Kridabhiramam* mentions oil prepared from *champaka* flowers for application to hair.

The people engaged themselves in games and amusements during their leisure times. We have copious references both in literature and sculptures such as *Ragunju Pogunjulaata* (tug of war), *Gudi-gudi gunjalata, Appalavindulata, Sarigunjulata, Sarabontalata, Chitla-potlu, Goranta, Dagudumutha,* etc. (Aata literally means game in Telugu). The other games were *Gummadikayalata, Cheruku pandemulu, Pokalata, Bantulata* etc. The game of dicing was equally popular as during the early periods. Swimming, water play with *jalayantras* (syringes) were the other favourite pastimes. *Meshayuddha* (Ram fight), *Tamarachuda vinoda* (cock fight), were the pastimes indulged on festive occasions.

Chalukya Somesvara describes the other fights llike the *Lavaka vinoda* (quails fight), *Syena vinoda*(hawk fight), *Gaja-vyaghra vinoda* (elephant-tiger fight), *Matsya vinoda* (fish fight).

Mrigaya vinoda or hunting was a popular amusement enjoyed by the royalty. *Simhasana Dvatrimsika*, a contemporary work mentions three varieties of hunting *Dipambu-veta, Damena-veta, Tera-veta*. Fishing, wrestling *(Mallayuddha)*, snake charming, bullock-dancing *(Gangireddulata)*, magic, playing on stilts, puppet shows, etc., were the other forms of amusements.

Conveyances played an important role in the march of civilisation of mankind. The earliest mode of conveyance was a wheeled cart drawn by oxen, and the same old tradition continued even in the Kakatiya society. Carts were used for carrying provisions even times or war. The draught animals were known as *Perikas* and those who maintained them were *Perika varu or Perikalu*. Another important beast of burden was horse. The depiction of horses in various postures is an essential theme in the Kakatiya sculptures. The horses are shown with rich strappings, trellised saddle, forehead band, check plate and nose band.

Elephants enjoyed a paramount position during the period under review. The *Gaja-sthara* (elephant friezes) on the temples at Warangal and other places consists of a series of elephants mounted by mahouts. Camels were also used for carrying loads, in spite of its rarity in sculpture. The contemporary literature recollects the use of camel to transport packed loads and tents to the place of war. Palanquins, carts, chariots, boats and ships were the main means of transport. A brisk maritime trade is attested by the inscription entitled "The Charter of Security" issued by Kakatiya Ganapathideva at Motupalli, a sea port town on the east coast.

The military achievements of Kakatiyas had equally matched their cultural achievements. In fact, weilding a weapon was the order of the day to show off their swordsmanship just as wearing a *makuta* to show off royalty.

The medieval literature is replete with allusions of a variety of weapons such as *Ankusa, Asi, Bindiwala, Bhusundi, Musundi, Gada, Chakra, Kadga, Karavala, Khetaka, Krakacha, Kshurika, Kuthara, Mudgara, Musala, Yasthi, Naaracha, Parigha, Parasu, Pattisa, Phalaka* etc.

The bows are classified into two categories namely those with a single curve or those of a composite type. The arrows are variously described in the literature as *Sili-mukha* (hawk- faced), *Sardula-mukha* (tiger-faced), *Ushtra-mukha* (Camel-faced), *Sukara-mukha* (boar-faced), *Uraga-mukha* (Serpent faced), *Karivairi-mukha* (lion faced). *Danti* (elephant faced), *Grudhra-mukha* (vulture faced), *Agni-mukha* (fire faced), *Ulka* (meteor) *Vidyun-mukha* (like lightning), *Graha-mukha* (planet or star shaped), *Mihira-Mukha* (water emanating), *Dahana-mukha* (burning), *Chandra-mukha* (crescentic) etc.

Besides the above weapons the swords were referred to by the terms such as *Asi, Khadga, Karavala, Kshurika* etc. The battle-axe, mace, discus, trident, spear *(tomara)*, Javelin (*Shakti*), shield (*Khetaka*), body armour (*Kavacha*) have been variously represented in the sculptures.

The Muslim chroniclers have given an interesting account of siege engines used at times of war. They are *Gargaz, Sabat, Manjaniques*, etc.

Various kinds of crops, plants, cereals, creepers, flowers, fruits, vegetables etc., which were in common use during the Kakatiya period, were recorded in literature. There are a good number of sculptural representations of the *pipal*. banyan, mango, banana, palmyra trees, sugar-cane, sitaphal, cactus and pineapple etc.

The birds like the parrot, peacock, duck, cock, swan and animals like elephant, horse, lion, wild boar, jackal, stag, monkey and domestic animals such as dog, bull, cow, ram etc., are seen in the figural depictions. Similarly, cobra is the commonest of all the reptiles. The other creatures mentioned are the crocodile, the fish , the tortoise etc.

Thus the study of the literary, epigraphical and more importantly the sculptural evidences of the period throw abundant light on the material culture of the commoners and the aristocracy in the Deccan of the Kakatiya epoch which may hold good to a large extent to all parts of India.

Fortunately, a large number of medieval literary works of Telugu have been carefully preserved from generation to generation mostly due to their religious contents rather than literary or cultural. No doubt the secular works like *Kridabhiramam, Chatuvulu,* are the true mirrors of the contemporary society and have survived due to their literary excellence interlaced by erotic narratives. The third category are the works extolling the achievements of political personalities like the *Prataparudriyam*. The sculpture of the period is the other prolific repository for the study of the Kakatiya society.

BIBLIOGRAPHY

Sanskrit and Telugu Works:

Abhinaya Darpana, Nandikeswara Ed Manmohan Ghosh 1934 Calcutta

Amarakosa of Amarasimha (Namalinganusasana), Ed., Sarma, H.D., and Sardesai, N.G., 1939.

Andhra Mahabharatam of Tikkana Somayaji, Ed., Lakshmiranjanam, K., Telugu Sahitya Academy, 1970.

Andhrula Charitra-Sanskriti, Lakshmiranjanam, K., Educational Publishers, Kurnool, 1951.

Bhaskara Ramayanam, Gona Buddhareddy, Ed., Ramaswami Sastry, V., Madras, 1916.

Basava Puranam, Palkurki Somantha, Ed., Subramanym. G.V., 1969.

Kakatiya Sanchika, Ed., Rama Rao, M., Andhra Historical Research Society, Rajahmundry, 1935.

Kanduri, Cholula Sasanamulu, Sastry B.N., Musi publications, Hyderbad, 1984.

Kautilyas Arthasastra, Ed., Shama Sastry, R., Government Press, Banglore.

Kridabhiramam of Vallabharaya and *Veedhi Nataka Chatuvulu*, Ed., Singaracharya, B.V., Sampradya Sahiti, Seshachalam & Co., Machilipatnam.

Kridabhiramam of Vallabharaya, Ed., Prabhakara Sastry, V., Manimanjari, Hyderbad, 1960.

Kumara Sambhavam (Telugu version) of Nannechoda, Ed., Ramaswami Sastry, V., Madras, 1961.

Kumara Sambhava of Kalidasa, Ed., Wilson, H,H., Indological Book House, Varanasi, 1966.

Mahabhagavatam (Telugu version) of Bommera Pothana, Ed., Bulusu Venkatatmanyya, 1964.

Manasollasa of King Somesvara, Ed., Shrigondekar, G.N., Oriental Institute, Baroda, 1939.

Neetisastra Muktavali of Baddena, Ed., Ramakrishna Kavi. M., Narendra Sahitya Mandali, Tanuku, 1962.

Nrutta Ratnavali, Jaya Senani, Ed., Raghavan, V., Govt., Oriental Manuscripts Library, Madras, 1965.

Palnati Viracharitra, Srinatha, Ed., Umakantha Pandita, Sri Rama Mudrakshara Sala, Madras, 1955.

Prataparudra Charitra, Ekamaranatha, Ed., Lakshmiranjanam, K., Narendra Sahitya Mandali, Tanuku, 1969.

Pratapa Rudriyam, Vidyanatha, Ed., Kumaraswami, K., Vavilla Ramaswamy Sastry & Sons, Madras, 1954.

Ramayana of Valmiki, Kishkindha Kanda, Telugu Trans. by Srinivasa Siromani, Triveni Publishers, Machilipatnam, 1956.

Ranganatha Ramayanam, Ranganatha, Ed. Rama Swamy Sastry,V., Madras, 1960.

Reddy Sanchika, Ed., Appa Rao, V., Andhra Itihasa Parisodhaka Mandali, Rajahmundry, 1947.

Rigveda Arylu, Rahul Sankrityayan, Trans. by Subba Rao,M., Vishalandhra Publishing House, Vijayawada, 1974.

Simhasana Dvatrimsika Parts I & II , Koravi Goparaju, Andhra Sahitya Parishad, Kakinada, 1960.

Sri Panditaradhya Charitra, Palkurki Somanatha, Ed. Narayana Rao, Ch., Andhra Patrika Press, Madras, 1974.

Sri Siddheswara Charitra, Kase Sarvappa, Ed. Lakshmiranajam,K., Andhra Rachayitala Sangham, Hyderabad, 1960.

Sivananda Lahiri of Sankaracharya, Ed., Narasimha Sastry,P.M., C.V.Krishna Book Depot, Madras. (with Telugu Commentary).

Somadeva Rajiyam, Kuchimanchi Jagga Kavi, Narendra Sahitya Mandali, *Tanuku, 1969.*

Sri Suryarayandhra Nighantuvu, Ed., Subbaiah Sastry, K., Andhra Sahitya Academy, Hyderabad.

Tripurantaka Devalaya Sasanamulu by Sastry. B.N., Musi Publications, Hyderabad, 1984.

Velugotivari Vamsavali, Ed., Venkataramanayya, N., Madras University, Madras, 1939.

Vikramankadeva Charitra of Bilhana, Ed., Buhler, G., Bombay, 1897.

General Books:

Agrawala, P.K., 1980 Aesthetic Principles of Indian Art, Prithvi Prakashan, Varanasi.

Agrwala, V.S., 1965 Studies in Indian Art, Vishwa Vidyalaya Prakashan, Varanasi.

Aiyer, A.K.Y.N., 1953 The Antiquity of Some Field and Forest Flora of India, Bangalore.

Altekar, A.S., 1959 The Position of Women in Hindu Civilization, Benaras.

Appa Dorai, A., 1936 Economic Conditions in Southern India 1000- 1500 A.D., Madras University Historical Series No.12, Madras.

Ashraf, K.M., 1969 Life and Conditions of the People of Hindustan, Delhi.

Banerjea, J., 1974 The Developent of Hindu Iconography, Munshiram Manoharlal Pvt.Ltd.,New Delhi.

Boner Alice, 1966 Ramachandra Kaulachara Silpa Prakasika, Leiden,E.J.Brill.

Briggs, John, 1910 History of the Rise of the Mohammedan Power, Calcutta.

Brown, Percy, 1956 Indian Architecture (Buddist and Hindu), Bombay.

Chakarborthy, S.K., 1973 A Study of Ancient Indian Numismatics, Varanasi.

Chakravarti, P.C., 1972 Art of War in Ancient India, Oriental Publishers, Delhi.

Claude Compbell, 1898 Glimpses of the Nizam's Dominion, Historical Publications, U.S.A.

Coomara Swamy, A.K., 1927 History of India and Indonesian Art, Hiersemann, Leipzig, New York.

1948 The Dance of Siva, Asia Publishing House, Bombay.

1969 Introduction to Indian Art, Musnshiram Manoharlal, Delhi.

Cousens, H., 1931 Medieval Temples of the Dakhan (A.S.I. Imperial Series Vol. XLVIII), Calcutta.

Cunningham, A., 1962 The Stupa of Bharhut, Varanasi.

Das, A.C., 1925 Rigvedic Culture, Calcutta.

Day, C.R., 1891 The Music and Musical Instruments of South India and the Deccan, London.

Desai, P.B., 1968 Basavesvara and His Times, Dharwar.

Dikshitar, V.R.R., 1927 The Art of War as Practised in South India, Bhandarkar Institure, Madras.

Dhaky, M.A., 1977 The Indian Temples in Karnataka Inscriptions and Architecture, New Delhi.

Dhavalikar, M.K., 1973 Ajanta - A Cultural Study, University of Poona, Poona.

Fergusson, J., 1910 The History of Indian and Eastern Architecture, London.

Gangoly, O.C., 1915 South Indian Bronzes, Indian Society of Oriental Art, Calcutta.

Gangoly, O.C., 1957 Indian Arts Heritage, Oxford Book & Stationery Co. New Delhi

Gangoly, O.C., 1973 Andhra Sculptures, Archaeological Series No.36, Govt. of A.P.,Hyderabad.

Ghurye, G.S., 1951 Indian Costumes, The Popular Book Depot., Bombay.

Gopalakrishna Murthy, S., 1964 The Sculpture of the Kakatiyas, Archaeological Series No.34, Govt. of A.P., Hyderabad.

Gopalan, S., 1952 Asvasastra of Nakula, Manuscript (unpublished), Nagpur Universiry, Nagpur.

Gopala Reddy Y. 1985 The Ghanpur Group of Temples, Archaeological Series No.60, Govt. of A.P., Hyderabad.

Gopinath Rao, 1968 Elements of Hindu Iconography, Motilal Banarsidas, Delhi.

Goswami, O., 1961 The Story of the Indian Music, Asia Publishing House, Bombay.

Gururaja Rao, B.K., 1972 Megalithic Culture in South India, Mysore.

Herold Newman, 1981 Dictionary of Jewellery, Thames and Hudson Ltd., London.

Havell, E.B., 1908 Indian Sculpture and Painting, John Murry & Co., London.

1920 The Ideals of Indian Art, John Murry & Co., London.

Herbert, A. Popley, 1950 Music of India, Calcutta.

Hugh Whistler, F.Z.S., 1914 Popular Handbook of India, Curney and Jackson, London.

Jamila Brij Bhushan, 1958 The Costumes and Textiles of India, D.B.Taraporevala Sons & Co.,Pvt.Ltd.,Bombay.

Indian Jewellery, Ornaments and Decorative Designs, D.B.Taraporevala Sons & Co., Bombay.

Jayakar, Pupul, 1956 Textiles and Ornaments of India, The Museum of Modern Art, New York.

Joshi, N.P., 1967 Life in Ancient Uttarapatha, Hindu Vishva Vidyalaya, Nepal Sanskrit Series, Benaras Universirty Press, Benaras.

Kamala S.Dongerkery. 1966 Indian Sari, R.G. Mundkar, All India Handicrafts Board, Industry, New Delhi.

Krishna Murthi, N.S., 1975 Andhra Dance Sculpture, A.P.Sangita Nataka Academy & Lalita Academy, Hyderabad.

Krishna Murthy, K., 1977 Nagarjunakonda - A Cultural Study, Concept Publishing Company, Delhi.

1982 Hair Styles in Ancient Indian Art, Sandeep Prakashan, Delhi.

1983 Material Culture of Sanchi, Sandeep Prakashan, New Delhi.

Krishna Sastry, V.V., 1983 Proto and Early Historical Cultures of Andhra Pradesh, Govt. of A.P., Hyderabad.

Macdonell & Keith, 1958 Vedic Index of Names and Subjects, Motilal Banarsidas, Varanasi.

Mahajan, V.D., 1968 Ancient India, Chand & Co., Delhi.

Mc Crindle, J.W., 1877 Ancient India as Discovered by Megasthanese and Arrian, Published by Chakravarti,

Moti Chandra, 1940 Cosmetics and Coiffure in Ancient India, Indian Society of Oriental Art.

1973 Costumes, Textiles, Cosmetics and Coiffure in Ancient and Mediaeval India, Oriental Publishers, Delhi.

Mulk Raj Anand, 1957 The Hindu View of Art, Asia Publishing House, Bombay.

1977 In Praise of Hoysala Art, Marg Puhlications, Bombay.

In Praise of Aihole, Badami, Mahakuta, Pattadakal, Marg Publications, Bomaby.

Homage to Kalamkari, Marg Publications, Bombay.

Nagaraja Rao, M.S., 1971 Protohistoric Cultures of the Tungabhadra Valley, Dharwar. 1983 The Chalukyas of Kalyana (Seminar Papers Ed. by Nagaraja Rao, M.S.), The Mythic Society, Bangalore.

Nagaswami, R., 1982 Tantric Cult of South India, Agam Kala Prakashan, Delhi.

Nigam, M.L., 1975 A Catalogue of Arms and Armour in the State Museum, Hyderabad, Govt. of A.P., Hyderabad.

Nilakanta Sastry, K.A., 1939 Foreign Notices of South India, University of Madras, Madras.

Oppert, G., 1880 On the Weapons, Army Organisation and Political Maxims.

Pal, M.K., 1970 Jewellery and Ornaments in India, Census of India, Office of the Registrar General, Ministry of Home Affairs,Delhi.

Pant, G.N., 1970 Studies in Indian Weapons and Warfare, Jagmohan Singh (Army Ed.), New Delhi.

1978 Indian Arms and Armour, S.Attar Singh, Army Educational Stores, New Delhi.

Parabrahma Sastry,P.V.,

1968 *Siddhodvaha*, Govt. of A.P.,Hyderabad.

1974 Insciptions of A.P.,Karimnagar District, Epigraphical Series No.8, Govt. of A.P.,Hyderabad.

1975 Kakatiya Coins and Measures, Museum Series No.14, Govt. of A.P., Hyderabad.

1978 The Kakatiyas, Archaeological Series No.52, Govt. of A.P., Hyderabad.

Pramod Chandra, 1985, The Sculpture of India 3000 B.C. to 1300 A.D., National Gallery of Art, Washington.

Radha Kamal Mukerjee, 1965, Cosmic Art of India, Allied Publishers, Hyderabad.

Ramachandra Rao, P.R., 1956, The Art of Nagarjunakonda, Rachana, Madras.

Rama Rao, M., 1966, Select Kakatiya Temples, Historical Series No.2, Sri Venkateswara University, Tirupati.

Ramesan, N., 1961, Glimpses of Buddhism, Archaeological Series No.2, Govt.of A.P., Hyderabad.

1970 Copper Plate Inscriptions of Andhra Pradesh Govt.Museum, Govt. Of A.P., Hyderabad.

Rhys Davids, C.A.F., 1910, Dighanikaya, Vol.II, Sacred Books of the Buddhist, Series-1, London.

Ritti, S.H., 1972, The Seunas of Devagiri, Dharwar.

Saletore, R.N., 1982, Vijayanagara Art, Sundeep Prakashan, Delhi.

Sarma, I.K., 1980, Coinage of the Satavahana Empire, Agam Kala Prakashan, Delhi. 1982 The Development of Early Saiva Art and Architecture, Delhi.

Sewell, Robert, 1924, A Forgotten Empire, London.

Shanti Swarup, 1957, The Arts and Crafts of India and Pakistan, Taraporevala, Bombay.

Sharma, M.S., 1948, The History of the Reddy Kingdom, Waltair.

Sherwani, H.K, 1968, Cultural Trends in Medieval India, Bombay.

Shukla, D.N., 1958, Vastu Sastra (Hindu Canons of Inconography & Painting), Gorakhpur University, Gorakhpur.

Sir George Watt, 1908, The Commercial Products of India, London.

Sir Monier Monier Williams, 1979, Sanskrit-English Dictionary, Oxford University Press,London.

Sitapati,. P., & Krishna Sastry, V.V., 1980, New Satavahana Sculptures from Andhra Amaravati, Archaeological Series No.54. of A.P., Hyderabad.

Sivarama Murthy, C., 1942, Amaravati Sculptures in the Madras Government Museum, Govt.Press, Madras.

1961 Indian Sculpture, Allied Publishers, New Delhi.

Srinivasachar, P., 1953, Ramappa and Other Temples at Palampet, Govt. of A.P., Hyderabad.

Stella Kramrisch, 1954, The Art of India, Traditons of Indian Sculpture, Painting and Architecture. The Phaidon Press, London.

1960 Indian Sculpture in the Philadelphia Museum of Art, University of Pennsylvania Press, Pennsylvania.

Stephen Fuch, 1973, Aboriginal Tribes of India, Macmillan,

Stephen P. Huyler, 1985, Village India, Abrams Inc., New York.

Soundara Rajan, K.V., 1965, Architecture of Andhra Pradesh, Archaeological Series No.21, Govt. Of A.P., Hyderabad.

1970 Indian Temple Styles, Munshiram Manoharlal, New Delhi.

Thomas Holbein, 1909, Indian Jewellery, W.Griggs & Sons Ltd., London

Thurston, E., 1909, Castes and Tribes of Southern India, Govt.Press, Madras.

Upadhyaya, S.C., 1963, Kama Sutra of Vatsyayana, Taraporevala Sons & Co., Bombay.

Videhi Krishna Murthy,A., 1970, Social and Economic Conditions in Eastern Deccan 1000-1250 A.D., Madras.

Vasudeva Sastry,V., 1973, Vastuguna Prakasika (Materia Medica) Rajahmundry.

Venkata Narayana Swamy & Venkata Rangayya Pantulu, 1936, Tandava Lakshanam or The Fundamentals of Ancient Hindu Dancing, G.S.Press, Madras.

Venkataramanayya, N., 1942, Early Muslim Expansion in South India, Historical Series No.17, Madras University, Madras.

1974 Inscriptions of Andhra Pradesh, Warangal District, Epigraphical Series No.6, Govt. of A.P.,Hyderabad.

Warmington, E.H., 1928, The Commerce Between the Roman Empire and India, Cambridge.

Yazdani, G., 1960 The Early History of the Deccan, Govt. of A.P., Hyderabad.

Yule & Cordier, 1903, The Book of Ser Marco Polo, Messrs John Murry, London.

Zimmer, Heinrich, 1954, The Art of Indian Asia; Its Mythology and Transformations, New York.

Epigraphy and other Periodicals:

Annual Reports on South Indian Epigraphy,

Andhra Pradesh Annual Reports on Epigraphy, 1965, 1966 & 1967.

Copper Plate Inscriptions of Andhra Pradesh Govt.Museum, By Ramesan, N., 1962.

Corpus of Kannada Inscriptions in the Districts of Hyderabad State by Desai, P.B., 1958.

Epigraphia Andhrica Vol.I, III, IV.,

Epigraphia Indica.

Hyderabad Archaeological Series - Corpus of Telingana Inscriptions, Hyderabad, I, II and III by Srinivasachar, P., 1940, 1958 IV by Somasekhara Sarma, M., 1973.

Inscriptions of Andhra Pradesh, Hyderabad, Warangal District, by Ven-Kataramanayya, N., 1974, Karimnagar District by Sastry,P.V.P., 1974.

South Indian Inscriptions, Archaeological Survey of India, vols. IV, V, VI, VII,IX and X.

Ancient India - Bulletin of the Archaeological Survey of India.

Annual Reports of the Archaeological Department of H.E.H. The Nizam's Dominions.

Annual Reports of the Dept. of Archaeology and Museums, A.P. Govt A.P. Hyderabad.

Journal of Archaeology, Govt. of A.P. Hyderabad.

Journal of Islamic culture, Hyderabad.

Itihas, Journal of State Archives, Andhra Pradesh, Hyderabad.

Journal of Andhra History and Culture, Guntur.

Journal of Andhra Historical Research Society, Rajahmundry.

Journal of All India Oriental Conference.

Journal of Asiatic Society, Bengal.

Journal of Andhra Sahitya Parishad, Kakinada.

Journal of Bombay Branch of Royal Asiatic Society.

Journal of Bihar and Orissa Research Society.

Journal of Deccan History and Culture, Hyderabad.

Journal of the Economic and Social History of the Orient, E.J.Brill, Leidon.

Journal of Indian History, Trivandrum.

Journal of Hyderabad Archaeological Society, Hyderabad.

Journal of Mythic Society, Bangalore.

Journal of the Music Academy, Madras.

Journal of Telugu Academy.

Journal of the University of Madras.

Memoirs of the Archaeological Survey of India.

Prachi Jyoti, Degest of Indological Studies.

Quarterly Journal of Mythic Society.

Description of Plates

1. Relief of pillared *mandapa* with multiple storeys.
2. A torana-gateway at Warangal fort.
3. Bikshatana Murthi from Yeleswaram, Nalgonda district, now exhibited in Khazana Building Museum, Golconda.
4. Chennakesava (a form of Vishnu); from Haveli Sayampet, Warangal District.
5. Gajasura Samhara Murthi on the ceiling of Ramappa temple at Palampet, Warangal District.
6. Idol of Annapurna with a ladle and pot distibuting food to the devotees; from Kasipet in Karimnagar district, now exhibited in the State Archaeological Museum at Hyderabad.
7. Nagini, a bracket figure at Ramappa temple, Palampet, Warangal District. The stark naked figure stands over a coiled serpent, *Nagabandha* with several other serpents over the body.
8. A figure of *Manini* from Ramappa temple. This bracket figure of *Manini* or the modest-lady is shown as being molested by a monkey pulling down her scanty under-garment.
9. A narrative scene depicting the episode of *'Taravilapa'* fom the Ramayana. The panel is from Nidikonda temple in Warangal district. The photograph is not clear due to lot of clay sticking to it.
10. Lord Krishna stealing away the garments of the Gopis, who were bathing naked in the river Yamuna. The panel is from the Ramappa temple, Palampet, Warangal district.
11. A triangular panel from the Surabhandesvara temple at Kondaparti, Warangal District depicting the Kakatiya Commander, Chaunda, triumphantly returning home on horse back after battle.

12.
13&
14. Life size Bracket figures of dancers from the temple of Ramappa at Palampet.

15. A dancer flanked by drummers inside rounded cusps. The various dancing gestures of the same dancer are shown in six rows, three in each. The panel is carved on the side screen of the main door of Ramappa temple.
16. Nataraja panel from Pachchala Sameswara temple. Panugal

17. Dancing Narasimha inside *Makara torana* found on the architrave of Thousand Pillared Temple at Hanumakonda, Warangal District.
18. Dancing Saraswati standing on *hamsa* flanked by garland and flywhisk bearers. This ceiling panel is from Ghanpur now in State Museum, Hyderabad.
19. Three dancers shown with two pairs of legs, in order to depict the vigorous gestures of the dancers, with sticks in their hands. The main dancers are flanked by stick wielders and musicians.
20. One more panel depicting the same theme as above.
21. Gold ear rings with coin type pendants decorated with seated figures of Lakshmi, the Goddess of wealth in the middle. The treasure trove was excavated from Narsipur, Warangal district.
22. A Bracket figure of *Madanika* (voluptuous lady) from Ghanpur, now exhibited in the office premises of the State Department of Archaeology and Museums, Hyderabad.
23. Gold beads with peripheral beaded decoration in the form of a *Nandipada*. There is also a central Pipal leaf pendant.
24. Torso of a male or female bedecked with exquisitely carved waistband having a central jewel and tassels suspended.
25. A chauri bearer wearing a beautiful coiffure, from the Thousand Pillared Temple, Hanumakonda, Warangal district.
26. A lady figure having a beautiful *dhamilla* type coiffure, form Pangal temple, Nalgonda district.
27. A lady wearing a *dhammilla* type coiffure also form Pangal temple.
28. A seated lady is dressing her hair and making it into a plait. Pangal, Nalgonda district.
29. A lady from Warangal Fort having a *Kesapasa* or loop type of hair style.
30. A wall panel showing wrestling bouts in different postures.
31. Another panel from Palampet showing a terrible wrestling scene.
32. A battle scene showing warriors mounted on chariots drawn by horses, depicted on a horizontal lintel which supports the ceiling, Nagulpadu temple, Nalgonda districts.
33. A panel depicting Siva as Tripurasura Samhara Murthi, standing on a chariot flanked by Brahma, Vishnu, Ganesa and Ganas;from Ramappa temple Palampet.
34. A panel showing the donor couple, probably Recherla Rudra and his consort, on a door jamb inside Ramappa Temple, Palampet, Warangal District.

35. A row of warriors carrying round and rectangular type shields and swords; from Nagulapadu, Nalgonda district.

36. A huntress is shown carrying a composite type of bow with a joint in the middle. An arrow is seen in her right hand. Ramappa temple, Palampet, Warangal District.

37. Tribal ladies wearing leaf graments, carry simple type of bows; from Bejjanki temple, Kareemnagar district.

38. A battle scene with warriors wielding swords, spears and a variety of shields;from Ramappa temple at Palampet.

39. A Suprrbly carved bull (Nandi) in Pachchala Someswara temple, Panugal.

INDEX

Fig. 1

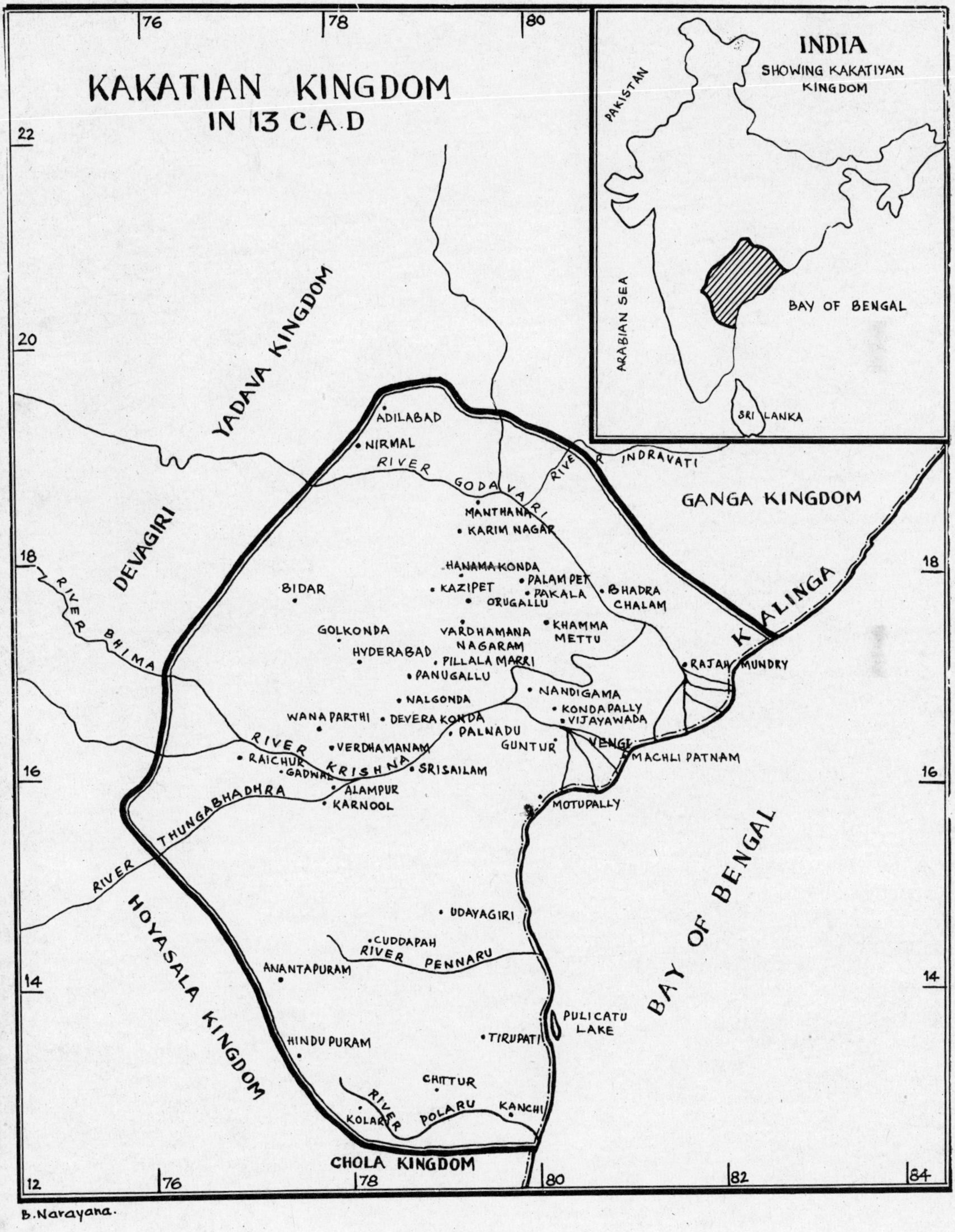

B. Narayana.

GENEALOGICAL TABLE OF THE KAKATIYAS

Family of Durjaya

Venna (Founder of the Kakatiya line)

Guṇḍa-I

Guṇḍa-II

Guṇḍa-III (who died sometime before 900 A.D.)

Erra

Betiya (Mentioned in the Mangallu grant only)

Guṇḍa-IV (assisted Danarnava; 955-995 A.D.)

Garuda Beta (Beta-I) (996-1051 A.D.)

Prola-I (1052-1076 A.D.)

Tribhuvanamalla (Beta-II) (1076-1108 A.D.)

- Tribhuvanamalla Durgarāja (1108-1116 A.D)
- Prola-II (1116-1157 A.D.) m.Muppama
  - Rudra (1158-1195 A.D.) Mahādeva m.Bayyama (1296-99 A.D.) established ṣoverein power in 1163 A.D.
    - Gaṇapatideva, m.Somaladevi (1199-1262 A.D.)
      - Ganapāṁba m.Koṭa Beta
      - Rudramadevi (1262-1289 A.D.) m.Chalukya Virabhadra
        - Mummadamba m.(Kakati) Mahadeva
          - Pratāparudradeva (1289-1323 A.D.)
        - Rudrama m.Yadava Prince Ellanadeva
        - Ruyyama m.Induluri Annaya-mantri
    - Mailāmba
    - Kuṅdāmba
  - Harihara
  - Gaṇapati
  - Repolla Durga

Fig. 3 **Architecture**

a b c d

B. Narayana, C.A.

Fig. 4 **Musical Instruments**

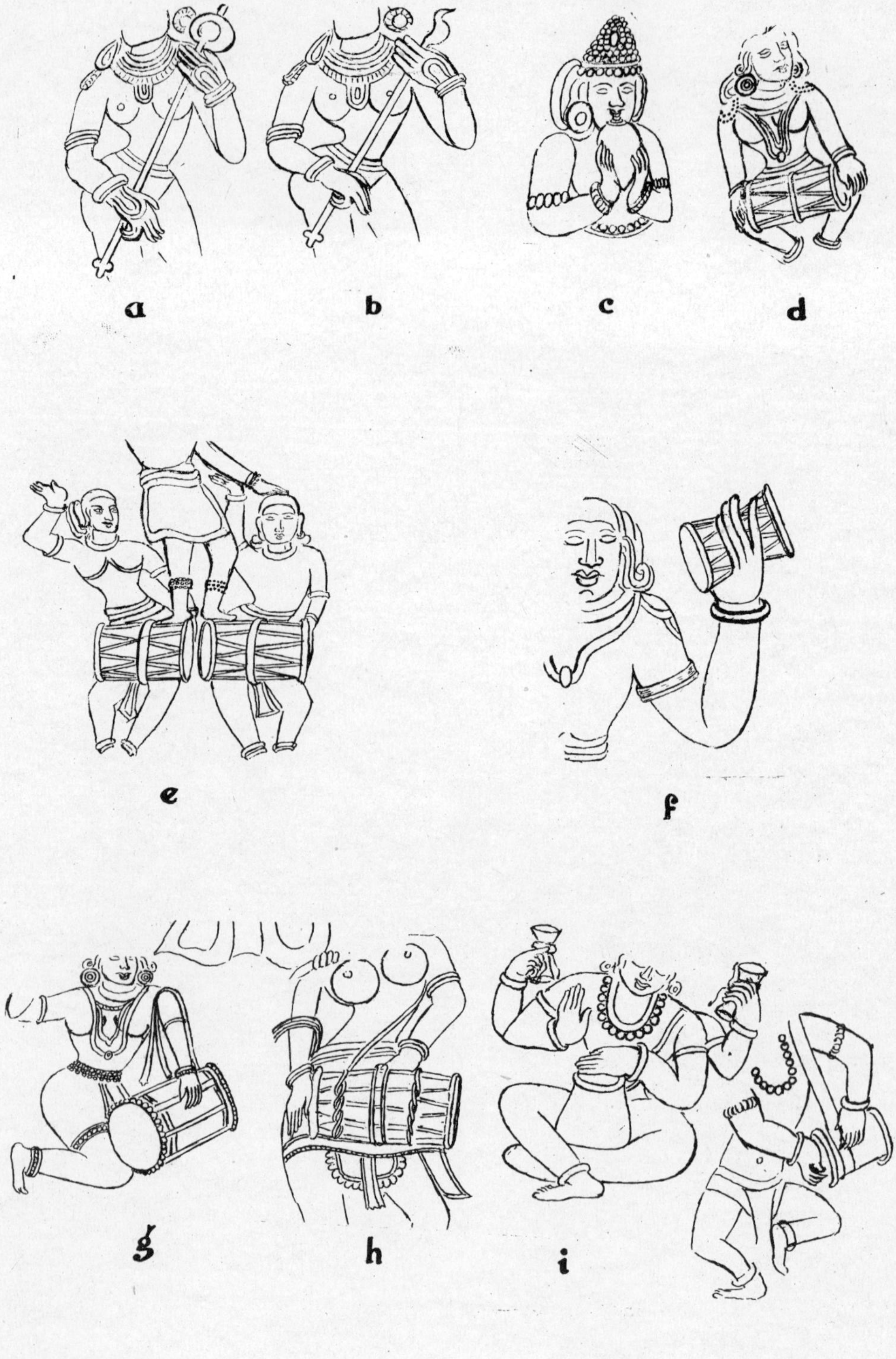

Fig. 4

Musical Instruments

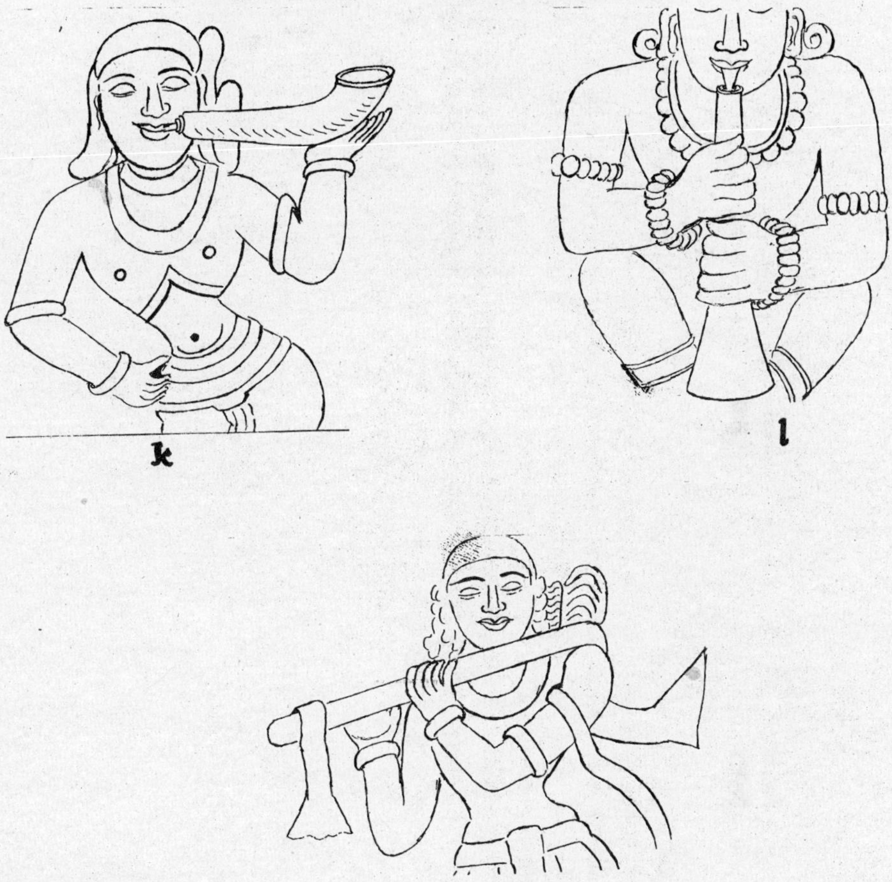

Fig. 5

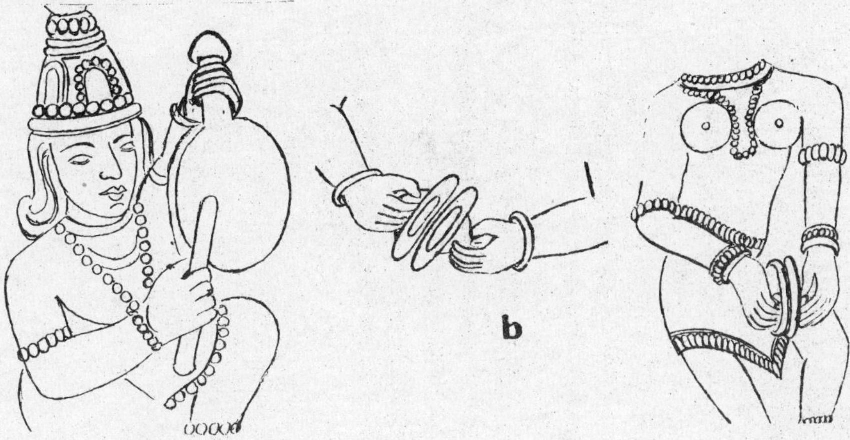

Fig. 6 Dancing Drama

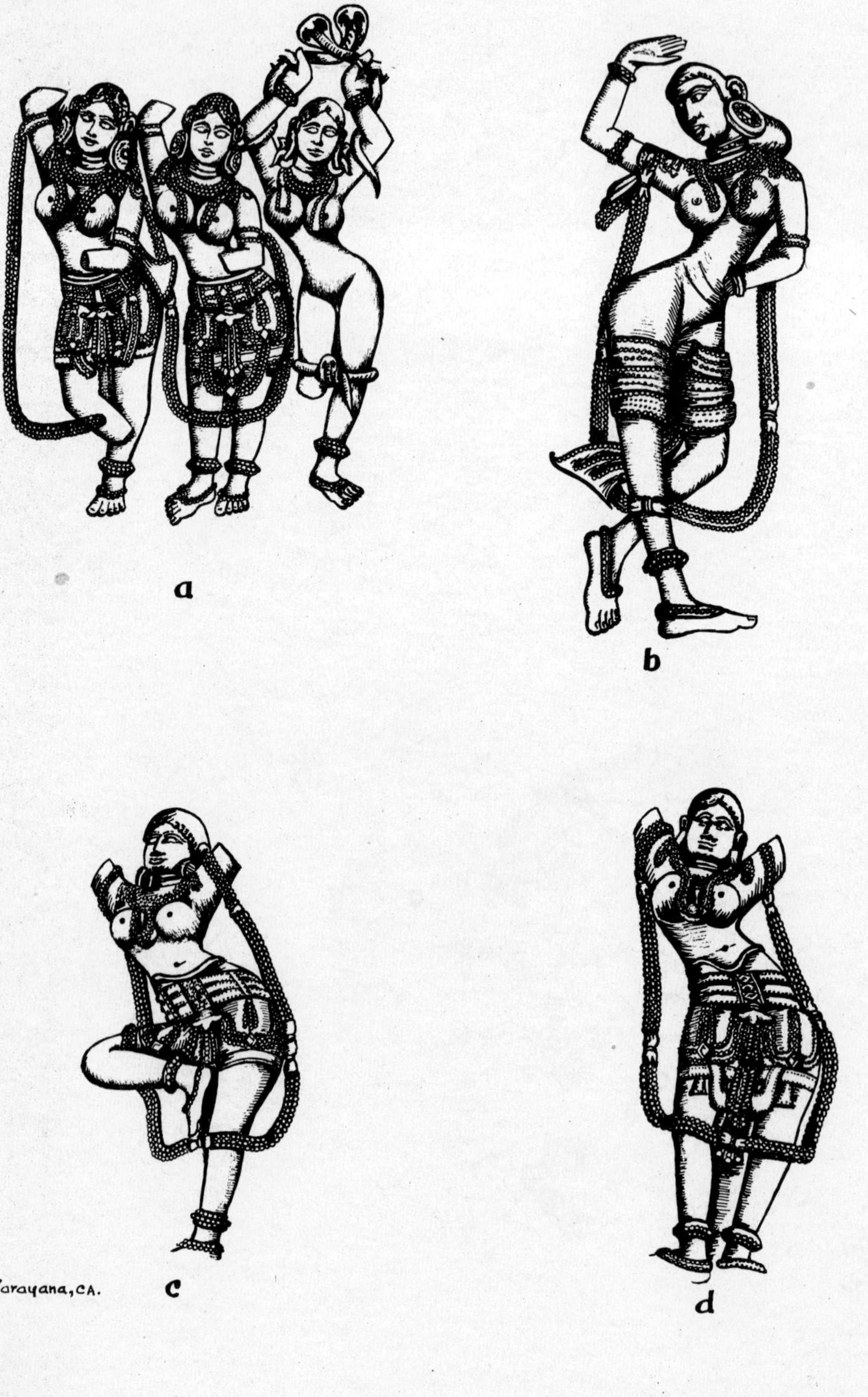

B. Narayana, CA.

Fig. 7 **Dancing Drama**

a

b

c

d

B. Narayana, C.A.

Fig. 8 Costumes

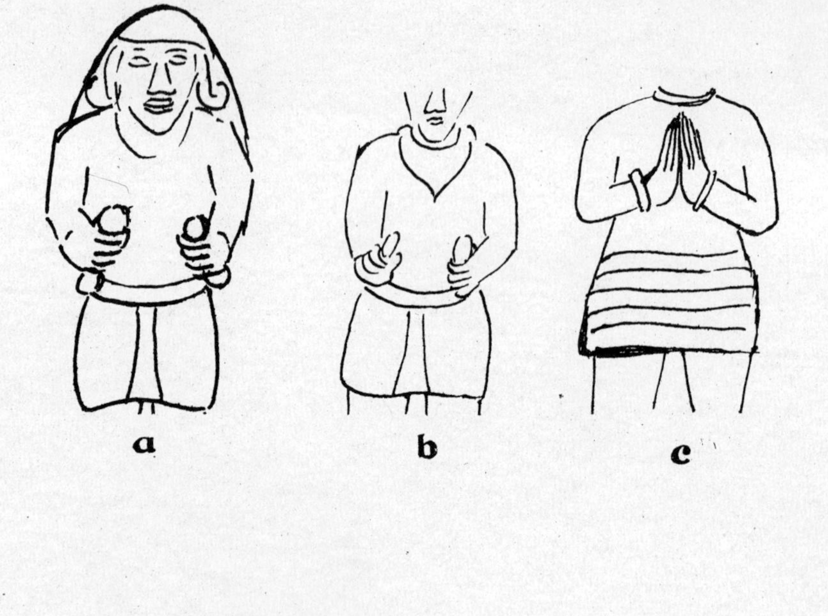

Fig. 9 **Costumes**

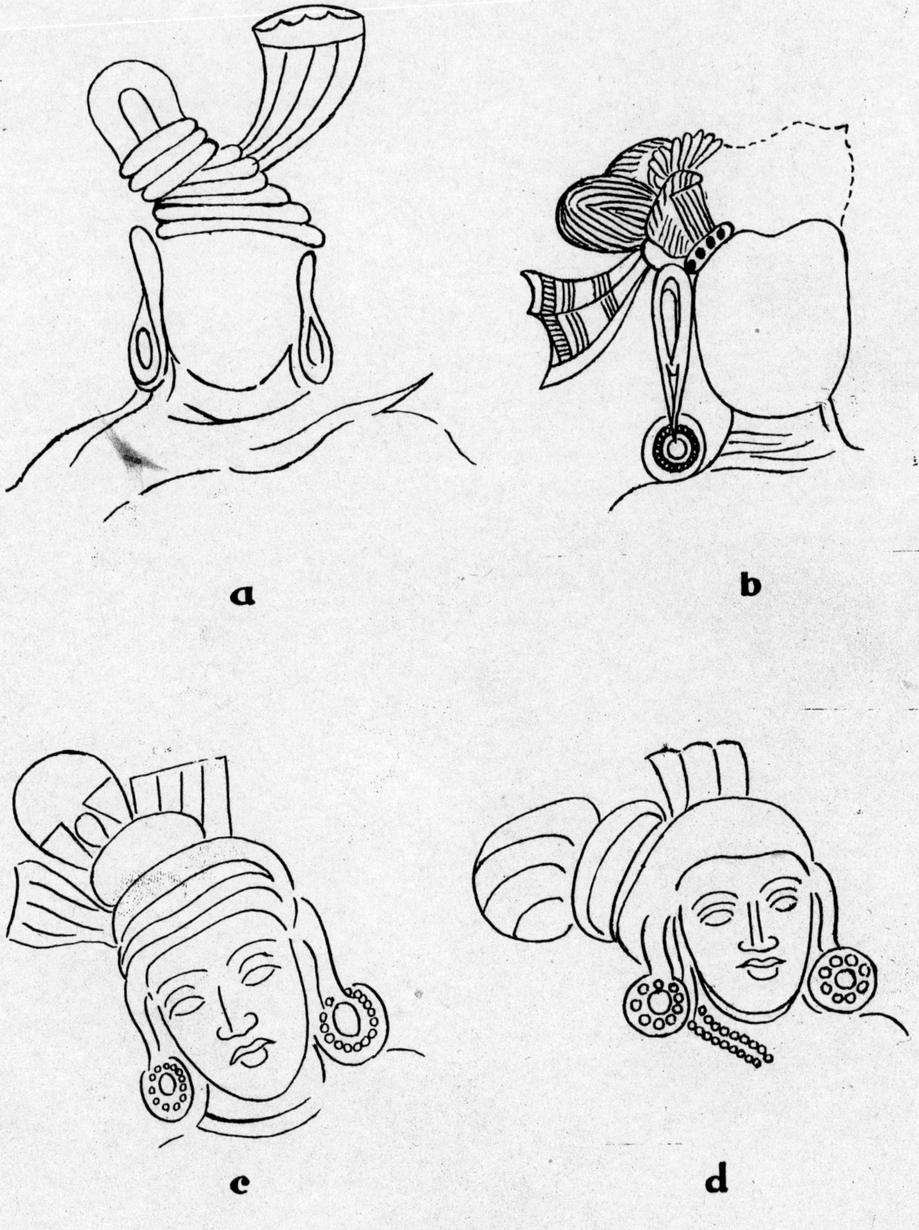

a b c d

Fig. 10 Costumes

Fig. 11 **Costumes**

Fig.12 Jewelry and Ornamentation

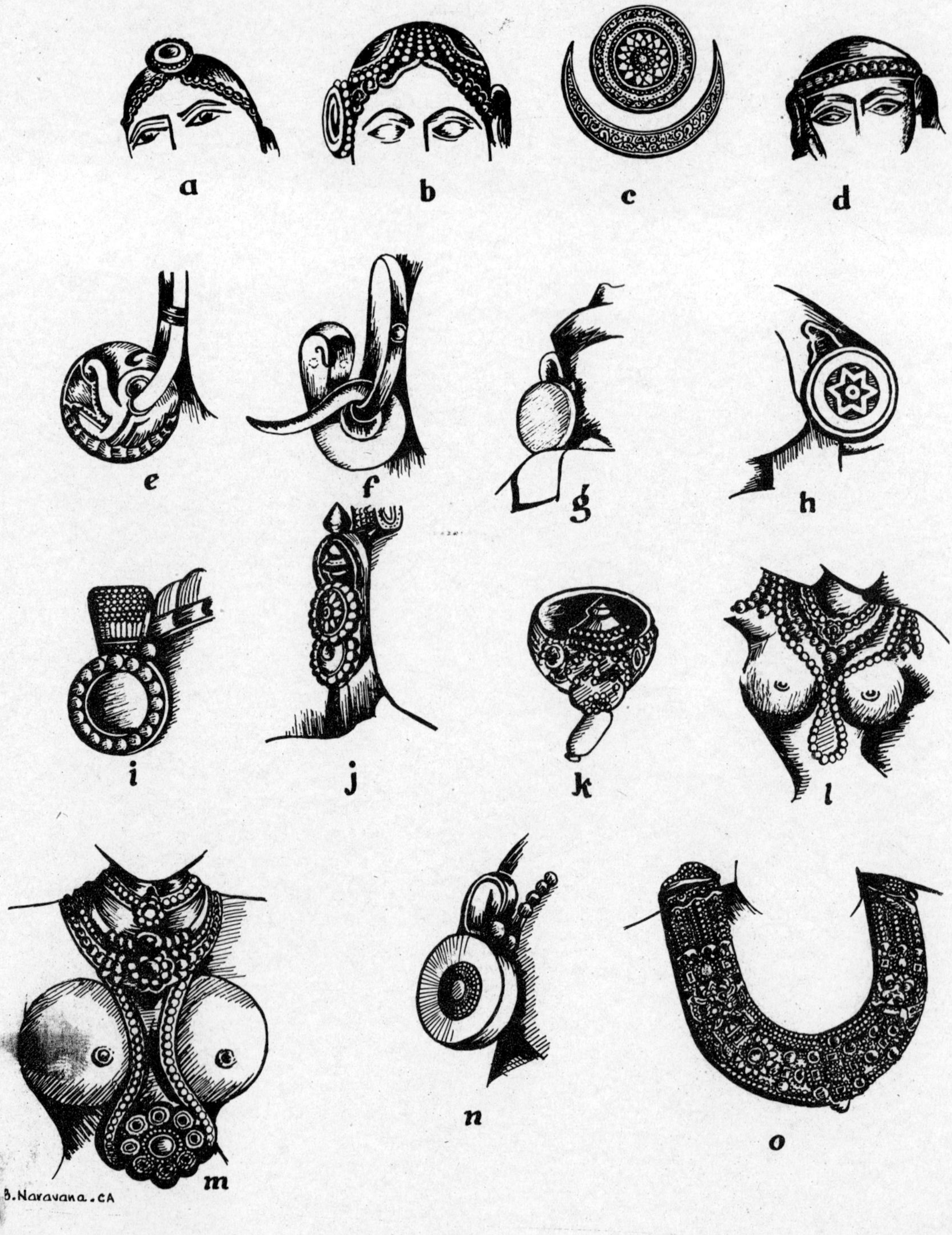

Fig. 13 **Jewelry and Ornamentation**

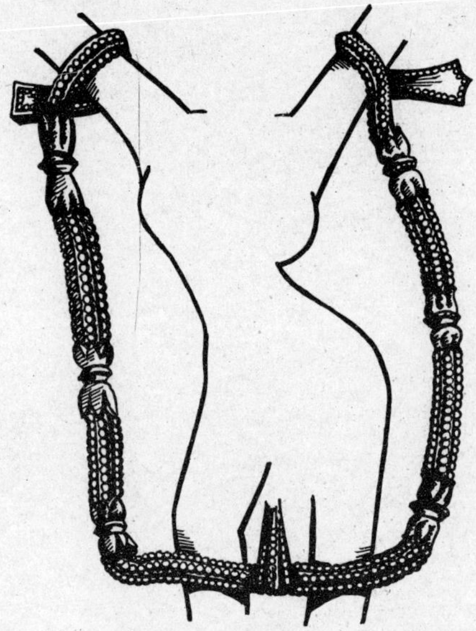

a

b

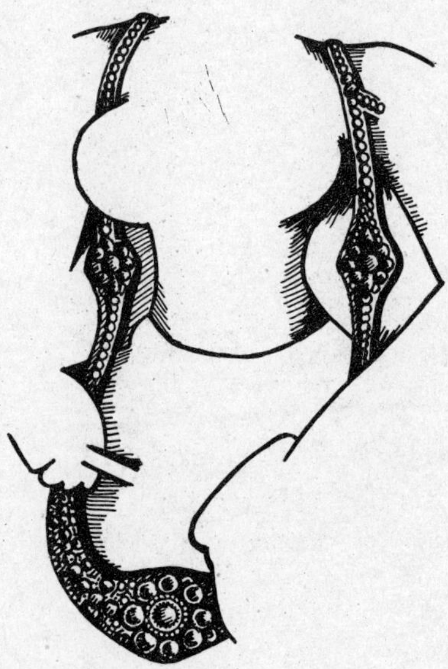

c

Fig. 14 **Jewelry and Ornamentation**

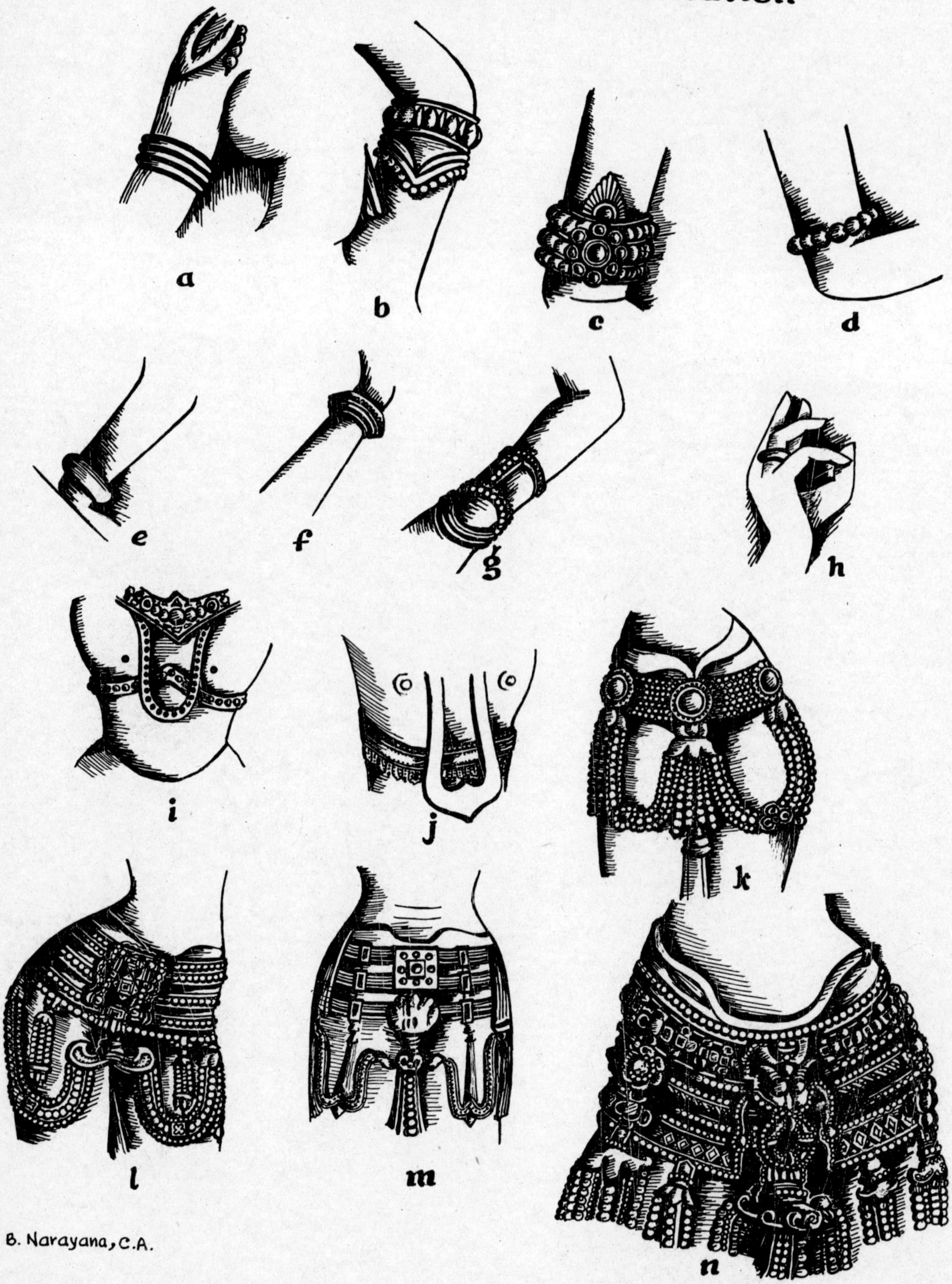

B. Narayana, C.A.

Fig. 15 Jewelry and Ornamentation

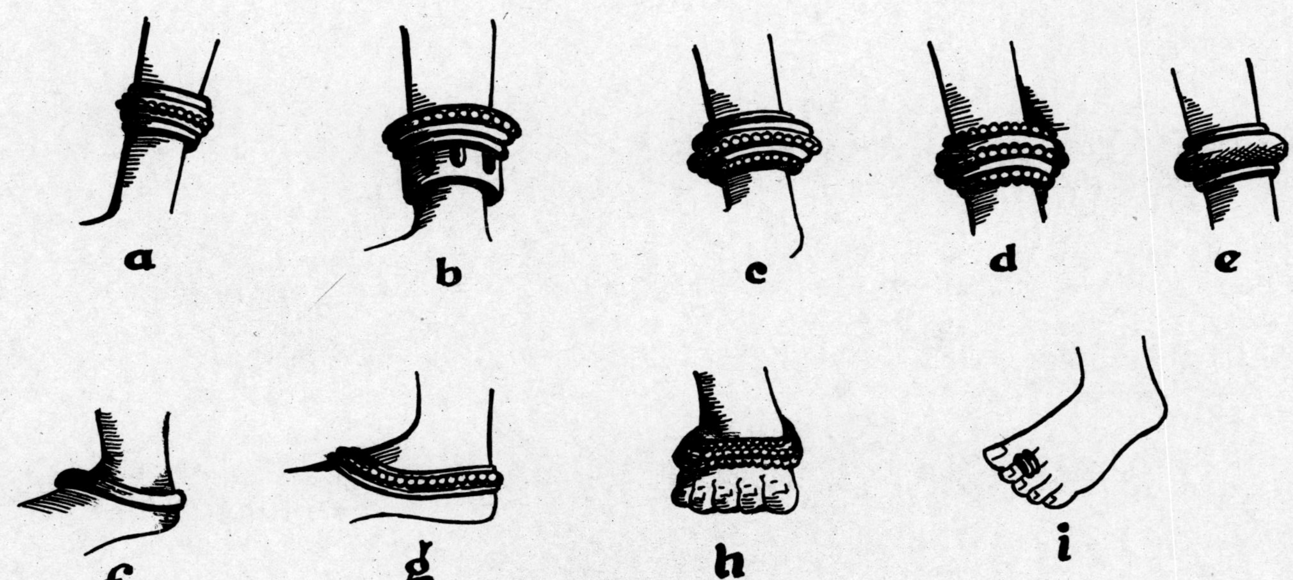

Fig. 16 Coiffure

Fig. 16 **Coiffure**

m n o p

Fig. 17

a b c

Fig.18 Conveyances

Conveyances

Fig. 19

Fig. 20

Fig. 21 **Weaponry**

Fig. 22 **Weaponry**

Fig. 22 **Weaponry**

m

n

l

p

o

q

Fig. 23 Weaponry

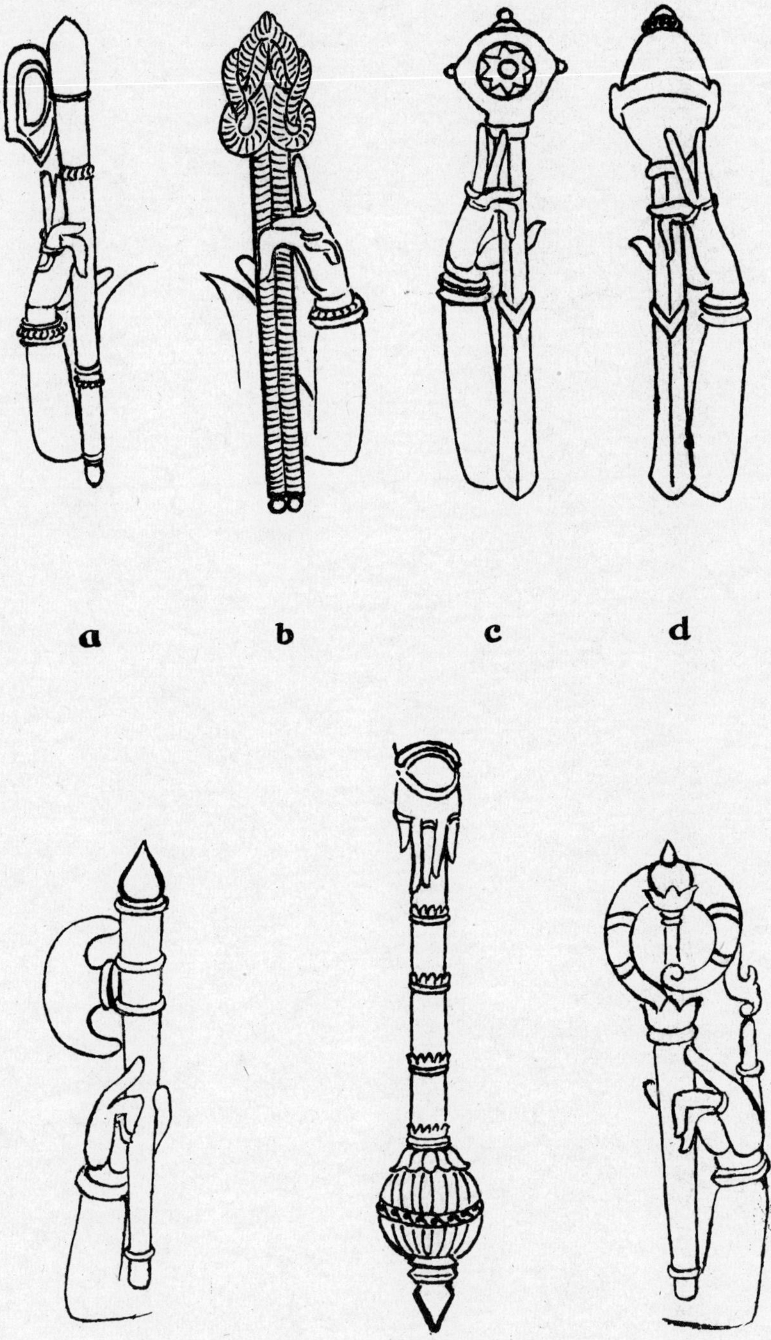

Fig. 23 Weaponry

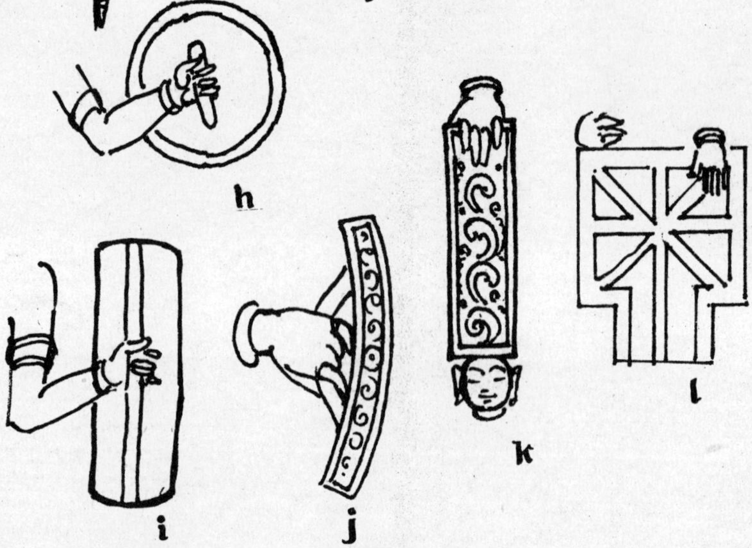

Fig. 24

Plate 1

Plate 2

Plate 3

Plate 4

Plate 5

Plate 7

Plate 6

Plate 8

Plate 9

Plate 10

Plate 11

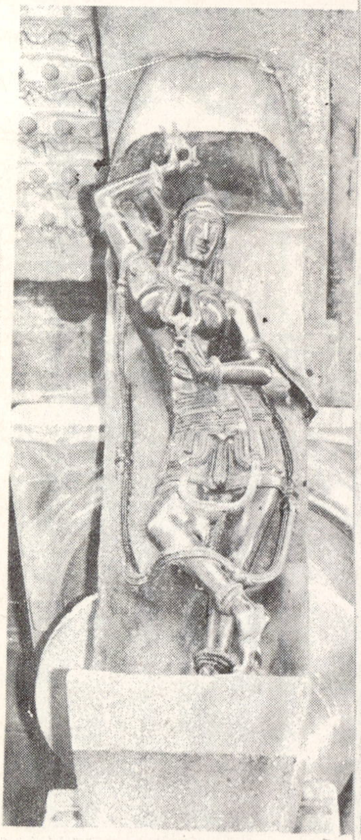

Plate 12

Plate 13

Plate 14

Plate 15

Plate 17

Plate 16

Plate 18

Plate 19

Plate 20

Plate 21

Plate 22

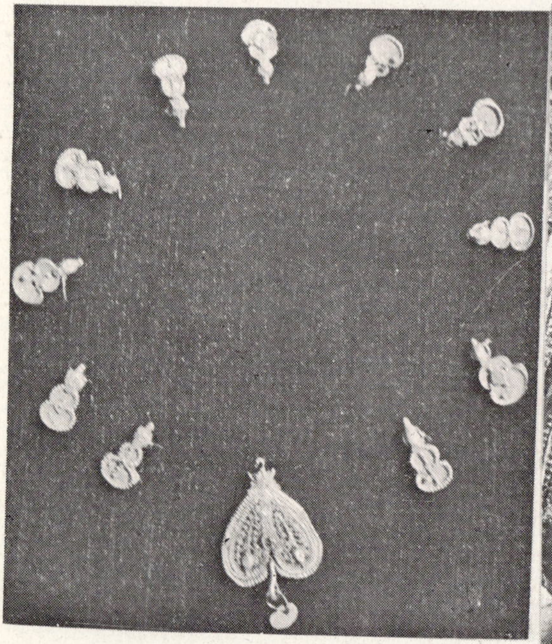

Plate 23

Plate 24

Plate 25

Plate 26

Plate 27

Plate 28

Plate 29

Plate 30

Plate 31

Plate 32

Plate 33

Plate 3[illegible]

Plate 35

Plate 37

Plate 36

Plate 38

Plate 39